1001 *The Sequel*
WAYS TO BE
ROMANTIC

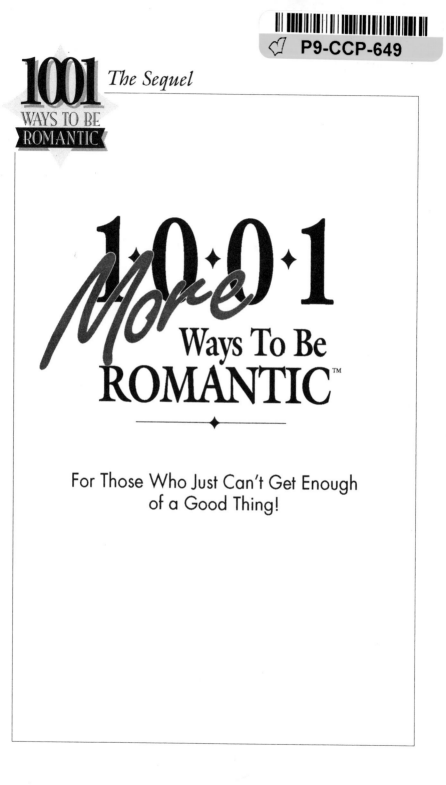

1·0·0·1
More
Ways To Be
ROMANTIC™

For Those Who Just Can't Get Enough
of a Good Thing!

Also by Gregory J.P. Godek
1001 Ways To Be Romantic

On its way
LoveStories—
Outrageous & Inspiring & *True* Romantic Stories

And one of these days
1001 Ways To Be Romantic—
The Novel

"*What's the number one complaint of otherwise happy wives in America?*
"My husband is not romantic anymore."
What's the number one complaint of husbands in America? "I don't have time to be romantic."
What's the number one way to solve both problems?
Pick up a copy of Gregory Godek's
clever and creative new guide for the romantic wannabes to oh-so-marrieds. **"**

~ Dave Kirby, *Troy Progress*

Casablanca Press,™ Inc.
Boston

Bookstore distribution: Login Publishers Consortium
800-626-4330

Giftstore distribution: Silver Visions
617-244-9504

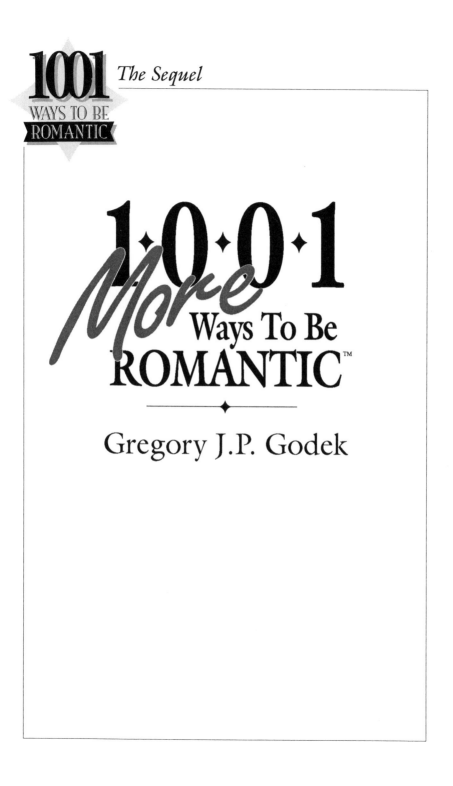

1001
WAYS TO BE
ROMANTIC

The Sequel

1·0·0·1
More
Ways To Be
ROMANTIC™

Gregory J.P. Godek

"1001 Ways To Be Romantic™" is a trademark of
Casablanca Press,™ Inc. and Gregory J.P. Godek, denoting a series of books
and products including newsletters, calendars, audio cassettes & videotapes.

Second printing.
Printed in the United States of America.
10 9 8 7 6 5 4 3 2

Published by:
Casablanca Press,™ Inc.
P.O. Box 226
Weymouth, Massachusetts 02188-0001
617-340-1300

Cover illustrations by Maria Thomas at Pendragon Ink , 508-234-6843
Book design by Bruce Jones Design, Inc., 617-350-6160
& Hannus Design, Inc., 617-227-3725

Publisher's Cataloging in Publication Data

Godek, Gregory J.P., 1955-
1001 *More* Ways To Be Romantic

Includes index.
1. Self-help. 2. Psychology. 3. Relationships. 4. How-to. I. Title.

Library of Congress Catalog Card Number
91-92118

ISBN 0-9629803-2-3 (softcover)
ISBN 0-9629803-3-1 (hardcover)

Dedications

This book is dedicated to the thousands of *wonderful* people
who've written or called me following the publication of
1001 Ways To Be Romantic.

And to the
hundreds of thousands of people who've bought the book.

And *also* to the many "reluctant recipients"
whose lovers used the book to send a Romantic Wake-Up Call!

And, of course, to my Bride . . .
I.S.I.L.W.Y.—W.E.C.I.D?

✦ Contents ✦

✦ Contents ✦

Acknowledgments

Tracey
Danielle LaFountaine
Courtney McGlynn
Josephine Fatta
Andy Pallotta
Mike Beard
Tom Blazej
La-La-La-La-Lola
Dominique & Mitch
Everyone who ever had anything to do with the Mac PowerBook
Maria Thomas & Pendragon, Ink
Craig Schreiber
Bill McHugh
Kim Molloy
Alice Donahue
Candy Means & Maureen Branca & Naomi Karten
Claire Stevens
Clare Saulnier & Steve Howard
Tim Corbett
Bruce Jones
Dale
H.S.
Kenn Brown
Sam and The Group
Wolfgang Amadeus Mozart

About the Author

Gregory J.P. Godek, author of *1001 Ways To Be Romantic,* has survived the success of his first book with his marriage intact. He now tempts Fate again with the sequel. (And yes, he's working on Book #3. —"What's the word for the sequel of a sequel?")

Greg confesses that he doesn't really "write" these books—they "happen" to him. "Sometimes it grabs me by the throat. More often it seduces me. Occasionally it sneaks up on me and *pounces*—the way Hobbes playfully yet violently attacks Calvin." This methodology, rarely employed by writers of stature, seems to work for him. It does, however, mean that there is rarely any logic behind his research. What ends-up in the book is rarely by design.

Greg received his advanced degree in Romance from The Good Old Fashioned School of Lover Boys. He credits his parents with his personality that is "just naturally romantic." From his mother he learned creativity and sensitivity, and from his father he inherited boundless energy and a passion for living. Otherwise, his suburban upbringing holds no clues to his pathological interest in Romance that borders on the obsessive. "I've always believed that the happiest people in the world were those who made no distinction between work and play. I'm now there, and I was right!" In his mind, this explains everything.

Greg presents keynote talks, seminars and workshops to groups nationwide. "My wish is to *truly* communicate with people. This means creating a *dialogue,* and not merely a *monologue.* This book is part of a Grand Conversation. I look forward to hearing from you."

Apology

To Mrs. Wilcox: I *know* that I break nearly every rule of good English— and proper punctuation. —And CAPITALIZATION. (*And* sentence structure.) I'm also rather *liberal* with my use of *italics* and stuff. This book probably would have flunked me out of your High School English class! But, Mrs. Wilcox, The Rules are just *too confining!* If only one could write words with the precision and control with which musicians write their scores. *Alas! Alas!* I'll let my pen (well, computer) follow my heart, and ask for your tolerance, if not your forgiveness.

~ Fondly, G.J.P.G.

Author's Note

As was the case in *1001 Ways To Be Romantic*, there are *not* really **1001** ways to be romantic in this book either—*there are 1,185!* [Those of you who've read the first book can skip directly to the note below, as the rest of this paragraph explains stuff that you already know.] *Why* are there more than 1001 Ways here? Because many of the numbered items include *several* concepts, ideas or gift suggestions. On the other hand, a few ideas and items appear *more than once* in the book. *I've done this on purpose.* Why?? Because most readers of this book skim and skip through it— as opposed to reading systematically from beginning to end—and I want to make sure they don't miss some of the things I consider most important (or most fun).

Note to new readers: *Welcome!* I think you're going to enjoy the book. I see it as the beginning of a *dialogue*, and not merely another long-winded monologue by some so-called "expert." I would *love* to hear from you: Romantic hideaways, unique gifts, romantic stories, wonderful gestures, great surprises, tales of how you met your lover, or how you got engaged, and anything *else* you think other romantics around the world would like to hear about! If I can't fit your stuff into one of my upcoming books, it may make its way into one of my seminars or speeches—or, it might end-up in my *Romance Newsletter*! [See page 295.]

Note to old readers: [—I don't mean *old* as in "old." *You* know what I mean. I didn't mean to *insult* you . . . Geez! I just wanted to welcome you back. Oh, *nevermind!*] *Welcome back!*

Aloha (see #1322),

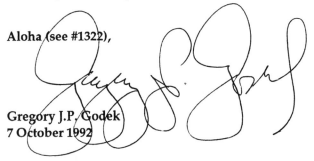

Gregory J.P. Godek
7 October 1992

Publisher's Note

Every effort has been made to ensure the accuracy of information in this book. Any errors or omissions will be gratefully corrected in the next printing. To express our gratitude, we'll send you a free copy of the first book, *1001 Ways To Be Romantic*, if you'll send us any corrections. Really!

Here We Go Again

1002

Romance is a state of being. It's about taking *action* on your feelings. It's a recognition that Love in the abstract has no real meaning at all.

Romance—love in action—is a daily, living, growing activity.

Romance often *starts* as a "state of mind" (#1 in *1001 Ways To Be Romantic*), but it must move *beyond* mere thoughts and intentions, and be communicated to your lover . . . through words, actions, gifts, gestures, or just a tender look.

1003

Romance is a **process**—*it's not an event.* It's not a one-time thing. It's not something that's "accomplished," and then forgotten. In order to work, it's got to be an ongoing thing—a part of the very fabric of your daily life. {Thanks to Phil Wexler, a business consultant and professional speaker who stresses that "Sales is a process—not an event."}

1004

There's hope for the "Romantically Impaired." Yes, modern science, combined with sophisticated psychological techniques and a loving whack upside the head will do the trick. I've heard the most wonderful tales of romance re-kindled during this past year. [Hey, I should write a book!] During my talks and seminars around the country, and from my appearances on many call-in radio talk shows, I've been constantly reinforced in my opinion that *deep down we're all the same*: Men and women, young and old, singles and marrieds—we all want to be loved, cared-for and appreciated. Yes, there *is* an appalling number of the Romantically Impaired among us, but I haven't yet met anyone who was beyond help or beyond hope.

1005

✳ "Pings"—as defined in *1001 Ways To Be Romantic*—are any habit or action that your partner does that you just know you couldn't live with for the rest of your life!

✳ "Bings"—as defined by comedian Robin Williams—are creative flashes.

✳ "Zings"—just now being defined—are *sexual Bings.*

1006

Know your lover's "Little Passions" and "Big Passions." Knowing them can spark your romantic imagination.

❤ "Big Passions" are interests that often run a person's life or define one's career. Some Big Passions include: An academic interest that leads to a teaching career; an interest in food that leads to a career as a chef or restaurant owner; an interest in children that leads to parenthood; an artistic or musical interest that leads to the poorhouse—no, no, just kidding!

❤ "Little Passions," on the other hand, don't dominate our lives—but they *do* bring joy and meaning to many of us. Some of my Little Passions include Mozart's music and collecting comics. Some of Tracey's include weird earrings and cool umbrellas. We often work these little passions into our romantic gestures.

"Men are motivated and empowered
when they feel needed . . .
Women are motivated and empowered
when they feel cherished."

~ John Gray, Ph.D.

1007

You can be yourself and it works! It's astonishing to me that so many people think that "being romantic" means something other than "being yourself." There are a lot of myths, misconceptions and outright lies being propagated in books, magazines and newspapers, school hallways, locker rooms and bars. Be careful who you listen to!

1008

Here, then, are the Top Ten Reasons Why You Should Be Romantic:

10. The Rose-Growers of America need your help.
9. You'll stay young-at-heart.
8. You need all the help you can get!
7. Love makes the world go 'round.
6. Your wife will let you back into the house.
5. Romantics lead more interesting lives than mere mortals.
4. Why *not?*
3. Your partner *wants* it—What more reason do you need??
2. You'll score points with your mother-in-law.
1. It will improve the quality of your life.

{With thanks and apologies to David Letterman.} Now, create your *own* list, and mail it to your stubborn partner.

1009

✳ Present him with a *written bill* for the next dinner you prepare for him: "Jean-Ann's Cafe: Bill for Services: Salad: 1 kiss. Entree: 8 kisses. Dessert: 3 kisses. Total bill: 12 kisses. (Tipping *is* encouraged.) You may want to take advantage of our Frequent Diner Program. See the manager. Thank you, come again!"
✳ Present her with a bill for the next time you change the oil in her car: "John's Garage: Bill for services: 6 quarts of oil: 1 kiss each. Oil filter: 1 kiss. Labor: 4 kisses. Total bill: 11 kisses. No checks accepted. Note: Special rates for customers who sleep with the mechanic!"

1010

Tips on getting the most out of this book (from readers of the first book):

➤ One California couple is reading the book "together"—she from the *front*, and he from the *back*. {Steve & Sharon Thompson, Petaluma, California.}

➤ One couple is reading it *aloud* to each other.

➤ One couple rates each of the 1001 items along the following scale:

1 = Personal favorites
2 = Things I want you to do for me
3 = Things I'll do for you
4 = Let's discuss
5 = *No way!*

1011

❧ He gave her a simple little music box that plays *As Time Goes By*. As she opened it, he said to her: "*As time goes by* I love you more and more."

❧ She gave him the key to her apartment in a jewelry box. As he opened it, she said, "It's the key to my heart, too. You've unlocked it—please don't break it."

❧ The real gift in each case was *what was said* in conjunction with the gift. Think about it!

1012

↦ Got a few minutes on your hands? Fill his *entire* answering machine tape with romantic songs! First message: "Hi, hon, it's me! This song reminded me of you, and I thought I'd share it with you." Then put the receiver up to the stereo and record 30 seconds of the song onto the message. Then, over the next couple of hours, whenever a great song comes on the radio, call his phone and just record another song segment. This may drive him crazy, but I guarantee he'll "get the message" that you're crazy about him!

↦ A variation on the theme: Turn it into a game of "Name That Tune" by playing 2-second segments of the songs!

Romance 101—Revisited

1013

A Test For True Romance (vs. Mere Manipulation and Smooth Moves):

Ask yourself: "Does the gift or gesture
1) Build intimacy and trust, or
2) Merely impress?"

Genuine romance has no ulterior motive other than the expression of love. Granted, this is a lofty goal that is only occasionally attained, but it's definitely a *worthy* goal. It's certainly fine if *some* romantic gestures impress. But beware of the lover whose romantic gestures never reveal much about himself, and are always extravagant, expensive, showy and glitzy.

1014

Romance resides in the *everyday*.

1015

Are you "Past-Oriented," "Now-Oriented" or "Future-Oriented"? Your "romantic style" is often determined by your "time orientation."

* Past-Oriented people tend toward the sentimental and nostalgic. They're into scrapbooks and saving things.

* Now-Oriented people are spontaneous and often extremely creative. They're into last-minute activities and adventures.

* Future-Oriented people are planners and listeners. They're into surprises and grand gestures.

1016

A great concept recently developed by a friend and colleague of mine is "24-Hour Communication." In fact, Ken has an entire presentation that details the concept. Here are the highlights: 24-Hour Communication is the realization that we are communicating *all the time*. You can't ever "turn it off"—from the moment you're born until the second you die. "You're even communicating in your sleep," Ken observes. Your body language, breathing patterns and whether or not you're a cover-stealer all communicate a lot about you! The point here is to increase your awareness of what you're communicating to your partner: By the things you say, the manner in which you say them, the way you dress, the way you touch her, the way you make love, etc. Too often, people are only aware of their communications at work, then leave those skills behind when they go home. Is it any wonder why so many businessmen are great successes at work, and miserable failures at home? {Ken West is a business consultant and professional speaker in the Boston area.}

1017

I've recently become aware of the amazing power of *little* gestures to communicate *volumes*. And when I say "little," I mean TINY: A look, a raised eyebrow, a touch on the elbow, the smallest hints of body language, can communicate volumes between two lovers who are in-tune with one another. Intimacy is built on such small things.

1018

The *anticipation* is often just as much fun as the event or gift itself.

1019

A relationship is a *learning experience*—it's not a static thing. If you haven't learned something *new* about your partner in the last month or so, you're not trying hard enough.

Monogamy— *Not* Monotony!

1020

Monogamy . . . This one word may very well define the Nineties. It encompasses a variety of values (*another* hot word this decade)— from commitment and family, to spirituality and personal growth.

1021-1030

And now . . . *Ten Rules for a Happy Marriage*

1. Compliment each other in public.
2. Cherish each others' uniqueness.
3. Pay attention to the *little* things—they can pile-up and sink you.
4. Fight fair when you must fight. (And *all* healthy couples fight!)
5. Talk. Listen. Share. Empathize. Repeat.
6. Celebrate your life together. Create special rituals.
7. Never go to bed mad.
8. Forgive one another. Then forgive yourself.
9. Never meet without an affectionate greeting.
10. Keep your relationship your Number One priority.

{Compiled from lists sent-in by Julie in Iowa, and Jim in Arkansas.}

1031

You can only be *truly known* in an intimate, long-term relationship.

1032

Conventional wisdom says that the American marriage is on the rocks. . . That the sexual revolution has shattered family values . . . And that infidelity is rampant, checked only by the fear of AIDS.

Conventional wisdom is wrong!

Here are some statistics that may shock—and then relieve—you:

Love and happiness: Most couples are more in love now than in the first years of their marriages. More than 60% describe their marriages as "very happy."

Fidelity: Most couples are faithful in their marriages. 90% say they have had only one sexual partner since they were married. Nearly half say they have had only one sexual partner in their entire life!

Sex: Most couples say sex is very important in holding a marriage together. Over 65% say their sex life is very satisfying.

Faith: Most couples say their religious faith helps their marriages. Two-thirds of all married couples pray together. And the couples with both a satisfying sex life and a strong religious faith are the most likely to remain married.

Want to see more? Get the book *Faithful Attraction*, by bestselling novelist and sociologist Andrew M. Greeley. Subtitled *Discovering Intimacy, Love and Fidelity in American Marriage*, the book shatters the negative myths popularized in the mass media, and affirms the continuing health and vitality of marriage in America today.

1033

Romance expresses love. Love creates intimacy. Intimacy enhances trust. Trust builds commitment. Commitment is the cornerstone of monogamy. Monogamy flourishes amid romance . . . Romance expresses love . . .

1034

Marriage Magazine—Celebrating the Potential of Marriage. This magazine is one of America's greatest little secrets. A spin-off from the well-respected Marriage Encounter organization, *Marriage* is not a religious magazine, but one that *does* include spirituality among the mix of relationship issues that confront us all. I'll let editor Krysta Eryn Kavenaugh describe it: "The purpose of *Marriage* is to share the vision of the infinite potential of marriage. We celebrate the ideal of a long-term, intimate, forever growing union. We also accept the reality of our imperfect, wonderful selves and relationships as they are now. We believe in the divine union of two; the necessity of individuality and a solid sense of self; the beauty of the individual's and couple's spiritual path; and the sharing of the marital love with family and community. We rejoice in the journey and sacred space that allows us to have a more fulfilling, deepening, and enriched life." A subscription is just $15. Write to 955 Lake Drive, St. Paul, Minnesota 55120, or call 612-454-6434.

1035

Nearly 45% of all marriages in America are *second* marriages. Hope springs eternal. Keep at it you guys, I give all of you lots of credit. Many readers have written to me, explaining that one of the major lessons they've learned is the importance of romance in their relationships.

You may want to peruse *The Second Time Around: Why Some Second Marriages Fail While Others Succeed*, by Louis Janda and Ellen MacCormack. Some insights from the book: Two-thirds of those remarried say that it's harder than they anticipated. The most difficult issues?—Children and money.

1036

The purpose of romance is to create intimacy. Intimacy ensures long-term relationships.

Help for the
Romantically Impaired

1037

(File under "If you want something done right, do it yourself!"): Can't get him to write you a love letter? Write it yourself! Create a fill-in-the-blank love letter and send it to him (along with a self-addressed, stamped envelope, of course).

1038

When all else fails—talking, bargaining, threatening, beating him with this book—*hypnotize him!* I'm *serious!* Look, there are many successful therapists who help people use the power of their own minds to stop smoking or lose weight. So why shouldn't they be able to help a reluctant/forgetful lover be more romantic?

A hypnotherapist friend of mine wants me to stress to you that there's nothing magical or mysterious about hypnosis. "It's simply a way for you to tap into the incredible power of your mind," says Douglas Tibbetts. "We all have a huge untapped reservoir of strengths and abilities that are accessible only through intensely focused consciousness." Hypnosis is simply a technique for inducing a state of deep relaxation during which the mind is cleared of random thoughts. Suggestions made to a calm mind seem to have more power. How good a candidate for hypnosis is your partner? Five to 10% of us are *highly* susceptible to hypnosis, 80% to 85% of us are *fairly* susceptible, and the remaining 5% aren't susceptible at all.

* Douglas can be reached at 603-627-7007.
* Terri Kaplan holds "Mind Over Matter" seminars. Call 800-945-MIND.
* For Do-It-Yourselfers: *Discovering the Power of Self-Hypnosis*, by Stanley Fisher, Ph.D.

1039

YOU MAY ALREADY BE A WINNER! The Publishers Clearinghouse Lovestakes has chosen *YOU* to be the recipient of AT LEAST 1,000,000 kisses—that's **ONE MILLION** kisses (and hugs!) Nothing to buy! No coupons to fill-out! What do you have to do in order to qualify for ONE MILLION kisses and hugs?!—Just bring home one bottle of champagne this Friday. That's all! But—if you want to qualify for the BIG BONUS PRIZE of 1,000 nights of passionate lovemaking, you'll have to bring home one red rose per week for the next year. A SMALL PRICE TO PAY, WOULDN'T YOU SAY—FOR 1,000 NIGHTS OF PASSIONATE LOVEMAKING!! (This offer expires the day after tomorrow.) So act *TODAY!*

(If junk mail can work for Ed McMahon, it can work for you!)

1040

Print-up a bunch of custom business cards, patterned after a doctor's appointment card:

YOUR NEXT APPOINTMENT WITH YOUR WIFE IS ON: _____
PROPER ATTIRE IS REQUIRED.
THE EVENING'S ACTIVITIES WILL BEGIN WITH _____
CONTINUE WITH _____
AND CONCLUDE WITH _____
NO CANCELLATIONS. ONLY ONE RE-SCHEDULING IS PERMITTED.

Fill-out several cards: Make one classically romantic, one outrageous, one sexy, one easy, one hard, one cheap, one expensive, one time-consuming, one quick, etc. Mail 'em one at a time to your lover.

1041

A major reason why some people aren't romantic is that *a lack of it doesn't affect them*. If you want him to be more romantic, but he's satisfied with the status quo . . . "Well, tough luck—that's *your* problem!" he says/thinks. The solution? Simple: *Make it his problem.* As consultant/speaker Lou Heckler says, "People only really solve problems that they see as *problems that relate to them*."

How do you "make it his problem"? Well, you start by telling him up-front *what* you want (more romance), and *how* you want it (circle your favorite items in this book!). Tell him what action you're going to take if he doesn't meet you half-way. Then select activities that you know will strike home with him: Withhold sex. Stop cooking dinner. Stop helping him with selected chores. Stop being romantic toward *him*.

He'll either get the message or leave. Either way, you win.

1042

Ya don't gotta be perfect—ya just gotta keep tryin'! Whoever set-up the "Perfection-Mindset-Thing" oughta be taken out and shot! Religious dogma that demands perfection is de-motivating. School grades are even more ridiculous and out-of-touch with reality. Here's what you learn in school:

- ✏ If you're right 90% of the time, you get an "A"—you're *excellent.*
- ✏ If you're right 80% of the time, you get a "B"—you're *fair.*
- ✏ If you're right 70% of the time, you get a "C"—you're *average.*
- ✏ If you're right 60% of the time, you get a "D"—you're *pretty dumb.*
- ✏ If you're right less than 60%, you get an "F"—you *fail.*

Now, let's compare this with Real Life.

- ★ A baseball player who bats .300 is a *star*!
- ★ In most life situations, you get more than *one* chance!
- ★ A businessperson who *never* fails at all is seen as too cautious.
- ★ Your true friends accept you as you are; they don't expect perfection.

Ya don't gotta be perfect—ya just gotta keep tryin'!

1043

Collect quotes on love. Write each one on a 3x5 card. When you've collected a hundred or so, begin a Campaign of Love by mailing them, posting them, hiding them and showering them on your lover. Continue this Campaign for weeks and months. If he doesn't get the hint, here are your options: 1) Get his eyes examined, 2) Get his head examined, 3) Get *your* head examined, 4) Grab the next stagecoach out of town.

Include some of your *own* quotes among those by Shakespeare, Thoreau, Godek, McCartney and Dickenson! {Tip 'o the hat to Susan Doremus, of Minnesota.}

Men & Women

1044

Are you stuck in a "Romantic Stalemate," in which each partner is waiting for the other to "start"? The solution?—Swallow your pride for one quick minute, "give-in," and start the romantic ball rolling. You'll gain more from this "surrender" than from "holding your ground." Romantic Stalemates are based in mistrust, mind-games, insecurity and/or immaturity. Breaking the stalemate is always growth-inducing. *Go for it!*

1045

Despite the section called "Letting Go of Romance," *A Book for Couples* is excellent. Authors Hugh and Gayle Prather are masters at viewing people and relationships practically yet spiritually. One of their themes is that "The two of you are not the relationship . . . something new now exists . . . it is part of your mind . . . and it will drain or strengthen you depending on whether you nurture it from your heart or your ego."

1046-1047

➤ Ladies, let's stop . . . male bashing . . . assuming that *all* men are Romantic Boneheads . . . feeling superior about your relationship skills (which often *are* superior) . . . putting-down the Men's Movement . . . being a martyr . . .

➤ And start . . . giving him the benefit of the doubt . . . appreciating his quirks . . . putting yourself in his shoes . . . sending him flowers.

1048-1049

➤ Guys, let's stop . . . stereotyping women . . . assuming we know what they think . . . feeling threatened by feminism . . . ignoring our feelings . . . acting superior . . .

➤ And start . . . being real . . . getting in touch . . . reviving gallantry . . . giving of yourself . . . making your relationship a top priority . . . listening more.

1050

Sigmund Freud's famous question "What do women want?" has puzzled men for years. I, too, have thought about this one. I do not have The Answer to the question, but I *do* have some opinions about the question itself. [But then again, I have opinions about just about *everything*, don't I?!] First, I believe that the question is, essentially, absurd. It is so broad as to be meaningless. The question also trivializes women, and turns them into objects of study, instead of individuals to be understood (and appreciated). I believe that the only relevant (and answerable) question is "What does *my* woman want?" We are all so fiercely individual and unique that I think it's much more helpful to focus your attention on *your* lover rather than on the theoretical Universal/Generic Woman.

1051

Although it may seem paradoxical, when two people explore and appreciate their *differences,* it can bring them closer than ever! (When, of course, the process is approached in a spirit of love.)

1052

A great way to gain understanding about yourself and your partner is through learning about your "Psychological Type." There are a variety of systems that define and explore them, some modern, and some ancient—everything from astrology to the Myers-Briggs test which seek to help us understand ourselves by categorizing our abilities, attitudes and temperaments by areas such as introversion vs. extroversion, logic vs. emotion, intuition vs. sensation, judging vs. perceiving.

An excellent book that contains a self-administered test to determine your "temperament," plus lots of detailed explanation, is *Please Understand Me: Character & Temperament Types,* by David Keirsey and Marilyn Bates. The following is a vast oversimplification of the "Four Temperaments" described in the book, but it will give you a flavor for it:

✦ **The Dionysian Temperament**: This person must be free; he won't be tied or confined or obligated. He can miss romantic nuances which may be apparent and precious to other types. Although he is the master of the grand gesture, he can forget a promised telephone call or word of affection.

✦ **The Epimethean Temperament**: This type is most comfortable as the giver, not the receiver; the caretaker, not the cared-for. These words describe the Epimethean type: Steadfast, dependable, stable, reliable, a pillar of strength.

✦ **The Promethean Temperament**: Power fascinates this type. Not power over people, but over things, situations, nature. The scientist, the engineer, the thinker—He has a passion for knowledge. For him, "Work is work, and play is work.

✦ **The Appollonian Temperament**: This type is people-oriented, not thing-oriented. They are not interested in, or not content with abstractions: They seek relationships. Interaction is extremely important to this person.

1053

Hey, you guys, *write her a love letter!* I know I've said this before, but it's a BIGGIE, and worth repeating. The most common reason/excuse for not writing love letters is that "I'm not eloquent. I'm no poet." Well, guess what, guys?—Your wives and girlfriends already *know* that you're not Shakespeare. They don't expect eloquence. (They can get eloquence from Billy Joel or Al Jarreau.) What they *do* expect is *you. Your* words expressing *your* feelings in *your* way. That's all! It doesn't have to be long. It doesn't have to be poetic. It don't even gotta be grammatically correct! [Sorry, Mrs. Wilcox.]

1054

Ladies, before you read this item, please read the item above. [Pause.]

Now, consider this: In the same way that you don't expect him to be Shakespeare, *your partner does not expect you to be a Playmate.* Hey, it's no *secret* to him that you're not built like Miss July, that you're not a Victoria's Secret model, or that you're maybe a tad overweight: He loves you *anyway*! And nine guys out of 10 would *still* be turned-on if you'd wear that frilly little thing, or surprise him with that garter belt/stockings/bra/panties & heels outfit. I *know* that this body-image thing is a big issue with a lot of women, and I know that there are no simple answers. But I think this may be a helpful little step along the way.

Love creates an "us" without destroying a "me."
~ *Leo Buscaglia*

Women & Men

1055

Romance Quiz Question: Guess which major magazine this quote is from:

". . . we *need* romance and sentimentality in our lives . . . Note that I say "we need"—*all* of us, men and women, right down to the most macho truck driver or professional mud wrestler. There was a general supposition a couple of decades ago, when women first banded together to seek "liberation," that one of the first casualties would be "romance," particularly in its more obvious and exploitative forms. Would Betty Friedan really expect a box of chocolates on February 14? Would Kate Millett wait for flowers? Would women, once they had become astronauts, weight lifters, firepersons, and entrepreneurs, and after becoming dependent on the Pill and sisterhood, still crave romance? And was not romance itself merely another of those many cultural traps that men had perfected for women over the centuries? As anyone could have predicted, romance won out, in fact was never in danger at all."

Where did this item appear? *Cosmo*? Nope. *Glamour*? Nope. *Reader's Digest*? Nope. *Penthouse*? Yup! (Written by Michael Korda, who isn't exactly known for his sentimental attitudes!)

1056

Every man's challenge is to incorporate the Warrior with the King, the Magician and the Lover, in order to achieve the fullest expression of our personalities. So say the authors of *The Warrior Within: Accessing the Knight in the Male Psyche*, Robert Moore and Douglas Gillette. This book provides some help for men (and for women who want to understand us better). *The Warrior Within* is the second in a projected series of four works on the structure of male archetypes. This study follows *The King Within*. The author's thesis is that the Warrior is an integral part of the male psyche, but one that must be socialized so it does not turn destructive.

1057

Even though my emphasis is on the similarities of men and women, I believe it's important to understand the differences between us, too. For example:

* 68% of men like the way they look naked; only 22% of women do.
* Women cry about 5 times as much as men. A male hormone may actually suppress tears!
* Women's bodies release stress and return to normal faster than men's.

These, and 57 additional differences are explored in a fun and accessible book called *He & She: 60 Significant Differences Between Men and Women*, by Cris Evatt. While there have been many books about gender differences, this is the first time the research has been brought together in one volume. Also included is a quiz to test how well you know men and women, and a "gender scale" to help you rate your own masculine and feminine qualities.

1058

Are you stuck in a "romantic stalemate"—where each partner is holding back, waiting for the other to make the first move? Here's a thought: "Making the first move" isn't giving-in—rather, it's the more aggressive, more loving, and riskier thing to do. [Doesn't look like a sign of weakness to me!]

1059

Is divorce becoming just another "rite of passage" for Americans in their 40s? I certainly hope not, but a number of people are viewing it this way. Mary Ann Nalbandian, adjunct professor of psychology, in Worcester, Massachusetts, has observed many people who seem to "expect" their marriages to break-up during this transitional decade in their lives. She notes that men's "mid-life crises" tend to coincide with career changes, while women's tend to coincide with their children becoming old enough to fend for themselves.

1060

Do you work with your lover? Over 90% of all businesses in the U.S. are family-owned. [I didn't know that!] Couples who work together face special challenges in their relationships that the rest of us don't have to deal with. [Of course, you also have some special opportunities for being romantic, too!—Like leaving love notes in his in-box; hiding special messages in his computer; love trysts in the middle of the afternoon!] Anyway . . . Here's a book just for you: *Working With the Ones You Love: Strategies for a Successful Family Business*, by Dennis Jaffe, Ph.D. This is the first book on family business by a psychotherapist. It provides new insights, information and practical tools for building communication, resolving conflict, and separating personal and business issues.

1061

Ladies: Do you really think that *he* thinks like *you* think?
Gentlemen: Do you really think that *she* thinks like *you* think?
Everyone: *Think again!*

➤ She gives him this book:
  * *What she means*: "This will improve our relationship."
  * *How he takes it*: "She's trying to turn me into someone else."

➤ He gives her some lingerie:
  * *What he means*: "You'd look great in this."
  * *How she takes it*: "He wants me to look like a slut!"

➤ She wants to go out for dinner and a movie:
  * *What she means*: "I want to go out for dinner and a movie."
  * *How he takes it*: "I'm going to go broke!"

➤ He gives her one red rose:
  * *What he means*: "This symbolizes my love for you."
  * *How she takes it*: "He's too cheap to buy a dozen."

1062

Where do your opinions about the opposite sex originate? Ideally, I would think they should be the result of combining your beliefs with your experiences. But I've observed that many people's opinions actually contradict their experience. Their opinions seem to be a mish-mashed conglomeration of their parents' attitudes, their experience of their parents' relationship, some fairy tales, some locker room banter, some movie scenes, some talk show host's opinions, some *Cosmo* articles, some *Penthouse* letters, and some bits and pieces from various comedians' routines. To me, this does not seem to be a wise foundation upon which to build one's Belief System about the opposite sex.

For Singles Only

1063

Think you're too smart to try personal ads in order to find a mate? Think again! Members of Mensa, the select society for the top 2% of the population with IQs of 132 and above, have newsletters in which members seek-out like-minded partners. More than a few marriages have resulted. Note: Two-thirds of Mensa members are male, and 52% of all members are single. Think you're smart enough? Call 800-666-3672, or write to American Mensa, Box V-92, 2626 East 14th Street, Brooklyn, New York 11235.

1064

A single man leaving to Fate
The question of finding a mate . . .
He sat in his room
Dressed-up like a groom
Saying "I wonder just why she's so late!"

Yes, I believe in serendipity and in Fate, but *ya gotta get out there*!

1065

For **Single Women Only**: If he's hopeless . . . if you've tried everything, and nothing works . . . *Maybe He's Just A Jerk*. That's the title of a book by Carol Rosen, founder of the "Jerkline," a call-in phone line, and a collector of tales about women involved with "jerks." She defines the jerk in all his guises: Con man, sleazy lover, charming scoundrel, married seducer, mama's boy, batterer, critic and addict. She relates stories that range from the humorous to the tragic. The book lists national hotlines and self-help groups.

1066

Have you tried all the dating/mating/matching services to no avail? Has your life in the single lane gone to the dogs? Maybe you should base your next date on your mutual interest in pets! A national quarterly newsletter called *Single Pet Lovers* matches compatible animal aficionados. [I swear—now I've heard everything!] Among other pet-oriented info, the newsletter lists biographies of members along with, of course, their pet preferences. A subscription is $9.95. Write to Post Office Box 487, La Guardia, New York 11371.

1067

One of the major Singles Events of the year is the "April In Paris" weekend held at Kutscher's, a wonderful resort in Monticello, New York. The event is a sellout every year, with about 1,000 singles from around New York and around the country. They have so many activities going on that you'd have to stay locked in your room in order *not* to have a good time! In addition to dancing, nightclub entertainment, cocktail parties, swimming and tennis, they publish a special "Getting To Know You" journal including personal ads of all the participants. The April In Paris weekend is usually held during the second week of April every year. Call 800-431-1273.

1068

"Think Like A Married Person: Strategy #1"
Intimacy

Although you can't *force* intimacy, you *can* make it a goal. When you think about it, many goals of single folks are *short-term* at best, and downright *shallow* at worst: Relieving loneliness, "scoring," finding a great dance partner. If, instead, intimacy is your goal, you'll share more of yourself sooner, you'll communicate honestly, and you'll listen to the other more attentively. {So says Martin G., of Pittsburgh, Pennsylvania.}

1069

"Think Like A Married Person: Strategy #2"
Long-term thinking

The single brain is consumed with short-term goals: This Friday night, this Saturday night, what will I wear?—Will he kiss me tonight?—Will she sleep with me on the second date? *Chill-out*, singles! A long-term mindset will relieve a lot of your stress, help you be more "yourself," and give you a better perspective on things.

1070

"Think Like A Married Person: Strategy #3"
Communicating

Have you ever noticed that single people often do a lot of talking without really communicating much? The single scene is often characterized by a lot of posturing, boasting and clever bantering. Those who get beyond these things the most quickly tend to end up in the best relationships. {According to Eli W. of South Bend, Indiana.}

1071

50 Ways to Find a Lover—Proven Techniques for Finding Someone Special, by Sharyn Wolf. This wonderful, specific, straightforward and practical book literally lists and explains 50 ways. Here are a few of them: Identify where you get stuck most often. Make your imagination your asset. Create a buddy system. Get out of your rut. Do some reality testing. Take a class. [I met Tracey in a Mozart class at the Boston Center for Adult Education!] Sharyn Wolf knows what she's talking about. I've been on TV with her, so I know she's a cool person, in addition to being a psychotherapist and teacher of the popular courses "50 Ways to Find a Lover" and "72 Ways to Flirt."

1072

If you'd rather work one-on-one with a professional matchmaker instead of hiring a larger organization, here's one of the best: Ms. Wenty Kelleher, Community Yentl. I met her on a TV talk show, and was impressed with her sensitivity, caring attitude and "spiritual depth." She focuses on four areas: 1) Resolving past relationships, 2) Creating a "Master Plan" for your life, 3) Attracting a *compatible* mate, and 4) Developing a long-term relationship. She notes that "Many people have an easy enough time *finding* someone, but they have a hard time getting them to *stay* in their lives." Wenty conducts personal consultations in-person and via phone. Call her at 800-333-3731. [And yes, her name really is "Wenty"—and not "Wendy."]

> *"We Wobegonians...even when we are in love—what to us is romantic passion—appears as only mild interest . . . Because we're low-key people."*
>
> ~ *Garrison Keillor*

1073

Several single people (and one "formerly-single" person) wrote to recommend these matchmaking services.

- ♥ Los Angeles: Debra Winkler Personal Search, 310-553-7000. Co-founder of the largest singles organization in California; knows 3,600 professional people personally; instrumental in 224 marriages.
- ♥ San Diego (and several other cities): J. Wingo International, 619-558-6934. They utilize executive search techniques to match-up people of "substance and style."
- ♥ Atlanta: Traditional Matchmakers, 404-237-8593. "Romance made the old-fashioned way." [Hey, I *like* that!] Ask for Beatrice Gruss.
- ♥ New York City: Denise Winston, 212-935-9350. Professional, dignified and discreet introductions.

1074

Would you like to know *why* you've chosen the partners you have—and how to make *better* choices? Would you like to know the 10 types of relationships that won't work? Would you like to avoid "Compatibility Time Bombs"? If so, pick-up a copy of *Are You The One For Me? Knowing Who's Right & Avoiding Who's Wrong,* by Barbara DeAngelis, Ph.D., who is also the author of the #1 bestseller *Secrets About Men Every Woman Should Know.* This woman really knows how people tick! (And she's *also* the author of *How To Make Love All the Time.*—This woman is *busy!*)

1075

Need a clever ice-breaker? Try creating your own, personalized Personality Quiz to hand-out to potential dates. Here's a portion of one written by Brian Wicker, of St. Paul, Minnesota.

Entertainment, Attitude & Philosophy Quiz: Relationships 101

Your answers to the following questions will reveal an elaborate psychological profile of yourself. We already know you're unbalanced enough to voluntarily hang out with me, so we're just trying to help you before it's too late. There are no right answers, which should horrify the perfectionists and thrill the delinquents among you. Drinking during the quiz is strictly encouraged.

1. Men . . .
  a) . . . make life worth living.
  b) . . . have their faults, but they are easier to train than dogs.
  c) . . . are only good for lawn care and vehicle maintenance.
  d) . . . should be shot on sight, no questions asked.

2. The best film in history is . . .
  a) . . . Citizen Kane
  b) . . . Gone With the Wind
  c) . . . It's A Wonderful Life
  d) . . . The Wizard of Oz
  e) . . . I Was a Teenage Werewolf
  f) . . . Other

3. The perfect man resembles . . .
  a) . . . Albert Einstein, but is a better dancer.
  b) . . . Arnold Schwarzenegger, with better diction.
  c) . . . Cary Grant, but not dead.
  d) . . . Donald Trump, but with fewer tabloid headlines.
  e) . . . Danny DeVito, except shorter and fatter.

For Marrieds Only

1076

A plain old vacation is *not* the same thing as a "second honeymoon"! There's a special feeling of magic and romance around a second honeymoon. How do you create one? You start planning about a year in advance (so the anticipation builds). You buy her a stack of brides magazines (that's where all the honeymoon destination ads are). Send travel brochures to her in the mail (with your personal notes and comments written-in). You buy special clothes. If you do this right, it'll really spice up your life—for a year or more!

1077

"Think Like A Single Person: Strategy #1"
Singles dances

If you're stuck in the "Marriage Rut," and fantasizing about how great it was to be single, here's an exercise for you and your spouse to do together: Go to a singles dance. ("Are you crazy, Godek?!" Perhaps—but give me a minute more.) While you're there, do two things: 1) Watch all the singles closely. (Don't just watch their bodies and outfits—watch their body language and their eyes.) Are they happy? Do they want to remain single? 2) Pretend that you're meeting your spouse for the first time. Act-out some variation of a pick-up fantasy. Then go home together and live happily ever after.

1078

"Think Like A Single Person: Strategy #2"
Flirting

When's the last time you actually flirted with your own husband? Try it the next time you're out at a party together. (Don't be surprised if he wants to leave the party early!)

1079

"Think Like A Single Person: Strategy #3"
Instant gratification

The typical mindset of a married person is *long-term*. The *positive* side of this is that long-term can mean security, commitment and comfort; the *negative* side is that it can also mean boredom, laziness and non-activity. One way to combat this negative side is to adopt the mindset of a single person: It's a mindset of **instant gratification**. Horny? Make love *now*. Thinking of her?—Call her *now*. Appreciate him?—Hug him *now*. Walking through a mall?—Pick up a little love-gift *now*.

1080

"Think Like A Single Person: Strategy #4"
Seduction

When's the last time you seduced your spouse? How often do you bother to "set the mood," play the music, dress the part, say the right words, do the little things? {Sara Gudinoff, of Fort Lee, New Jersey, says her husband Stan is a "Master of Marital Seduction."}

1081

FYI, I carry my wedding license in my wallet at all times. Here's the way I figure it: I'm required to carry my driver's license, to prove I'm a legal driver—so why not carry this reminder of my legal/emotional/spiritual commitments to the Most Important Person In My World?! [Yes, I know I'm a little strange. It's been said before.]

1082

How well do you *really* know your spouse? If you're like many married people, you're sometimes a little bored with your partner, and you're secretly afraid that if you got to know him or her *better*, you'd be even *more* bored! Here's what Dr. Jane Shaw, the newspaper advice columnist says: "Far from producing boredom, a thorough understanding of another's inner life can lead to ever more rewarding exchanges, particularly if you've chosen your partner well." There's a Reason you're together, and the better you know one another, the more exciting your lives can become.

1083

Here's another "frame-it" idea: Frame the lyrics from a favorite song, from "Your Song," or from songs played at your wedding—as did Karen Garcia, of Fort Atkinson, Wisconsin.

Common Sense

1084

Be real. Be genuine. "To fake emotion is to sap all life and spontaneity from a connection," says Dr. Jane Shaw, newspaper advice columnist.

1085

Don't settle for a relationship that doesn't provide for all of your needs: Emotional and spiritual as well as practical and financial. When you "settle," you diminish the entire quality of your life; you de-value yourself. *No one* should "settle"! We all deserve wonderful, loving, expressive, growing relationships.

Getting what you deserve requires confidence, positive self-esteem, and a willingness to take responsibility for the state of your relationship. Passive people never have passionate lives.

1086

Buy an answering machine for your phone. I'm serious! Most of us are so conditioned to answer a ringing phone that we'd interrupt foreplay to answer the stupid thing! *Let it ring!* What in the world could be more important than giving your undivided attention to your partner— regardless of whether you're talking, dining, lazing or loving?!

1087

Use your strengths, talents, interests and abilities in creating romantic gifts, gestures, surprises and scenarios. Are you a singer, writer, baker, shopper, talker, listener, organizer, maker, runner, creator, finder . . . ?

1088

I believe that the best relationships are *well-balanced*. I'm not talking about a *delicate* balance. And I'm not talking about a *static* balance. I'm talking about a *dynamic, ever-changing* balance. "Love isn't weighed and dispensed in equal measures," says Leo Buscaglia, in *Born For Love.* "It is not possible, nor even desirable, that two people completely balance each other. Imbalance creates the challenge and motivation for growth."

Good relationships balance *over time.* This means that at any particular point in time, the relationship may appear to be quite *unbalanced*—One partner may be more nurturing; one may be more needy; one may be providing all the financial support, etc.—but if both partners are loving, understanding, giving, dedicated and flexible, then the relationship can handle all kinds of ups and downs, and still be strong, exciting—and, yes, romantic!

> *Women will forgive almost anything except being taken for granted—or ignored on Valentine's Day.*
>
> ~ *Michael Korda*

*Un*Common Sense

1089

Climbing trees can help you be more romantic!" exclaims Jason E., of Canandaigua, New York. He goes on to explain that he and his girlfriend of six years spent a week on an Outward Bound adventure, and it "helped both of us look at our lives differently. Among other things, we realized just how important we were to each other. We're now engaged!" While we can't promise you'll end up *engaged*, we *can* promise that Outward Bound will increase your self-confidence and boost your self-esteem! Call 'em at 800-243-8520.

1090

One therapist poses this pointed question to couples in marriage counseling: "What is your mistress?" She explains that she's not referring to infidelity, or even to a person. "*What* is your mistress? What activity are you passionate about that competes for your time?" Your work? Your golf? Your cars? Your hobbies? Your causes? Your sports?

She's not suggesting that you *give up* your mistress—just that you identify it, acknowledge it, and discuss it with your partner. She uses the word "mistress" instead of "interest" or even "passion" precisely because it's such an emotionally-charged word. It grabs your attention and makes you think.

I know it made *me* think. I realized that throughout my whole life—until recently—I've never had a mistress. This made it *easy* for me to focus a lot of romantic attention on the woman in my life. But recently—and ironically—*these books on romance have become my mistresses*! I'm able to put most of the rest of my life "on hold" in order to work on these books. I *love* doing this work! But sometimes I even put *Tracey* on hold. Needless to say, this is hard on our relationship. But we're workin' on it! We fight a little, talk a little, love a little. Actually, we fight a little, talk a *lot*, and love a *whole bunch*!

1091

I just recently learned about Great Hill—the Lovers Lane of my town. I've lived here 10 years, and I've *never* gone necking. [I must be slipping!]

If you no longer live in the town where you grew up, you probably don't know the great "make-out" spots in your town, either. Here's what you do: Find a teenager who isn't wearing a Walkman, and ask him. If they all play dumb—and bribery doesn't work—call your local police department, pose as a concerned parent looking for your wayward teenage daughter, and they'll tell you where it is! (The police are no fools—they know all the kids' hangouts!)

1092

You don't need to have Romance on your mind all the time in order to actually *be* Romantic. Some people are naturally inquisitive and childlike—they appreciate the wonder of every day. Other people are in-tune with the importance of learning and changing. Some folks don't see what all the fuss is about: They're just thoughtful and considerate. Other people are naturally sensitive and empathic. Some people live all of their lives in a passionate manner. Others are simply expressive. While some place great importance on creativity in their lives. Some people live their spiritual values. My guess is that all of these kinds of people live Romantic lives.

1093

If there ever was any doubt that romance was beneath the intelligentsia, let the doubters beware! The respected author and intellectual Susan Sontag has written a romance novel! The "intellectual champion of modernism"—author of such books as *Against Interpretation, Styles of Radical Will*, and *AIDS and Its Metaphors*—has written a romance called *The Volcano Lover*. [I *love* it when people defy the labels that others attach to them!] Described by *The New York Times Magazine* as "a hybrid of reason and romance," Sontag has given renewed respectability to a genre of books that, while very popular, are not exactly regarded as great literature. *Three cheers for romance*—in *any* of its forms!

1094

Make an *appointment* to make love. Hey, sometimes you just gotta schedule these things in!

1095

Stereotype-Busting:

☞ *Men aren't in touch with their feelings.* If that's true, why are rock stars from Paul McCartney to Elvis Costello, and Michael Jackson to Jackson Brown, pouring their hearts out in their songs?

☞ *Women aren't as tough or as strong as men.* If that's true, I know a couple of female graduates of West Point and Annapolis that I'd like to introduce you to.

1096

The Golden Rule doesn't always work! "Do unto others as you would have them do unto you" would lead clothes-lovers to buy their partners outfits; workaholics to buy their partners briefcases; and handymen to buy their wives tools! Try **The Platinum Rule**: "Do unto others as they want to be done unto." Think about it.

The Golden Rule leads you to buying *presents*, while the Platinum Rule leads you to buying *gifts*. [See the definitions of "gifts" and "presents" in the *Bonus Chapter: Highlights from the First Book*.]

1097-1103

How many different ways can you think of to communicate with your lover?

* You could learn sign language—You *could* learn just the sign for "Love," or you could both learn to "speak" in sign language, which would allow you to say all kinds of outrageous things to each other across crowded rooms!
* You could learn a foreign language (one of the *Romance* languages!)
* You could learn Morse Code!
* You can communicate through comics, lovesongs and newspaper articles.
* You can send messages via fax, mail, modem, Western Union or Federal Express.
* You can write notes, letters, poems and limericks.
* You can send a message with a book title or album title.

Lovesongs

1104-1105

- Romantic movie classics from a well-known favorite: The CD or cassette *As Time Goes By—And other Classic Movie Love Songs* by Henry Mancini and the Mancini Pops Orchestra. 15 songs total, including timeless movie love songs like "Everything I Do" and "Unchained Melody."

- New music from a romantic newcomer: Warren Hill, with his album *Kiss Under the Moon*. Great, jazzy, romantic, clarinet-led instrumentals. (Warren opened for Natalie Cole during her "Unforgettable" tour.)

1106

For the rock music fan—*and* for the classical music aficionado: A very clever concept and a great recording: **What If Mozart Wrote "Born To Be Wild."** The cassette goes for $10.95, and the CD for $16.95. Call the Wireless Catalog at 800-669-9999.

1107-1108

❦ An instant romantic classic: *Unforgettable*—Natalie Cole sings the greatest hits of her father, Nat King Cole.

❦ Original romantic classics: *Nat King Cole and the King Cole Trio* are captured in this set of original recordings from the 1940s. The 78 selections include "Paper Moon," "I Got Rhythm," "I Can't Give You Anything But Love," and dozens more. Over 3-1/2 hours of music. Five cassettes for $19.95, or five CDs for $36.95. Call the *Wireless Catalog* at 800-669-9999.

1109

Bruce Springsteen, during opening night of his American Tour 1992 in East Rutherford, New Jersey, July 23: "We have a sponsor tonight. I'm not going to sell you beer or sell you sneakers. Our sponsor is *love*. This next section of the show is for lovers only." There followed several new songs—the powerful "Leap of Faith" (about having "the guts" to fall in love), the R&B version of "Man's Job" and the rollicking "Roll of the Dice."

1110

The World's largest CD catalog: *BOSE Express Music.* 75,000 titles! It's the ultimate CD, tape and video sourcebook in the world. Includes over 1,000 independent labels (including impossible to find labels like Cheskey, Pausa and Alligator!) Only $6, refunded with your first order. Free updates! 800-451-BOSE; The Mountain, Framingham, Massachusetts 01701.

1111

Tracey introduced me to the music of Jon Gailmor, and I'll always be grateful. Our favorite album is *Generations*, which is a "theme album" of songs revolving around family relationships. Some of these songs will bring tears to your eyes. Jon Gailmor is a Vermont folk hero with a devoted following. I invite you to join us. Membership is just $8.50 (for the cassette) or $15 (for the CD). Call Green Linnett Records at 800-468-6644 or 203-730-0333, or write for a catalog: 43 Beaver Brook Road, Danbury, Connecticut 06810. (The catalog also features a wide variety of World Music, with artists from a variety of traditions and cultures.)

1112-1114

Say, "Hello, Love," in three different ways, courtesy of the *Wireless Catalog*!

* Garrison Keillor's *Hello Love* video: A salute to love by Garrison and guests Doc Watson, Emmylou Harris, Kate MacKenzie and Leo Kottke. Music and humor, including Keillor's own mock-epic love poem "The Finn Who Would Not Take a Sauna," and a special Valentine's Day edition of "The News from Lake Wobegon." ($19.95)

* Two albums for lovers and lovers of opera:
    * *Amore* (as reported in *1001 Ways To Be Romantic*) is a collection of 23 of the most romantic love songs ever written, magnificently performed by Luciano Pavarotti, Kiri Te Kanawa, Richard Tucker and other opera stars.
    * And now . . . a new album called . . . *More Amore* features eight passionate duets from Aida, Don Giovanni, Otello, Tosca and other operas. Each is available on cassette ($8.95) and CD ($12.95) from the *Wireless Catalog*: Call 800-669-9999.

1115

And speaking of *duets* . . . Here are some of more recent vintage:

- ❖ *Almost Paradise*, Reno & Wilson
- ❖ *Always*, Atlantic Starr
- ❖ *Don't Know Much*, Ronstadt & Neville
- ❖ *I Got You Babe*, Sonny & Cher
- ❖ *Islands in the Stream*, Parton & Rogers
- ❖ *Love Makes Things Happen*, Pebbles & Babyface
- ❖ *Nothing's Gonna Stop Us Now*, Starship
- ❖ *Opposites Attract*, Paula Abdul & MC Skat Cat
- ❖ *Somewhere Out There*, Ronstadt & Ingram
- ❖ *Time of My Life*, Dirty Dancing

1116

Some favorite songs from readers.

- ☆ *Shelter of Your Love*, Jimmy Cliff
- ☆ *I'll Always Love You*, Tayler Dayne
- ☆ *True Love*, Bing Crosby
- ☆ *Suddenly*, Billy Ocean
- ☆ *Take My Breath Away*, Berlin
- ☆ *Rambling Rose*, Nat King Cole
- ☆ *I (Who Have Nothing)*, Tom Jones
- ☆ *In Your Eyes*, Peter Gabriel
- ☆ *You're My World*, Helen Reddy
- ☆ *To Be With You*, Mister Big
- ☆ *Time In a Bottle*, Jim Croce
- ☆ *Dream On*, Oak Ridge Boys
- ☆ *Wonderful Tonite*, Eric Clapton
- ☆ *Overjoyed*, Stevie Wonder
- ☆ *Have I Told You Lately That I Love You*, Van Morrison
- ☆ *Evergreen*, Barbra Streisand
- ☆ *Lady*, Kenny Rogers

1117

One musically-oriented couple has ongoing written conversations that consist entirely of song titles! One of them will start a conversation by jotting down an expressive song title and either mailing it to the other, or attaching it to the refrigerator, or tucking it into the other's briefcase. Some sample conversations:

Him: *You are my lady.*
Her: *You are the sunshine of my life.*
Him: *I'm so excited!*
Her: *Great balls of fire!*
Him: *I got you, babe.*
Her: *I feel good!*

Her: *I'm in the mood for love.*
Him: *Some enchanted evening.*
Her: *I want to hold your hand.*
Him: *I can't give you anything but love.*
Her: *Why do I love you?*
Him: *Opposites attract!*

Him: *Don't wanna lose you.*
Her: *Girls just wanna have fun.*
Him: *I wanna dance with somebody.*
Her: *Walk like an Egyptian.*
Him: *Love me tender.*
Her: *You'll always be the one I love.*
Him: *My one and only love.*
Her: *You're nobody 'til somebody loves you.*

Him: *Let's spend the night together.*
Her: *We've only just begun.*
Him: *I can't get no–satisfaction!*
Her: *You can't always get what you want!*

1118

Is there an Al Jarreau Fan Club out there somewhere? [If not, there *should* be!] I've gotten 53 letters (so far) chastising me for omitting him from the first book. All right, all *right!*—I'm sorry! For those of you unfamiliar with the romantic warbling songmeister, here are some of his albums:

- ❖ *Breakin' Away*
- ❖ *High Crime*
- ❖ *All Fly Home*
- ❖ *Hearts Horizon*
- ❖ *Heaven & Earth*

- ❖ *In London*
- ❖ *Jarreau*
- ❖ *L is for Lover*
- ❖ *Look to the Rainbow*
- ❖ *This Time*

Love Stories

1119

[I *swear* that this one is true! It was told to me by a reliable eyewitness.] "Jim" has a flair for the dramatic, and he knew that "Sue" wasn't exactly the shy type. (It's a good thing!) Here's how he proposed marriage to her: They were at a community theatre showing of "Peter Pan." During the intermission, Peter Pan suddenly appeared on stage and told the audience that he had an announcement to make. He began talking about a "special couple" in the audience. Meanwhile, Tinkerbell flew out over the audience, landed in front of Sue, and presented her with a diamond ring from Jim. (A little fairy dust never hurt anyone's relationship!)

1120

Barbara Lazear Ascher's husband lay in a hospital bed dying. Here's what she wrote:

"When you look in the face of death, what becomes perfectly clear and suddenly simple is that there is only one priority. And that is love . . . We had set about our lives together to make certain that they would be just that—together. Our offices were within walking distance of our home so that we could eat three meals a day in each other's company. We had slept in the same bed each night, even when there had been a terrible fight and one of us would have preferred the solitary comfort of another room. In sleep there is forgiveness—and an arm or leg that would reach out to find solace in touch. Ours had not been a romance full of extravagant gifts, frequent roses, or nights of dancing. There was a lot of hard work and routine. There was also 'I love you,' first thing in the morning and last thing at night." [Surprise happy ending: Baffling the doctors, he had a miraculous recovery.]

Barbara Lazear Ascher is an essayist and the author of *Landscape Without Gravity: A Memoir of Grief.* The above quote is from *Redbook,* February 1992.

1121

She was in theatre; he was in the French and Indian War. Well, actually, he's into 18th Century battle reenactments. She was acting in a "traveling medicine show" at the Penn's Colony Festival, in Prospect, Pennsylvania; he was in uniform as part of the Festival. The maiden bumped into the soldier. Sparks flew. He cooked dinner for her over a campfire. They talked of life. They talked about families and children. They had a *lot* in common. The soldier said, "If you could put-up with this hobby of mine—which keeps me busy every summer—and you're interested in marriage and a family, then I'll love you forever." Six months later they were engaged. {The maiden is played by Deborah Jarecki, of Butler, Pennsylvania; the soldier is played by Dave Bybee, of Harrisburg.}

1122

Here's a little story of how I changed a romantic surprise mid-stream, and how I *still* managed to incorporate a surprise into the event. Tracey had fallen in love with Natalie Cole's album "Unforgettable." One day in the Sunday *New York Times* I see an ad for Natalie Cole in concert at Radio City Music Hall. So of course I immediately call for tickets and then rip the evidence out of the paper. I tell Tracey to reserve the date—two months hence—but tell her it's a surprise. About two weeks later it occurs to me that with many events—like Christmas—the *anticipation* is just as much fun as the event itself. So I told Tracey about the concert. Actually, I wrapped-up the tickets and presented them to her. [Why not add a little flair?!] She was thrilled, and had great fun looking forward to the concert. There was, however, one *little* piece of information that I held back: The fact that we had *front row seats*!

1123

Charlie Pellett and his girlfriend Randi Minsky were seated side-by-side in First Class aboard Continental Airlines flight 191 from Newark to San Francisco. "I have an important announcement for the lady in seat 3-L," said the pilot over the intercom. "Will you marry the gentleman in seat 3-K? If the answer is *yes*, press the call button for the flight attendant." As Randi burst into tears, Charlie kept saying "Push the button!" When she did, a flight attendant came along carrying a silver tray with two glasses of wine and the ring! {Charlie, a news writer at WINS-Radio in New York City, is also a plane nut who collects airport postcards. His wife Randi is a schoolteacher.}

1124

Tom arrived home from running some errands one Saturday morning to find his wife, Susan, gone. His daughter handed him a note from her: "Go to the drug store. See the pharmacist." Even though his first reaction was, "Why? Who's sick?" he went along—What else *could* he do but follow instructions? When he started up the car, a tape of romantic music was set to play. ("Ah, ha! I think something's going on here!") The pharmacist had a card for him: "Happy Anniversary!—Now, head for the liquor store!" A bottle of champagne was waiting for him there, along with another note: "Ready to celebrate? Not yet! On to the men's shop first!" A monogrammed shirt was his surprise there. The note was no longer a surprise: "Almost done! But first, please stop at the grocery store." A picnic basket packed with goodies was ready to go. The last note simply had an address on it. It led him to a romantic little bed and breakfast, where Susan was waiting for him. The rest, as they say, is history!

*The anticipation is often just as much fun
as the event or gift itself.*

1125

Sometimes you just have to tell these guys *exactly* what to do. (Ah, but when you *do*, you usually get *exactly what you want!*) She planned the whole vacation to Paris—just one week in advance! Here are some selections from her note to him: "Once you complete OPERATION PASSPORT, your next Mission, should you decide to accept it, is to pick-up your traveling papers from a tall, 'perky' brunette with brown eyes in the City of Brookline, USA. You will be traveling under the code name VALENTINE. When you meet her, you will be carrying a single flower. You will give her this flower and whisper 'sweet nothings' in her left ear. She will then know that you are VALENTINE." {Concept courtesy of the creative mind of Julie Gouldman, Brookline, Massachusetts.}

Words of Love

1126

"Your words should be like *little silver boxes*," says professional speaker Florence Littauer. She uses this vivid image in a wonderful, inspiring talk that reminds us how important our words are. What we say has powerful effects on those around us, especially on those we love the most. Are your words precious gifts, or are they careless, hurtful, judgmental attacks? Your words have *power*: Use them to heal, to connect, to warm, to love! (One of Florence's listeners put little wrapped boxes in every room of her house to remind her!)

1127

* A book of daily thoughts/affirmations/reflections on love: *A Garland of Love: Daily Reflections on the Magic and Meaning of Love*, by Daphne Rose Kingma.
* And a nice little book of thoughts and suggestions for making your relationship "sweeter, deeper and more passionate": *True Love*, also by Daphne Rose Kingma.

1128

In *1001 Ways To Be Romantic* I told you how to say "I love you" in 15 different languages. Today's language lesson is how to say "Newlywed" in 11 languages. Why would you want to know that? Because newlyweds often get extra-special treatment when traveling in foreign countries! (Maybe someone should invent the Newlywed Card: "Don't leave home without it"—Good for hotel rooms with a view and better tables in restaurants around the world!"

- ❂ Italian: *Novelli sposi* (no-VEL-ee SPOZ-ee)
- ❂ French: *Nouveaux marie's* (noo-VOH mahr-ee-AY)
- ❂ Spanish: *Recie'n casado* (ray-SYEHN kah-SAH-doh)
- ❂ German: *Hochzeitspaar* (HOK-tsites-par)
- ❂ Greek: *Nionymphi* (nyo-NIM-fee)
- ❂ Danish: *Nygifte* (nye-YIFT-ah)
- ❂ Swedish: *Nygifta* (nye-YIFT-ah)
- ❂ Japanese: *Shin kon* (shin kone)
- ❂ Chinese: *Xin hun* (shing hoon)
- ❂ Portuguese: *Re'cem casados* (RAY-seem ka-SAH-thos)
- ❂ Russian: *Novobrachnoe* (no-vo-BRACH-noy-eh)

{Thanks to *Glamour Magazine* and Harlequin.}

1129

Words that men love to hear:

- ✦ "I believe in you."
- ✦ "I want you."
- ✦ "You're the greatest."

Words that women love to hear:

- ➤ "I cherish you."
- ➤ "I need you."
- ➤ "I adore you."

1130

The "Stream-of-Consciousness Letter"—or "Zubey Letter," named after its creator. Get a sheet of paper (lined or blank, tablet-sized or poster-sized). Print her name in the center in large block letters. Then, starting in the upper left corner, start writing anything that comes into your mind that has to do with her, you, or your relationship. Anything is fine: Complete sentences, sentence fragments, single words, places, things, ideas, memories, etc. Keep writing until you fill the entire page! Take several days or weeks to complete it, if necessary. Have fun! *Tracey Ellen. The Saint Bonaventure. Maureen's wedding. The apple orchard. Gary's car. Hungry i. Wolfgang Amadeus Mozart. The John B. Hynes Veterans Memorial Convention Center. Jupiter! "I like a man with a VCR." What else can I do?— I'm so in love with you. I.L.Y.—A.D.Y.F.I.(F.A.S!). Mars—Needs—Women. You can leave your hat on.* {Thanks to Jason Zubey!}

1131

When all else fails, *hire a professional—even* when it comes to love! Martine Greber, founder of Love Letters Ink, will write *custom* love letters for you, based on your input! They'll then render the letter in calligraphy on fine paper, from delicate handmade florals to exotic Japanese. Your love letter is then rolled, tied with a satin ribbon, sealed in a protective tube, and delivered. Martine also writes wedding letters, holiday letters, get-well letters, and just about anything else you can think of. She also has a catalog of pre-written letters that can be personalized for you in a flash! Prices start around $16.95. Overnight delivery is, of course, available. Martine understands all about those "romantic emergencies"! Write to 329 North Wetherly Drive, Suite 102, Beverly Hills, California 90211, or call 213-275-8441 or 800-448-WORD.

1132

Get her a wristwatch. Inscribe it with: *I always have time for you.*

1133

Communication between lovers must occur on *parallel channels* in order for it to be successful. Everyday communication takes place *head-to-head*. But *intimate* communication takes place *heart-to-heart*. Things get messed-up when you try to talk heart-to-head. Suzy Sutton, a very insightful professional speaker, notes that talking head-to-head is safer; but that talking heart-to-heart has the potential to build true intimacy. It's worth the risk!

(There *is* one *additional* channel of communication that can *really* mess things up: That's groin-to-groin communication. Parallel communication here is truly ecstatic!—But the groin-to-heart connection is the stuff of soap operas!)

Potpourri

1134

Tim and Tammy Smith, of Dallas, Texas, have created a "Romance Credit Card." Here's how it works: They've created their own "bank" which issues two types of credit: Money and time. On a quarterly basis the bank's officers (Tim and Tammy) meet to establish their credit limits. When cash is tight, they provide for more time. [Great concept!] They keep their credit card balances on a chart on the refrigerator, and they each carry a "Romance Credit Card" in their wallets as a reminder that they have an obligation to spend a little time and money on their relationship on a regular basis. [I wish I'd thought-up this one.]

1135

And now . . . some *pet-oriented* catalogs and products for you animal lovers.

☞ *Pedigrees*—"The catalog for pets with personality." Free catalog: Newsweek Reader Service Program, Post Office Box 5283, Pittsfield, Massachusetts 01203-9978.

☞ *The Artful Fish*—"A catalog of fine fish exotica for true 'afishionados'!" Free catalog: Post Office Box 40-a, Santa Cruz, California 95063, or call 800-525-6777.

☞ *The Crazy Cat Lady Catalog*—"High-style alternatives to the typical tacky-looking cat supplies." $1 to Box 691920, Los Angeles, California 90069.

☞ *Hep Cat*, a catalog of gifts for cat lovers. Just $1 to Department 7, Post Office Box 120122, Nashville, Tennessee 37212.

☞ *Passports for Pets* are great little gifts for the dog-lover or cat-fancier in your life. "Feline Passports" and "Canine Passports" are little, official-looking books that include helpful facts and fun trivia, plus space to record important info and memorable moments in your pet's life! These "Permits to Health & Happiness" are available from PetTrackers for just $4.95 each! Call 800-345-VETS.

1136

If your partner is a fan of one of the people/characters below, you could get him or her a "Lifesize Standup":

➤ Madonna	➤ Janet Jackson	➤ Larry Bird
➤ Marilyn Monroe	➤ Kiefer Sutherland	➤ Clint Eastwood
➤ John Wayne	➤ James Dean	➤ Barbara Bush
➤ President Bush	➤ Betty Grable	➤ Albert Einstein
➤ Robo Cop	➤ Michael Jackson	➤ Archie
➤ Magic Johnson	➤ Frankenstein	➤ Captain Kirk
➤ Jughead	➤ Bugs Bunny	➤ Dr. McCoy
➤ Santa Claus	➤ Michael Jordan	➤ Mr. Spock
➤ Wayne Gretzky	➤ Wade Boggs	

These things are free-standing, full-color, full-sized (even Larry Bird!) laminated cardboard cut-outs. Very cool! They range in price from about $20 to $30. Call Advanced Graphics at 510-370-9200, or write to 982 Howe Road, Martinez, California 94553.

1137

Always have at least one set of tickets for an upcoming event tacked to your bulletin board. It's always good to have some special event to look forward to. (The anticipation is half the fun!)

1138

Bouquets of flowers are fine . . . but creative romantics have reported . . .

- Homemade bouquets of cookies. {Diane C., New Castle, Delaware.}
- Homemade bouquets of $10 bills. {Bob S., Grundy, Iowa.}
- Homemade bouquets of tea bags. {Sidney M., Franklin, Louisiana.}
- Homemade bouquets of autumn leaves. {Andrea R., Boston.}

1139

Hand-crafted gifts that not only bring joy to the recipient, but also bring dignity and autonomy to craftspeople in developing regions around the world—are available from the *SERRV—Self-Help Handcrafts Catalog*. SERRV is a non-profit organization representing over 3,000 products from 40 countries. A very small sampling includes: Hand-carved wooden boxes and animals; baskets, brass and bags; pillows, pottery and paintings; chimes, coffee, clothing and chocolate; linens; wall hangings; toys; dolls and ornaments. Write to New Windsor Service Center 500 Main Street, Post Office Box 365, New Windsor, Maryland 21776-0365, or call 800-423-0071.

1140

Don't just "do it"—do it with *flair!*

1141

And then, of course, there's always the *umbrella-built-for-two!*

Awakening Your Senses

1142

"The Complete Musical Massage" is a complete package for your senses of touch, smell and hearing. Start by learning the art of massage with the 20-page Massage Booklet. Then reach for the bottle of fragrant massage oil. And complete the soothing environment with an hour of tranquil instrumental music, including Pachelbel's *Canon*. Just $24.95, through the *Signals Catalog*. Call 800-669-9696.

1143

The "Fragrance Ring" is one of my *favorite* discoveries of the past year. It's a way to fill your home with a delicate aroma that's longer-lasting than flowers, yet not as overpowering as incense can be. The Fragrance Ring is an aluminum ring that you place on a light bulb. You place several drops of this *Environmental Fragrance Oil* stuff into the ring. Then, when the light is switched-on, the ring heats-up, vaporizing the fragrant oil, which perfumes the whole room for hours. A variety of fragrances are available, including Southhampton Rose, Fairhaven Peach, Spring Rain, Nantucket Briar, Veranda, and Noel! The ring is just $3, and the fragrance oils are around $5 each—from Crabtree & Evelyn. Visit a boutique or call 800-289-1222.

1144

A Natural History of the Senses is an unusual book that will heighten your appreciation of *all* your senses. It's an erudite grand tour of the senses. It includes conversations with an iceberg in Antarctica and a professional nose in New York. There are dissertations on kisses and tattoos. And reflections on the music played by the planet Earth. Author Diane Ackerman has a flair for poetic prose, itself a feast for the senses!

1145

Hold a conversation with your lover *in the dark*. Shut out inputs from your other senses, and focus on the *sound* of your partner's voice: Its ups and downs, its unique qualities and quirks. Listen for the love behind the words. Listen. *Listen. Listen!*

1146

Try a little "foot reflexology." It's a form of foot massage based on the premise that there is a specific relationship between areas of the feet and other parts of the body. [It's kind-of like chiropractic, I think.] But aside from the health benefits—it just feels *great!* Your partner will appreciate your touch and your attention, especially at the end of a long, hard day on his or her feet! To get you started: *The Complete Guide to Foot Reflexology*, by Kevin and Barbara Kunz.

1147

I n c o g n i t o — O b s e s s i o n — P o i s o n — P a s s i o n
O p i u m — T a b u — T r o p i c s — U n f o r g e t t a b l e
I m p u l s e — B a b e — N a r c i s s e — D e s t i n y
P h e r m o n e — E t e r n i t y — E s c a p e — V o l u p t e
S p e l l b o u n d — A n i m a l e — S a f a r i — R e d — P r i m o

They're not only perfumes—they're *messages*. Attach a note. Write a poem. Create a fantasy. Combine with other gifts. Use your imagination!

1148

Create a "Five-Sense Evening," during which you and your lover stimulate *all five* of each other's senses. Enjoy!

1149-1152

Use more than one sense in your romantic communications. Because our sense of smell is our most under-utilized sense, here are some ways of adding some sensuous aroma to your lover's life:

- ✦ Don't just send a love letter—Send a *perfumed* love letter!

- ✦ Don't just buy any old bouquet of flowers—ask your FTD florist to suggest some especially fragrant flowers. Here's a start: Freesia, lilacs, stock, gardenias, Casablanca lilies, Rubrum lilies and Stephanotis.

- ✦ Don't just hide some lingerie in his briefcase—add a dash of his favorite perfume.

- ✦ Perfume his pillow as a signal that you want to make love tonight.

{Thanks to Christine Cafasso, of Redding, Connecticut.}

1153

In the process of getting to know one another, people in *new* relationships tend to utilize *all* of their senses. It's largely an unconscious thing. They touch one another a lot; they snuggle close and smell the other's unique odors; they gaze at one another; they listen to one another; and they kiss and taste one another. The use of all five senses helps you learn about the other person, and it enhances, deepens and speeds the process of building intimacy.

People in *established* relationships tend to fall into patterns of focusing on just one or two senses and virtually ignoring the others. One way of getting "back in touch" (pun intended) with your partner is to re-introduce the missing senses. An enhanced appreciation of the senses parallels an enhanced appreciation of your lover.

1154

People tend to have "dominant modes" in their use of the senses: Most people's modes are Visual, Auditory, or Kinesthetic. The *good* news is that you can utilize your dominant mode as a natural way of generating romantic ideas. The *bad* news is that partners who have *different* dominant modes often miscommunicate. The *good* news is that you can learn a lot from your partner, if you're not too pig-headed. {Thanks to professional speaker Greg Fitzgerald.}

Simple & Quick Ideas

1155

"*Balance*—is that what you find yourself hungering for? Do you search for calm and quiet while feeling overwhelmed by the daily pressures of our fast-paced society? . . . Has your life become your to-do list?" If so, do yourself a favor and pick-up *Delights, Dilemmas and Decisions—The Gift of Living Lightly*, by Maggie Bedrosian. This guidebook is designed to help you give yourself a break. It includes a Life Balance Inventory, to help you assess how much balance you have in seven zones of life: Health, career, finance, community, family, spirit and self. Rather than offering the perfect blueprint for balance that everyone can follow, the stories invite you to revisit your own choices, your own values, your own flaws, talents, hopes and dreams.

1156

Grab a calculator. Figure out how much money you spend on beer in an average month. Take that money to your local FTD florist and buy as many flowers as you can. (Some of you may need to rent a U-Haul to carry all the flowers back home.) [Hey, quit yer grumblin'—You could probably stand to skip the beer and lose a few pounds anyway.]

1157

Pick up the phone. Call your travel agent. Book a weekend in the Bahamas. [That was easy, wasn't it?]

1158

Head for the nearest mall. Enter the record store. Buy everything ever recorded by Al Jarreau and Luther Vandross. And George Winston. Oh, and George Benson. —Don't forget William Ackerman. And, as long as you're there, grab everything by David Lanz, too.

1159

Write "I Love You" on the driveway with chalk.

1160

Don't have time to dilly-dally over selecting just the right flowers for her? Here's a simple two-step solution: 1) Call 800-SEND-FTD, 2) Ask for the "Basket of Love," "You Send Me," or "Cherished Expressions."

1161

Give her a face massage. Give him a foot massage.

1162-1163

✓ Look through your wedding album together. Re-live the memories. (Then re-live your honeymoon!)

✓ Take a favorite photo from your wedding album—or from any album—attach a "cartoon balloon" to it, and mail it to him at work.

Complicated &
Time-Consuming Ideas

1164

The theatrically-oriented among you—or the just plain hams—may want to . . .

☞ . . . Follow Larry D's lead and act-out a scene from a favorite movie or play. "This requires both partners to be playful, creative, and flexible," Larry advises. Larry and Ms. X (he won't let me name her) from Boston have played Romeo and Juliet; Harry and Sally (from the movie *When Harry Met Sally*); and Rick and Ilsa in a variety of scenes from *Casablanca*.

☞ Howard and Janet B., of St. Paul, Minnesota, don't act-out movie scenes, but they do sometimes "do crazy things" with costumes at home. Most of their adventures start with homemade costumes. They rented costumes only once: "My tin-foil creation looked more like a robot from Dr. Who than a Knight In Shining Armor, so I broke down and rented a suit of armor from a local theatre company."

1165

Howard T., from "Somewhere east of the Mississippi, and south of Memphis" has a "very time-consuming and dirty way of communicating my love to my wife. And I mean 'dirty' as in dirt, not as in X-rated!" [Why are all of my readers punsters?!] You see, Howard is an avid gardener. Loves flowers. About 12 years ago, he designed his garden into letters spelling "I LOVE YOU." The message can only be read from their second-story bedroom window; the letters aren't recognizable from street level. "When my wife first noticed it, she nearly fell out of the window!" Howard reports. Anyway, Howard's gardens are usually complete messages. But for their 25th wedding anniversary, Howard simply designed the numbers "25" and presented his wife with an original, hand-written poem. [Way-to-go, Howard!]

1166

Use your (or your lover's) favorite TV show as the inspiration to create a date, a dinner . . . or a dinner theatre! . . .

The Star Trek Dinner Theater

A breakthrough in interplanetary dining, *Star Trek Dinner Theater* provides out-of-this-world food and entertainment at starbase prices. Where else can you toss back a Saurian brandy or a glass of Tranya while waiting for your meal and watching a favorite *Star Trek* episode?

What they're saying around the universe about the *Star Trek Dinner Theater*:

➤ *"I find the concept fascinating."* ~ Mr. Spock

➤ *"They don't put enough salt on the food."* ~ The M113 Creature

➤ *"We cruise the lounge whenever we're in this quadrant looking for husbands."* ~ Mudd's Women

This week's specials:

* *Vulcan Barbecued Chicken*: This would be Mr. Spock's favorite, if he weren't a vegetarian. A popular choice among the lizard-like Gorns, who occasionally wait until the chicken is dead before eating it.
* *Klingon Lemon Glazed Ribs*: This delicacy is one of the few concessions the Klingons make to fine dining, normally preferring to drink T.J. Swann and cruise around the galaxy stealing hubcaps off parked Federation shuttlecrafts.
* *The Bacon-Hamburger-Bean-Wrath of Khan Hotdish*: An old family favorite of Hkan Noonian Singh, who brought the recipe with him into space from the Eugenics Wars on Earth in the 1990s. Not served when *Fantasy Island* is showing in the lounge, no matter how much anyone begs.

[This concept is easily transferrable to *any* favorite TV show (or movie). Imagine the possibilities!—*A Cosby Cookout*—*The Roseanne Restaurant*—*The Lucy Luncheonette*—*The Seinfeld Comedy Club*—*The Oprah Lounge*—*The Donahue Diner!*] {This outpouring of creativity is from Brian Wicker, St. Paul, Minnesota, who sends his love across time and space to his girlfriend Joan Guilfoyle.}

1167

I'm quite familiar with "surprise birthday parties"—but a "surprise wedding"?! This one comes from John S., who related this idea to me and about a million other people in New Jersey and Metro New York, on NJ-101.5-radio in Trenton. For his 20th wedding anniversary, John surprised his wife by creating the following wedding scene . . . Officiating: The priest who originally married them! Guests: About 25 friends and family. Location: The chapel in the hospital where their two children were born. [Cool, huh?] Needless to say, John pulled-off one of the biggest (and most appreciated) surprises of the decade.

1168

When most people decorate or re-design their homes, they plan and sketch; they read home improvement magazines; they hire interior designers; they spend Big Bucks; they consider color, space, texture and style—but how many of them consider "romance" as a design element or a goal of the entire project? Why not design a home with "romance" as its guiding principle?

1169

Nora S., of Franklin, Alabama, has a husband who tinkers with his car "incessantly." This used to bother Nora, until she decided to make that car her medium for communicating with hubby. Her most time-consuming project was a love note attached to the end of the car's oil dip stick! She had a tiny slip of metal engraved with "I love you, Dave! Your Nora" and then carefully wired it to the end of the dip stick. Ol' Dave couldn't believe his squinting eyes! (And then, of course, there was the time that Nora was waiting for him in the back seat of the car, dressed "provocatively, shall we say?! I'd better leave it at that!" she says. *Vroom!*)

Oh, Canada!

1170

Newfoundland & Labrador—800-563-6353

* Visit villages with names like Heart's Delight, Come By Chance and Ha Ha Bay.
* Go whalewatching. Visit the first Viking settlement in North America at L'Anse Aux Meadows National Park.
* If you like birds, you must visit Bird Rock at Cape St. Mary's Ecological Reserve, on the Avalon Peninsula.

1171

St. John's—709-576-8106

* "St. John's is a city that combines Dublin and San Francisco", says Eileen B., of Chicago.
* Enjoy the oldest annual sports event in North America: St. John's Regatta, every August on Quidi Vidi Lake.

1172

Nova Scotia—800-341-6096

* If you like the ocean, you'll *love* Nova Scotia. No matter where you travel in this province, you're never more than 35 miles from the sea!
* Mile after mile of sandy, uncrowded beaches.
* Apple blossoms scent the air every spring in Annapolis Valley.
* Nova Scotia hosts over 350 festivals every year, celebrating everything from lobsters to Scottish culture!

1173

Prince Edward Island—800-565-0267

✴ Beach lovers *love* Prince Edward Island—it has the warmest waters north of Florida, thanks to the Gulf Stream!
✴ Fishermen looking for trout and Atlantic salmon come in droves.
✴ Also, wonderful arts and crafts.
✴ Visit the farmhouse that was the setting for Lucy Maud Montgomery's novel *Anne of Green Gables*, in Cavendish.

1174

Quebec—800-363-7777

✴ Take a romantic cruise on the Richelieu River, in Monteregie, the "Garden of Quebec."
✴ Visit the spectacular Montmorency Falls—one-and-a-half times higher than Niagara Falls.
✴ And, of course, there's Montreal—the Paris of North America—the second-largest French speaking city in the world: Host to the largest jazz festival in the world; over 4,000 restaurants and outdoor cafes; and haute couture on Rue Sainte-Catherine, trendy fashions on Boulevard Saint-Laurent, and antiques on Rue Notre-Dame.
✴ Did you know that Quebec City stages the biggest winter carnival in the world?
✴ Orford for watersports and horseback riding. North Hatley for lovely country inns, art galleries and antique shops. Dunham for Victorian style amid numerous vineyards.

1175

New Brunswick—800-561-0123

✴ The Saint John River plunges at Grand Falls, creating the second largest falls east of Niagara Falls.
✴ Vast evergreen forests, majestic rivers and lakes, and over 1,200 miles of warm, sandy beaches and sheltered coves.
✴ Watch whales at Passamaquoddy Bay. Watch birds at Grand Manan Island.

1176

Ontario—800-ONTARIO

* Shakespeare in Stratford!
* Oktoberfest in Kitchener—the largest such celebration outside of Germany.
* Toronto: 130 theatre companies; the CN Tower's revolving restaurant.
* Thunder Bay: A superior outdoor wonderland along Lake Superior.
* Legend has it that Napoleon's brother traveled by stage coach all the way from New Orleans to Niagara Falls for his honeymoon, thereby starting a tradition that still lives today!

1177-1182

Manitoba—800-665-0040

* Lakes for water sports. Northern Lights for your viewing pleasure.

Saskatchewan—800-667-7191

* Healing mineral waters at Little Manitou Lake. Plus 100,000 more lakes!

Alberta—800-661-8888

* The spectacular Canadian Rockies. Falher, the honey capital of the world.

British Columbia—800-663-6000

* The Pacific Coast. The Rocky Mountains. Whistler Resort: Ranked the #1 ski resort in North America!

Northwest Territories—800-661-0788

* Adventure vacations, anyone? Cruise the Northwest Passage amid icebergs.

Yukon—403-667-5340

* The highest mountains in North America! Pan for gold in Dawson City!

America, America!

1183

Did you know that America has 263 tourist rail lines? Here are a few favorites among the well-trained:

☆ North Conway, New Hampshire: Conway Scenic Railroad. Open observation cars, 11-mile trip. 800-356-5251.

☆ Strasburg, Pennsylvania: Strasburg Rail Road. Steam engine, wooden coaches, 9-mile trip through Amish farms. 717-687-7522.

☆ Chattanooga, Tennessee: Tennessee Valley Railroad. A 6-mile trip through Civil War country. 615-894-8028.

☆ Jamestown, California: Railtown 1897. Scenic rides of 14, 32 or 38 miles through gorgeous countryside. 209-984-3953.

If you're interested in the 259 other tourist rail lines, get a copy of the *Steam Passenger Service Directory*. Call 800-356-0246.

1184

Here's a twist—See the fall foliage aboard a *cruise ship!* Avoid the crowded highways, and leave the driving to someone else. Here are some of the cruise lines that offer leaf-peeping cruises:

★ Seabourne Cruise Line: 800-351-9595
★ Crystal Cruises: 800-446-6645
★ Princess Cruises: 800-LOVEBOAT
★ Crown Cruise Line: 800-832-1122
★ Royal Viking Line: 800-422-8000

1185

There are other ways to get your adrenaline pumping besides—well, you know. One of the most fun is white water rafting. What else can you do that combines togetherness, a little danger, the great outdoors, and lots of water?

☆ The Colorado River in Arizona: A rampaging trip through the Grand Canyon. Some people call it "The Ultimate" in white water rafting experiences.

☆ The Salmon River of central Idaho: One of the West's wildest and most picturesque rivers. Through a mile-deep gorge.

☆ The Gauley River, in West Virginia: 60 major rapids—with names like "Heaven Help You" and "Pure Screaming Hell"—along a 30-mile stretch.

1186

Only in America . . . could you go on safari in *air-conditioned tents*. Really! The only wildlife safari in North America is in Texas, at the Foothills Safari Camp at Fossil Rim. It's an outdoor adventure for those who prefer their travel to be luxurious. [Perfect for my mother-in-law. Are you listening, Judy?!] The 3,000-acre preserve is home to herds of giraffes, zebras and rhinos—and nearly a thousand exotic and endangered animals. You'll view these beasts from the comfort of your tent—a tent with a private bath, no less! Meals are served in a glass pavilion or on the veranda overlooking a game-filled meadow. (Meals include filet mignon and chocolate souffle'.) Safaris run year-round, with a new one starting each week. Call 'em at 800-245-0771.

1187

And then, of course, there's always the *Gone With the Wind* fall pilgrimage tours in Natchez, Mississippi. Elegant Antebellum homes, scrumptious plantation dinners, quaint bed-and-breakfasts, Southern Hospitality! Call 800-647-6742.

1188

What is America's most romantic city? My unscientific poll of readers and Romance Class participants indicates that the two top contenders are New Orleans and San Francisco—by about 60/40.

Other contenders include Boston, New York and Pittsburgh. [*Pittsburgh?!*]

1189

Go parking!

○ Dial-A-Park, the National Park Service's 24-hour events line: 202-619-PARK.

○ Do you *love* the great outdoors but *hate* the crowds and traffic of the most popular national parks? Try these less-frequented, but no less dramatic, national parks:

➤ Arches National Park: With more than 1,500 natural rock arches.
➤ Badlands National Park: If you saw *Dances With Wolves*, you saw this park's dramatic scenery.
➤ Canyonlands National Park: A beautiful wilderness of mesas and canyons.
➤ Jewel Cave National Monument: The world's fourth-longest cave!
➤ Voyageurs National Park: With 30 lakes!
➤ North Cascades National Park: With more than 300 glaciers!

○ By far the best book on America's parks is *The Complete Guide to America's National Parks*. It describes all 358 national parks; it provides specific weather information in month-by-month charts; it lists camping and hiking permits and fees; it has maps, phone numbers and lodging info. What more could you ask for? Well, all proceeds go to benefit the non-profit National Park Foundation! Just $12.95!— Call 800-285-2448.

1190

For all you Elvis fans out there . . .

★ If your lover loves you almost as much as she loves Elvis, I hope that you're using Elvis Stamps when mailing all your cards and love letters!
★ Have you taken her to Graceland yet?

1191

Train buffs, history buffs, and those who just like quiet little towns and beautiful scenery, will enjoy Durango, Colorado. Four impeccably restored, coal-fired, steam-operated, vintage locomotives run every day through the San Juan Mountains, giving visitors a grand view and a grand time. Quieter rides are available via horse-drawn buggy.

1192

Do you know how long California's coastline is? Neither do I . . . but here's an indispensable guide to it: *The Hidden Coast of California*. Without it, you'd never be able to find the best scenic drives, the numerous parks, the most romantic places, the hottest nightclubs, the scads of historic sites, and its revealing nude beaches (!). In bookstores, or call 415-601-8301.

And speaking of California, two of its best caterers/party planners are:

★ Mercy & Associates, in Palm Springs. They specialize in wedding and romantic events, and add a touch of elegance to any public or private affair. Call 619-779-4839.
★ The Creative Concierge, on North Rodeo Drive in Beverly Hills. They'll help you with anything from planning a romantic rendezvous to shopping for that one-of-a-kind gift! Call 310-546-8966.

Around the World

1193

Take a thirteenth century French chateau. Add 200 craftsmen, money (lots), style, and love . . . and you get a wonderful, romantic place to stay in the Beaujolais Region. The Chateau de Bagnols is grand yet cozy. It was built as a fortress (it has a moat, drawbridge, and arrow slits), and yet inside its Gothic arches it has . . . how you say . . . *esprit d'ambiance.*

The chateau has only 20 apartments, and is open year-round. Write to 69620 Bagnols, France, or call 33-74-71-40-00.

1194

Champagne has probably been an instrumental part of your life if you're living the romantic life-style. Why not visit the home of the bubbly: France's Champagne Region. Picturesque Champagne is dotted with 250 wine-producing villages and 110 champagne houses, many of which offer free tastings and tours deep into the caves where the champagne matures. Most of the houses are small and don't produce enough for export— so you're likely to experience some novel, undiscovered champagnes. But of course, you'll find some instantly-recognizable labels, too: Moet et Chandon, Mumm, Taittinger. FYI, Dom Perignon is produced by Moet et Chandon in Epernay.

1195

FYI, the largest international street performers festival *in the world* is in Nova Scotia, Canada. The Halifax International BuskerFest is held annually early in August.

1196

Have you ever heard of "boatels"? [I guess I don't get around enough.] Not surprisingly, they're floating hotels. Stockholm, Sweden—a beautiful city covering 14 small islands—boasts many wonderful boatels. Some are converted yachts, and others are various classic vessels. Call the Swedish Tourist Board at 212-949-2333, or write to 655 Third Avenue, New York City, New York 10017.

1197

Venice. Gondolas. Romance. Go. Now.

1198

Verona. *Romeo and Juliet*. Voted the **Number One, Without-A-Doubt, Best, Most Fantastic, Wonderfully Romantic City In The World**. {Way too many people to list. Thanks to all.}

1199

For you Francophiles, the French Government Tourist Office has created *Club France*—making one of the world's most romantic countries more accessible than ever before. Here a just a few of the benefits of membership:

- ❖ The French Embassy's quarterly *France Magazine*
- ❖ 1- to 3-day Paris Museum Pass
- ❖ Rental car upgrades
- ❖ Up to 50% discount on rooms in Paris' Abotel (Tradotel) Properties
- ❖ Priority reservations at nightclubs
- ❖ Discounts on Cooking School and Language Courses
- ❖ Quarterly newsletter *Club France*

A Club France membership is just $65. Write to the French Government Tourist Office, 610 Fifth Avenue, New York City, New York 10020, or call 212-757-0229.

1200

Passport is the quintessential newsletter about interesting places that have yet to be "discovered." London's intimate (yet affordable) hotels near the best shops and theatres. The best little bistros in Paris. The San Francisco most people never see. Write or call for a free preview issue: 350 West Hubbard, Suite 440, Chicago, Illinois 60610, or call 800-999-9006.

Intimacy

1201

Intimacy—a great album by Walter Beasley. Great, great mood music!

1202

Real intimacy involves risk, not reciprocity. (*Huh?!*) Many couples strive to maintain a "balance" in their intimacy: They only *give* when they know they'll *get* something in return. This is understandable, because it's difficult to reveal some emotions or insecurities if your partner doesn't reciprocate. But reducing intimacy to an "I will if you will" level creates dependency, not intimacy. David Schnarch, Ph.D., author of *Constructing the Sexual Crucible*, says that if you expect reinforcement or validation for every intimate disclosure, you're creating a "surefire recipe for sabotaging intimacy as the relationship progresses. As your partner becomes more important to you, you become less willing to risk rejection or disapproval. It allows the person with the weakest desire for intimacy to control that aspect of the relationship."

True intimacy involves opening up and revealing all of your personality to your partner, not just the "nice" parts. This process is the catalyst for intimacy. The *bad* news is that you risk rejection; the *good* news is that you open the door for profound inner growth.

1203

Are you familiar with the concept of the "Intimate Island"? Here's how therapist Jacqui Stratton describes it in her excellent publication *Duos*:

"Although many intimate moments are spontaneous, they are most often a result of ritually creating an 'Intimate Island,' a paradise in time and space where lovers can experience each other unencumbered. By investing energy to create such an environment and circumstance, joy and fulfillment are given the opportunity to make an appearance... Rituals are mini-performances that lovers can develop to uplift the ways in which they interact so that the interaction becomes magical, and enhances how they feel about themselves, each other, and their lives together. Rituals are tools that bridge the gap between the mundane and the sacred, turning ordinary activities into beautiful and profound small wonders."

She then talks about the "entryway" to the Intimate Island, and the importance of the setting. These are important concepts for today's lovers. Duos is a series of publications that help couples develop satisfying and pleasurable relationships. Seven issues are $25. Write to Stratton & Company, 3125 North Main Street, Soquel, California 95073, or call 408-464-1780.

1204

Keeping a "Couples Journal" is a way to open a new channel of communication between the two of you, and build intimacy in the process. You can create your own notebook, or purchase a wonderful book called *Secrets: An Intimate Journal for Two*. It's exquisitely illustrated with hand-tinted photographs, to help set the mood; it poses gently probing questions that help couples share their most private thoughts; and it suggests some fantasies to encourage flights of imagination.

1205

"Intimacy is not required 24 hours a day—but it *is* required *some time* during the 24-hour period." {Thanks, Sam.}

1206

Advice about intimacy and communication is often too-darn serious, don't you think? I've always found that *humor* is a wonderful way to connect with other people. My best relationships have always been with women with whom I've laughed the best. Some of the most special, intimate times I've spent with Tracey have been when we share some private joke. I've learned that there are many kinds and levels of intimacy: Sexual, spiritual, intellectual, and humoral. ["Humoral"—newly-defined by me.—Sorry, Mrs. Wilcox.]

1207

Private jokes. Silly messages. Your Song. Secret codes. Pet names. —They're all little but significant building blocks of intimacy.

Creativity

1208

Do you need some *really specific* strategies for being more **creative**? Why didn't you *say so?!* Here's the answer: The book *A Whack on the Side of the Head—How You Can Be More Creative,* by Roger von Oech. *Whack* breaks through your mental locks and opens your mind for innovative thinking. It's filled with provocative puzzles, anecdotes, exercises, metaphors, stories and helpful hints. A quick sampling: • Be foolish • Break the rules • Be impractical • Get out of your box • Look for "wrong" answers • Seek ambiguity • Make mistakes!

1209

The Patented Do-It-Yourself Romantic Idea Item! Tell your lover *specifically* what you find romantic; what turns you on; what you're going to do for him or her; what your favorite fantasy is . . .

_____

_____

_____

_____

_____

1210

Want to be more creative? Get back in touch with the Child inside you. We all have a host of inborn qualities that are often overlooked, suppressed, ridiculed or just plain forgotten: Curiosity, spontaneity, innocence, wonder, openness to new ideas, unwillingness to be bored, living in the Now.

1211

If your lover was a good student in school, maybe he'll be motivated by a "Romance Report Card." Grade him A+ through F- in these categories:

- ✦ Thoughtfulness
- ✦ Little Gestures
- ✦ Birthdays
- ✦ Surprises
- ✦ Intimacy
- ✦ Creativity

- ✦ Timeliness
- ✦ Big Gestures
- ✦ Flowers
- ✦ Sensuality
- ✦ "Extracurricular Activities"

- ✦ Communication
- ✦ Anniversaries
- ✦ Vacations
- ✦ Gifts
- ✦ (Add your *own* categories!)

1212

Let me introduce you to Linda Weltner. She's well-known and loved in New England for her weekly column in *The Boston Globe* called "Ever So Humble." Her sensitive and thought-provoking essays are inspirational as well as entertaining. Here are a few selections to spur your romantic imagination.

"I've driven our poor dog around to local landmarks and made him pose for pictures just so I could doctor them up with cartoon balloons which divulged the imaginary contents of his unconscious. "You're overdue. I'm missing you," he mutters in front of the public library.

"Julie and Chris' decision to get married in July, however, has inspired me to even greater leaps of fancy. These days I buy the National Enquirer because its editors have a perverse fascination with unusual weddings. I cut the stories out, then taking scissors to a pile of discarded photos, I send Julie and Chris doctored pictures of the two of them jumping off a diving board in formal wedding attire, riding to church on a tractor shovel, or standing at the altar, the bride (who has Julie's face) resplendent in a wedding gown made from human hair."

Linda Weltner is also the author of a wonderful book, *No Place Like Home: Rooms and Reflections from One Family's Life.*

1213

The "Don't-Be-Cheap—Call Me Long-Distance! Coupon Booklet": Take 100 brand new, crisp one dollar bills in a neat stack. Dip the top edge in Elmer's Glue. Apply two or three layers of glue. This creates a tear-off pad of money! Attach an appropriate note. *Voila!*

1214

For newlyweds-to-be who don't know whose last name to choose: Consider combining your names to create a new last name! This is what Michael Flaherty and Valerie Silverman did. They combined their names to create "Flaherman." "We wanted to share a name without being sexist or hyphenating two names," Michael said. {Reported in *U.S. News & World Report*.}

Sexuality

1215

Exercise! A growing number of studies confirm a correlation between regular aerobic exercise (3 or more 30-minute sessions a week) and libido. In a poll of more than 8,000 women, 31% reported having sex more often after they began a regular exercise program; and 40% noted an increase in their ability to become aroused. Studies of swimmers, cyclists, and runners show similar results, but experts have yet to determine the actual reason for this phenomenon. [Who *cares* what the reasons are!] From sex therapist Linda De Villers, Ph.D. {This helpful, healthful tip is from *To Us!—The Newsletter for Committed Couples*.}

1216

The Wonderful Little Sex Book, by William Ashoka Ross, aims to restore freshness and innocence to sex. Each page offers a thought-provoking tidbit to help improve your sex life by going beyond mere technique, and viewing sex as a potent means of connection.

1217

Talking about sex can be just as important to your love life as *having* it! Studies show that lack of communication about sex tends to decrease a couple's satisfaction and increase performance anxiety. (All you guys who aren't "into" communication, take note!)
{From "ISD: Inhibited Sexual Desire," by Dr. Jennifer Knopf & Dr. Michael Seiler, via the *To Us!* Newsletter.}

1218

How did we all manage to deal with sex before there was Dr. Ruth?! Her latest: *Dr. Ruth's Guide to Erotic & Sensuous Pleasures.* Helpful and frank, as always!

1219

And then there was the young couple who kept their "sex toys" in an old toy box. (They added a padlock after Junior discovered the toys one day and thought that some of them made great little rockets—"They make *great* humming sounds!") {Amy C.}

1220

And now, a *new* feature: "Aphrodisiac Update," with your host, Greg Godek! "First, for men only: *Playboy* reports that something called "yohimbine" *does* exhibit some characteristics of a male aphrodisiac. For centuries, the African yohimbe tree has enjoyed a reputation as a powerful male sex stimulant. Recent scientific studies have shown that an extract of the fabled tree's bark stimulated erections in a significant proportion of impotent men, apparently by increasing blood flow to the penis. Yohimbine is available as a prescription treatment under the brand name Yocon. And now, some news about an aphrodisiac for women: The herb Damiana. Try it—you'll like it! And last-but-not-least, our "Book Corner" features *A Dictionary of Aphrodisiacs*, by Harry E. Wedeck. This nifty book is a collection of potions, herbs, prescriptions and recipes—all wrapped around folk traditions, superstitions and quotes on our favorite subject. Well, that's our news for tonight. Stay tuned tomorrow, when my guests will be Dr. Ruth, The Church Lady, and Wilt Chamberlain."

1221

When researchers asked people "Why do you have sex?" here's what they said: Women 22 to 35 said *love* was the prime reason; women 36 to 57 said *pleasure* was the main motive. And for men . . . ? The answers were flipped.

1222

What's the *longest* lovemaking session you've ever had? C'mon, be honest! Fifteen minutes? An hour? *Three* hours?

1223

We all know that there are 1001 ways to be romantic . . . But did you know that there are "101 Ways to Excite Your Lover"? That's the title of a videotape from *Playboy* and *The Sharper Image Catalog*. Learn how sight, scent and sound can act as aphrodisiacs to intensify your pleasure. Your teachers are beautiful nude couples. Puritans need not apply. Just $49.95 from the *Playboy Catalog*. Call 800-423-9494.

1224

I don't mean to get personal here, but—*When* do you usually make love? If you're like *most* Americans, you leave lovemaking until the very end of the evening—when you're tired from getting everything *else* done, and when you're probably, and understandably, more interested in sleeping.

Two couples wrote to me, sharing a technique that helped them spend more time making love, and less time making excuses: They set a goal to have at least one two-hour lovemaking session every month. This forces them to plan, to schedule-in time for each other, or, at the very least, to think about it more! "We didn't always make our goal, but it sure was fun trying! Having a goal may sound too contrived to some people, but as they say, 'Don't knock it 'til you've tried it!'" {T. & B., K. & R.}

No Soap, Radio!

1225-1227

Three off-the-wall—or rather "on the wall" ideas. [Sorry, I couldn't pass-up the pun.]

✦ The "Love Room," a creation of Juanita and Teddy F., of Long Island, New York. "It started as a bulletin board where we tacked-up mementos; it overflowed onto the wall, and eventually took over our entire den. It's a mosaic of our life together!"

✦ The "Memory Wall," a dynamic project of the Elliot's. They prefer to frame their items.

✦ The "Wine Wall," a modest suggestion of my own. How about creating your own "wallpaper" out of wine labels?

1228

Find the item number in this book that corresponds with your lover's birthday or with your anniversary—and do it!

1229

And now, *another* new feature, called "Health Corner." Here's a tip for all you weight-watchers out there: An extremely passionate, one-minute kiss burns about 26 calories. [This is the kind of exciting, life-altering information that you look to me for, isn't it?]

1230

One way of bringing more romance into the world is to help *another couple's* relationship. Here's what one loving (and sly) mother-in-law did: Her daughter had married a very fine fellow with just one little flaw. You guessed it: He didn't have a romantic bone in his body. One day a dozen roses show-up for the young wife, allegedly from the husband—but really sent in secret by the girl's mother. (Got it?) Husband shows-up at home; wife throws arms around him lovingly; he's bewildered; can't admit the roses aren't from him; he basks in romantic warmth—gets a hint of why romance might benefit him. Same thing happens the next week. But *not* the third week. Husband finally picks-up the romantic ball and keeps it rolling. Couple lives happily ever after.

1231

Find an empty bottle of prescription pills. Create a custom label!

> Patient: (Your lover's name)
> Medication: LIBIDO LIBERATOR
> Dosage: TAKE ONE PILL DAILY UNTIL WE'RE TOGETHER
> Contents: Fill the bottle with green **m&ms**

{Thanks to Alan Lippart, of Markesan, Wisconsin!}

1232

Want to pique his interest? Send him a pair of oven mitts in the mail with a note attached: "I'm going to be *too hot to handle* tonight, so wear these!"

1233

Men & women tend to operate at different "speeds" when it comes to sex. To use a music analogy: Men are like 45s: They're single-minded and fast! Women prefer the longer-playing and slower speed of 33-1/3. [Note to our children's children's children: I know this analogy will be meaningless to you. Look in your history books under "Beatles" or maybe "Hi-Fi."] {Courtesy of DJ Rick Barber, on KOA-AM radio, in Denver.}

1234

Stage shows of possible interest!

✦ *Isn't It Romantic?* A contemporary comedy, by Wendy Wasserstein.
✦ *Romance Romance.* Winner of 5 Tony Awards, by Keith Hermann & Barry Harman.

1235

Just because you *speak* better than you *write*, that's *not* an acceptable excuse for not writing her a love letter! Compose an *Audio Love Letter:* Tape a short message to her. Here's how to get over your awkwardness: Some evening when she's not around for about two hours, gather these materials: A tape recorder, a blank tape, some cards and letters she's sent you, some photos of the two of you, paper and pen, some music that reminds you of her, and a glass of your favorite wine. Spend about half an hour looking through the memorabilia of your relationship, while sipping wine and listening to the music. Jot a few notes to yourself about your feelings for her. Then take microphone in hand, and *just talk to her* for five to ten minutes. Warning: Don't listen to the tape when you're done!—You'll be overcome with an irresistible urge to edit yourself and "do it perfectly." Don't! Now, wrap the tape and mail it to her, or insert it in her car stereo, or give it to her inside a Walkman.

1236

1+1=1 Two becoming One.

1+1=2 Two balancing independence and interdependence.

1+1=3 Oops!—And baby makes three!

Food, Glorious Food!

1237

The *Edibles* calendar is a celebration of the sensuous nature of food. *Edibles* is the favorite annual project of photographer Robert Kaufman, whose dozen or so wall calendars range from food to cats, and beaches to babies. If your favorite gift shop is out of them, call Silver Visions at 617-244-9504, or write to 301 Elliot Street, Newton, Massachusetts 02164.

1238

If your lover has a sophisticated sweet tooth, you've *got* to send for the confectionery catalog from Attivo Gourmet Confections. Mmmmm! Caramel apples like you've never seen them before! Chocolate covered *raspberries*! Write to 1165 Park Avenue, Emeryville, California 94608, or call 800-3-ATTIVO.

1239

A celebration of contemporary French food as interpreted by arguably the best chef in France, Joel Robuchon: The cookbook, *Simply French*, by Patricia Wells and Joel Robuchon. Some elaborate dishes will keep even an expert cook busy for hours, but most of the recipes require no special dexterity and can be prepared in less than an hour. The 368-page book includes gorgeous photographs and wine recommendations, too.

1240

Love Food (luv' food) 1. A special meal that comforts or brings a smile to your lover. 2. Any food that you prepare especially for your partner, or serve to him or her that says "I love you."

It doesn't have to be fancy. Mine is pizza. Tracey's is ice cream or Pad Thai. {Love food, defined by my good friends Clare Saulnier and Steve Howard.}

1241

How about ice creams and sorbets made from flowers and herbs!? Rosemary Ice Cream. Red Rose Blossom Sorbet. Peach and Champagne Sorbet with Mint. Dark Chocolate Sorbet with Orange Mint. Both the sorbets and ice creams combine the petals of edible flowers with fresh fruits, herbs, spices and wines. Yummmmmm! Call to order any of their 42 flavors: Out of a Flower at 800-743-4696.

1242

There's a lot more to food than just its taste. Properly approached, a meal can be a total five-sense experience. Those who appreciate the truly sensuous nature of food also tend to recognize the sensuous in other areas of their lives.

1243

And what's more romantic than a great wine with your elegant (or simple!) meal? One of my favorites is *Herman Wente Estate Reserve Chardonne.* (Wente Brothers' Grande Brut sparkling wines ain't bad, either!) Those clever and talented winemakers at Wente Brothers Winery, of Livermore, California, have recognized the importance of romance, and are working closely with the International Association du Romance. (See the "Romantic Resources" chapter for more info on the Int'l Assoc. du Romance!) And stay tuned for more great wines and some intriguing romantic developments from Wente Brothers!

1244

I was grocery shopping last week and almost crashed my shopping cart when I happened to notice "Romance Brand Pastas & Sauces"! I've since learned that this company is *really* into the romance scene. They have a newsletter with recipes for romantic dishes ("Romance Chicken Marinara"), romance trivia, ideas for picnics—and money-saving coupons, too! For a copy of their free Romance newsletter, write to Romance Foods, 5814 77th Street, Kenosha, Wisconsin 53142.

You Must Remember This

1245

💜 February is "Creative Romance Month." The goal is "to encourage couples to be more *creative* in their approach to romance. While research indicates that both men and women think that *time spent together* is the most romantic gift they could receive, many couples opt for cards, flowers and jewelry due to advertising and the ease of execution. Creative Romance Month is designed to remind couples that variety is an important ingredient of romance."

💜 August is "Romance Awareness Month." The goal is "to encourage couples to make romance an important part of daily living. Why? Because all too often the pressures of family and career responsibilities cause romance to seem frivolous rather than an important ingredient of a fulfilling relationship."

💜 For more info, call Celebrate Romance, at 800-36-TRYST.

1246

"Men are motivated and empowered
when they feel needed ...
Women are motivated and empowered
when they feel cherished."

Think about it. These wise words are from John Gray, Ph.D., from his wonderful book *Men Are From Mars, Women Are From Venus.*

1247

An excerpt from a great writer and columnist Sydney J. Harris:

Why do so many persons seem to pick disappointing lovers and inadequate mates, so deliberately, so stubbornly, so obviously doomed to failure? It is largely, I think, because romance, like liquor, feeds on its own delusion: the more we consume, the more intoxicated and distorted our judgement becomes.

One of the best and truest tests of a real affinity—though one not congenial to the youthful passions—may have been provided by St. Bernard of Clairvaux, when he said: "We find rest in those we love, and we provide a resting place in ourselves for those who love us."

When the infatuation has run its course, as it always does, the feeling that remains must include repose at its core; a quality much neglected and overlooked in most romantic literature and lore ...

Marriage, of course, does not change people; it merely unmasks them. It strips off the strangeness, the glamor, the appearance of strength, the fascination of novelty, the treacherous sense of uniqueness that every couple feels at first ...

A resting place is what we need as we grow older. A place not to gaze at each other in mutual fascination , but to look out at the world together from much the same angle of vision. A harbor, a shelter, a refuge, a source of nourishment and support. This is not what creates a marriage; but it is what sustains it.

[Tracey and I had this piece read during our wedding ceremony.]

1248-1250

Here are some handy memory techniques that can help you remember to be more romantic!

✦ Create an acronym—a word formed from the initial letters of a group of other words, phrases or concepts—to help you remember to be more thoughtful of your partner. If, for example, your lover's name is—oh, let's say "Tracey" (just to choose a name at random), you turn TRACEY into an acronym.

> **T**ea! She loves tea. Bring her a cup of Earl Grey every night.
>
> **R**emember to call her at work once a day. Maybe twice!
>
> **A**nniversary is August 25th.
>
> **C**ards: Send one every Monday from work.
>
> **E**scape on the weekends: Day-trips!
>
> **Y**ellow is her favorite color.

✦ Use the rooms of your house as a "memory blueprint." Picture the rooms or spaces of your home as you would walk through them: Porch, front hallway, den, living room, kitchen, bathroom, dining room, your bedroom, guest bedroom, bathroom. Now, whenever you need to memorize a series of items or ideas, visualize each one in a different room.

✦ These, and many other memory techniques are described in a great little book called *Blueprints for Memory*, by William D. Hersey, a consultant and professional speaker. Bill, at 82+ years old, proves that aging doesn't have to weaken your memory, as he memorizes names and data on *hundreds* of audience members for each of his speeches! (He also memorized the first 100 items in *1001 Ways To Be Romantic* in three days. You can call-out a number, and he knows which romantic idea it is!)

1251

How does one know if it's True Love or a Clever Imitation? I think that you need to listen very carefully to that little Voice inside you that tells you the Truth. The difficulty is that we all hear this Voice differently, and it's nearly impossible for someone else to interpret Its messages for you. Some people describe having a "Sixth Sense" about another person. {George F., Sidney J., Janis Z.} Others get a "funny feeling" in the pit of their stomach when something's wrong, and a "warm glow" when something's right. {Gary M., Meg F.} Some people know it's "right" when they "feel like I've known him/her forever." {Jim H., Sally J., Carol C., Jan B.} Calling each other pet names. {Sally S., Greg J.P.G.} Having the same sense of humor. {Waldo W., Barb. G.}

1252

Do you want him to call you more often? Try leaving subtle hints, like hundreds of Post-It Notes with your phone number stuck all over the place: In his briefcase, on the underside of the toilet lid, in his desk drawers at work, in his calendar, in the medicine chest, on his steering wheel, on the lawnmower, on the front door, on his pillow, in his socks . . .

1253

The single best piece of advice I've ever heard for ensuring a happy, fulfilling, loving, growing, romantic relationship:

Choose well.

That's it. *Choose well.* With the right partner, life can be a joy. With the wrong partner, life can be, well—pure living hell! So perhaps some folks need to pay more attention to choosing their lovers well, rather than trying to "make things work out" with the wrong person. I'm not saying this is easy. Far from it. Heck, I didn't get married until I was 35 years old! I waited until I found the right woman for me. And I definitely had some unhappy years in there. So—here's to waiting patiently, working diligently, and choosing well!

A Kiss is Just a Kiss

1254

Did you know that it's not uncommon for people to be dissatisfied with their partner's kissing style? (Too wet, too impersonal, too wimpy, too aggressive.) Most of us (especially men) assume that after all these years of experience, we're Expert Kissers. Why don't you ask your lover about it? It could lead to an eye-opening discussion—and to some enjoyable experimentation!

1255

"The Ultimate Kiss: A Sensual Guide to Oral Lovemaking" kind-of says it all, I think. This videotape-and-book kit from *Playboy* is "A sensual guide to the pleasures of oral lovemaking for men and women." [Not recommended for first-date viewing.] $27.95 from the *Playboy Catalog,* call 800-423-9494.

1256

K.I.S.S.

"Keep It Sentimental & Sweet." (Formerly "Keep It Simple, Stupid.")

1257

Butterfly kisses! I can't *believe* that I didn't include *butterfly kisses* in the first book! —*What*!? You don't know what butterfly kisses are? [Author rolls eyes heavenward here.] You're butterfly kissing when your face is very close to your lover's cheek (or whatever), and you blink your eye rapidly, softly grazing your eyelashes against her skin. Sensuous. Sometimes ticklish. Always fun. {Thanks to Jean Antonello, who, by the way, is the author of *The Anti-Diet Book—How to be Naturally Thin by Eating More*. [And I thought *I* had a great book title!]}

1258

Favorite romantic scenes from the movies (submitted by readers):

☆ *Picnic*: "The scene in which Kim Novak and William Holden dance." {John W. Bentz, Boston, Massachusetts.}

☆ *Funny Girl*: "Comic, but romantic. Especially Omar Sharif's seduction of a hilariously naive Barbra Streisand to the song, 'You Are Woman, I Am Man'." {John again.}

☆ *The Way We Were*: "When Streisand and Redford kiss in front of her fireplace. Very, very romantic!" {Ed Grimley.}

☆ *An Unmarried Woman*: "Jill Clayburgh and Alan Bates dancing to Billie Holiday in a moonlit SoHo loft." {Amy's husband.}

☆ *Out of Africa*: "When Redford and Streep fly in his bi-plane over the breathtaking Masai Valley." {Sam & Jesse's stepfather.}

☆ *Casablanca*: "The parting scene at the end. The best romantic scene of all time." {Paraphrase from dozens of letters. Thanks to M. & B. in Houston; B. Howard in San Francisco; Jim and Deb in Boston; B.J. & T.J. in St. Louis; Tina somewhere in Texas.}

☆ *Gone With The Wind*: "When Rhett steals a major kiss from Scarlett, as he's helping her escape Atlanta. The city burns, the sun sets in a blaze of red—hot, hot, hot!" {C.S., Boston.}

Creating Sacred Spaces

1259

When most people go on vacation, they're searching for adventure, they're searching for something exotic, or they're searching for something to write home about. While *some* people go *soul searching*. "Spiritual Getaways" are becoming increasingly popular. More and more people seem to be seeking quiet, solace and spirituality. Couples who take meditation retreats, spiritual journeys and religious holidays find themselves refreshed, renewed and more in love than ever before.

1260

The Hidden Power of the Heart: How to Create a More Loving Environment for Yourself and Others, by Sara Paddison. This is the kind of book you can sample when you feel the need. It not only addresses the day-to-day situations that cause anxiety and frustration in our fast-paced world, but it shows you how to gain peace in the moment by using the power of your own heart.

1261

If you believe that practicing forgiveness and learning to achieve a holy relationship just might improve your life, then you may want to check-out the spiritual and educational getaways that are available from the Foundation for "A Course In Miracles." The Retreat Center is situated on 95 tranquil acres in the Catskill Mountains, about 120 miles from New York City. Seminars, workshops and retreats focus on the themes of "holy relationships," "forgiveness," and "inner peace." Many sessions are taught by Dr. Kenneth Wapnick, editor and collaborator of *A Course in Miracles.* Write for a free newsletter and more info: Tennanah Lake Road, R.R. 2, Box 71, Roscoe, New York 12776-9506, or call 607-498-4116.

1262-1263

Romance involves many *pairs* of attributes and attitudes. The happiest couples recognize and make room for *all* of these in their relationship:

♥ Passion and peace.
♥ Excitement and repose.
♥ Fighting and loving.
♥ Communication and quiet.
♥ Spontaneity and planning.

♥ Give and take.
♥ Differences and similarities.
♥ Forgiving and forgetting.
♥ Surprises and reassurance.
♥ Gifts and gestures.

1264

Many couples report fond memories of the time and place that they first met; some of them visit their meeting place yearly; and many of them make a pilgrimage on their 10th, 20th, 25th, 30th, or 40th anniversaries. Even the most seemingly unromantic spots hold special meaning if you met "that certain someone" there. The Gottleib's of Nashville, Tennessee, ride in "*their* elevator" every five years; the Nortons of Geneva, New York, visit the grammar school where they met every year; and the Samuelsons of Nevada visit "a certain sidewalk square in SoHo where we bumped into each other (literally) in New York City over 50 years ago!"

1265

How do you *find* love? How do you *keep* love? One way is through *A Return to Love*, the best-seller from Marianne Williamson. Her warm, humorous, loving and down-to-earth style has allowed her to touch the hearts of millions of people. Her message is simple yet profound: Forgiveness is the key to love, happiness, freedom and peace.

1266

One of the best instruments for creating a romantic environment: Acoustic guitar. One of the best composers and players: William Ackerman. Some of his wonderful albums:

- ❦ *Past Light Visiting*
- ❦ *Passages*
- ❦ *It Takes a Year*

- ❦ *Conferring with the Moon*
- ❦ *Childhood and Memory*
- ❦ *The Opening of Doors*

1267

"An unholy relationship is based on differences, where each one thinks the other has what he has not . . . A holy relationship starts from a different premise. Each one has looked within and seen no lack. Accepting his completion, he would extend it by joining with another, whole as himself. He sees no difference between these selves, for differences are only of the body." Sounds like Truth to me! {From *A Course In Miracles*.}

*Do **you** have a great LoveStory to share?*
How did you get engaged?
What's the most outrageous gift you've ever given?
What's the best surprise you've ever pulled?

*Would you like to be in the **next** book?*
See page 295!

1268

If you look hard enough, you can find sacred spaces in the most *unexpected* of places. Hidden in the midst of an industrial park in Los Angeles is a Poetry Garden, created by public artist Siah Armajani. It's a beautiful little haven for lovers of verse and nature. The poetic oasis was commissioned by the Lannan Foundation, a supporter of the arts, for visitors to its galleries. High-backed armchairs welcome guests in the garden, which has podiums for readings among the lush greenery. You'll find the Poetry Garden at 5401 McConnell Avenue; 310-306-1004.

Communicating Feelings

1269

Run down to your local bookstore. Buy one of those books of blank pages. Every day or every other day, write down your thoughts about her, about your relationship, about your lives together. Some days you'll just jot a quick "I love you"—other days you may be inspired to write for 10 minutes or more. Do this for an entire year!—Then present it to her on your anniversary or her birthday. (You could do this year-after-year!) {Many thanks to Steve, who shared this idea with me on the *Deborah Norville Show* on ABC-Radio. Steve, a World Class Romantic, hung-up before we could get more info on him . . . So Steve, if you read this, call me, and I'll add your hometown to the next printing of the book!}

1270-1273

You'll be able to communicate your feelings much more effectively if you understand your—and your partner's—"Personality Type": Are you Traditional, Adventurous, Reserved or Ritualistic? Which description below fits you best?

Traditional

I am imaginative, insightful, communicative, affectionate, harmonious and supportive. I see potential and possibilities all around me, and I have a strong desire to encourage others to lead more significant lives. People look to me as a source of inspiration, as I am adept at motivating others. I bring drama, warmth and empathy to my relationships. I believe that one can fall in love and live happily ever after. People frequently call me the "The Ultimate Romantic" as I value the traditional symbols of romance: Flowers, candlelight, music, holding hands, poetry, love notes and cards. I cherish small gestures of love, and I enjoy romantic movies, novels and intimate dinners.

Adventurous

I am spontaneous, adventuresome, optimistic, witty, charming and generous. I thrive on fun, variety and excitement. I live in the moment, rather than the future. I like action and I am challenged to take risks and test the limits of life. I love to explore new things. I value independence; therefore, anything that is routine and structured can leave me bored and restless. I need to feel "Free to be me." For me, a romantic experience is special if it provides excitement, adventure and variety. I love extravagant gifts and surprises.

Reserved

I am inventive, curious, logical, competent, wise, intellectual and knowledgeable. I thrive in an environment that is predictable and controllable. I am an abstract, conceptual and independent thinker. I have a low tolerance for what I perceive as illogical and/or emotional thinking. I am often viewed as "unromantic" because I am not comfortable with public displays of affection and don't often verbalize my feelings. I enjoy the simple things in life done in a creative, private manner. I don't like surprises. Gifts are unimportant to me, as I purchase what I need. However, I do enjoy receiving creative cards that have messages with double meanings. I view romantic getaways (expensive hotels, limousines, fancy restaurants) as a waste of money.

Ritualistic

I am responsible, practical, punctual, organized, caring and loyal. You can count on me to get the job done, as I work hard, and always finish my work before I play, even if I have to work overtime. I thrive in a structured environment with established routines. I'm organized, and have an ability to handle details efficiently. I have a strong sense of right and wrong, and feel rules and regulations are important. I am careful with my time, money and possessions. My home and family are especially important to me, as I am parental and nurturing by nature. I have traditional, conservative views of love and marriage. I demonstrate love and affection through the practical things I do for my loved ones and by verbalizing expressions of love in ritualistic language. Birthday and anniversary celebrations are important to me. I like lasting and meaningful gifts—things like jewelry, artwork and framed verses.

{Thanks to Eileen Buchheim, of Celebrate Romance. Call 800-36-TRYST for romance kits, romantic suggestions, and all kinds of fun stuff! }

Hey, Big Spender!

1274

The "full-length mink coat" of cruises is the round-the-world cruise. If you've got about 100 days free, and anywhere from $18,000 to $50,000 to spare, go for it! The Holland America Line's Rotterdam makes an around-the-world cruise every winter. Write to 300 Elliott Avenue West, Seattle, Washington 98119.

1275

If your lover is *really* into massages, do-it-up right!—Get a professional massage table! Just $485. Or, for those who lack the funds, but are still serious about their massages—you've *got* to get a padded "face cradle"— just $75. Call the *Playboy Catalog* at 800-423-9494.

1276

"Give me a rich coat made of fur."
"But my wife, I just cannot concur!"
Though the price was sky-high
He saved-up to buy,
And a surprise was thus given to her!

{Thanks to Chris Marros, who related his sneaky tale of love over the radio on NJ 101.5-FM radio one night!}

1277

How about the "Gold Vacation" package at the Sandy Lane Hotel in Barbados? A Rolls Royce picks you up at the airport, champagne accompanies nearly everything, you get an airplane tour and a submarine ride! Just $4,000 per couple for a week of indulgence! Call 800-535-3426.

1278

A little "Bedroom Romance" for those who take their sleep very seriously. A rather exclusive shop in Los Angeles called Bonbon Collection sells accouterments such as $1,500 Egyptian-cotton sheets, $1,295 paisley cashmere blankets, $1,100 silk charmeuse and crepe de chine covers filled with layers of silk floss, and $2,200 Porthault linens. Bring your charge card and browse at 466 North Robertson Boulevard, or call 310-657-5600.

1279

A little three-part excursion, utilizing three very romantic modes of transportation!

1. You start with a 14-day train tour from Los Angeles to New York aboard a refurbished vintage rail car.
2. Then you cruise to London aboard the QE2.
3. And then you return on the Concorde.
   Prices start at $11,950 per person. Call Abercrombie & Kent at 800-323-7308.

1280

Around the world in . . . 36 days. With stops in Buenos Aires, Easter Island, Fiji, Beijing, India and Egypt. Included is a balloon ride over Kenya's Masai Mara. Just $43,500 per person. (For those of you on a budget, you can sign-up for a 17 or 24-day segment for $22,500 or $29,500.) Call Travcoa at 800-992-2003.

1281-1283

❖ Gift certificates to Tiffany's.

❖ A one-hour, no-limit shopping spree in her favorite mall. (On your mark, get set, *go!*)

❖ Dinner in each of the finest restaurants in America.

Low-Budget Romance

1284

Take him out on a classy date that won't cost you a dime: The New York Philharmonic's Free Parks Concerts. Usually held during early August. Call for more info: 800-992-8997.

1285

A lot of interviewers ask me what effect the recession (of the late 1980s and early 1990s) has had on romance, assuming that it's had a negative effect. On the contrary, I believe that *the recession is one of the best things that ever happened to romance!* Why? Because it's no longer so easy to simply "throw money at the problem!" People are thinking twice before buying roses, theatre tickets or gifts. And when you can't spend *money* to express your feelings, what do you do? You give of yourself, use your creativity, and spend more time with your lover. This seems to *me* to be a Good Thing.

1286

Hard economic times have spurred romance before. Remember all those great romantic movies from the Depression years of the 1930s? *Holiday, Lost Horizon, It Happened One Night, Wuthering Heights, Camille, Red Dust, Intermezzo, Gone With the Wind.*

1287

The Affordable CARIBBEAN—The Newsletter for the Value-Conscious Traveler. A year of monthly issues for $39. Write to Post Office Box 2054, Marion, Ohio 43306-2154.

1288

Perhaps the world's cheapest vacation resort is The Presidential Inn at Poland Spring, Maine. Two beautifully restored Victorian-style inns look out on the breathtaking scenery of southern Maine's Androscoggin Valley toward the White Mountains in the distance. The price? $20 to $40 a day! For this you get a room with private bath, buffet-style meals, and an entertainment program! Owners Mel and Cyndi Robbins disclose their secrets: "We keep it simple. There are no waiters in our dining room—everything is buffet style. There are no bellboys. Guests must bring their own soap and towels. There are no phones in the rooms." And yet, this isn't a Spartan vacation. They do offer band concerts under the stars, summer theater, cabaret theater, live country music, live big band music, and dancing! Call them at 207-998-4351, or write to Inns at Poland Spring, Poland Spring, Maine 04274.

1289-1290

Take your pick:

➨ "Our budget-vacation strategy is to spend as *little as possible* on accommodations, and as *much as possible* on dining out! Frankly, our lives revolve around food, and this approach works perfectly for us!" {Dolores & Bob Simmer.} Their "Bible" is The U.S. & Worldwide Travel Accommodations Guide, which lists hundreds of university dorms, hostels, and miscellaneous rooms available that would be nearly impossible to find any other way. Just $13, from Campus Travel Service, Post Office Box 8355, Newport Beach, California 92660.

➨ "When my husband and I travel, we pamper ourselves with the most luxurious room we can find! But we save money by not dining out, not going to expensive tourist traps, and not buying silly souvenirs. Instead, we create a 'love nest' for ourselves, and settle-in for a week of loving, reading, talking and sleeping!" {Cynthia & Doug Lambert, Montreal, Canada.}

1291

These firms sell cruises at a discount: Cruises of Distinction: 800-634-3445 White Travel Services: 800-547-4790. The Cruise Line: 800-327-3021. Cruises International: 800-ALL-SHIPS. Cruise Specialists: 800-544-AHOY. The Travel Company: 800-367-6090.

High-Tech Romance

1292

And then there was the wife who used a phone pager to call her hubby home during the most fertile time of her cycle. She liked the system so well that even *after* the baby arrived, she continued using the beeper to call her husband to let him know when she was "in the mood"!

1293

Lovers who have portable phones tend to call one another more often than the rest of us do.

1294

A brief lesson from the high-tech world of computers: "Multi-tasking"— or doing several things at the same time. Scan magazines in the bathroom; jot a quick love note while you're "on hold" on the telephone; pick-up a handful of greeting cards whenever you're at the drug store; think-up romantic ideas on your commute into work!

1295

Does your partner gaze passionately for hours...at his computer screen?! You *can't* beat 'em, so *join* 'em! Make the computer your friend, instead of your enemy! Why not use the computer *itself* as a way to communicate with him? If you're computer illiterate, get a friend to help you create a special "Message Disk" that you can send to him. If you're more familiar with computers, you could hide messages in various places on his hard disk, or create custom messages to appear on his screen-saver, or create a loving greeting that opens automatically when he boots-up. (Just don't mess with his system software.)

1296

Here's a true story. Once upon a time there was a writer who got so wrapped-up in his book projects that he had a difficult time giving his wife the attention he knew she deserved (even though he was *quite* a romantic guy). Then one day the wizards in Apple Land created a magic box called the Macintosh PowerBook. The writer got one of these magic boxes, and it transformed his life! Previously, whenever he traveled to exotic lands on business, he traveled alone and returned home as quickly as possible. But with his magic box by his side, he found he could combine business and pleasure. He thus sent a flying coach to bring his bride to his side more often. And, so I hear, they're living happily ever after.

1297

[You techies *already* know about Online services, but many folks *don't* . . .] There's a *whole world* of communication going on out there that allows computer users to "reach out and touch someone" in ways that Ma Bell never imagined! With a computer, modem, a little software, a small user-fee and a few keystrokes, you can tap into any of several Online services that let you access bulletin boards, ongoing conversations with several people, singles services, and all kinds of things! There's CompuServe, America Online, Prodigy and Genie. Call your local computer whiz, or grab one of these books: The *ABCs of On-Line Services; America Online Membership Kit & Tour Guide; Up & Running with CompuServe; Prodigy Made Easy.*

1298

Think of the romantic possibilities! . . . Now you can make gorgeous full-color photos from any image on your television—from a video cassette, your own camcorder movies, or directly from broadcast TV. It's a little steep, but if you're into electronic gadgets, it's probably par for the course: $999, from the *Hammacher Schlemmer Catalog.* Call 800-543-3366.

1299

Coffeehouse culture has been crossed with computer technology, and the result is a new way of meeting people and holding conversations. SF Net employs computer screens built into tables that are located in several coffeehouses around San Francisco. Just pop two quarters into the slot to purchase 20 minutes of time to chat or argue with people on the other end of the network. Many regular users of SF Net say that it's helped them overcome shyness and insecurities about meeting new people. It's added a new dimension to the social intercourse that coffeehouses are known for. The center of this activity is the Horse Shoe, on lower Haight Street in San Francisco. Log on!

Long-Lasting Relationships

1300

Warning! Even if you're pretty romantic, it's possible to get stuck in a rut! Don't make *every* gesture a surprise. Don't bring her the *same kind* of flowers every time (*even* if they're her favorites). Don't make every card *sentimental*. Over time, your romantic gifts and gestures should inspire, excite, amuse, surprise, console, connect, build understanding, reveal yourself, and deepen intimacy.

1301

Get re-married (to the same person) every year! You'll be a newlywed forever!

1302

One older couple in the Detroit area has devised a "Five-Year Cycle" that they've used to keep their relationship exciting for more than four decades. Perhaps you'd like to personalize this concept to suit *your* relationship:

- ♥ Year 1: *Dating*
- ♥ Year 2: *Courting*
- ♥ Year 3: *Engagement*
- ♥ Year 4: *Wedding*
- ♥ Year 5: *Honeymoon*

And then they start the cycle over again! They say it keeps them from getting stuck in a rut.

1303

★ A *bad* relationship is an anchor around your neck.
★ A *good* relationship is a safe harbor in the sea of change that characterizes our lives.
★ A *great* relationship provides a sail and rudder, allowing you to challenge the waves and live an exhilarating life.

1304

If you *like* each other, the details won't get in the way. If you *dislike* each other, the details will be insurmountable." This advice from Jim Hennig, a business consultant and professional speaker, is part of his seminar on negotiating tactics and business relationships. It applies amazingly well to *personal relationships* too, don't you think?!

1305

Successful long-term relationships don't "just happen," they're the result of *long-term thinking*. A long-term mindset will help you overcome many relationship difficulties and help you maintain some perspective. *Short-term* thinking, with its focus on instant gratification and its lack of any real goals, dooms many relationships that start out with great potential.

This reminds me of the comparison that is often made of American business versus Japanese business. Many U.S. firms fail because of their short-term orientation: All they care about is the current quarter's financial results. Everything is sacrificed to make a short-term profit, including product quality, employee morale and customer satisfaction. Many Japanese firms enjoy success and profitability over many years because they are directed by a long-term philosophy.

1306

"Because romantic moments are charged with emotion they create positive memories that last a lifetime. An accumulation of romantic experiences and memories binds couples together. This bonding enables couples to meet difficult times together, and sustains them through crises," says Eileen Buchheim, creator of Celebrate Romance, an organization that has a Romantic Idea Hotline (800-36-TRYST), and offers boxed Romance Adventures!

1307

It's okay, *early* in a relationship, to "test" your partner to see if he or she truly loves you. (It's an evaluation process to see if he or she truly listens to you; gives to you unselfishly; is confident enough to let you change and grow; is faithful, thoughtful and trustworthy.) But it's *not* okay to keep testing your partner *forever*! Healthy relationships reach a point of trust where you *know* that the other loves you deeply. Once you have reached this level, the two of you are on the verge of experiencing an unimagined level of intimacy, peace, strength, flexibility and love.

Jewelry

1308

Sometimes one concept can provide a *lifetime* of gift-giving opportunities. My friend Jerry Pallotta bought his wife Linda a modest diamond necklace one year. He's been adding one diamond a year for—well, for quite a while! (The necklace is no longer *modest*.) {Besides being a romantic devil, Jerry is the author of *The Icky Bug Alphabet Book*. It's not exactly romantic, but your kids will love it—and they might be so enthralled with it that the two of you might be able to sneak-off to your bedroom for a little of your *own* "Quality Time"!}

1309

Especially for diamond-lovers, science fiction fans, astrology fans, amateur astronomers or lovers-of-elegant-and-unusual-items: **Diamond Astrological Pins!** Jewelry designer A.G.A. Correa has created an incredible collection of constellation pins. Based on star charts, the pins are not only elegant, they're *accurate*: Each diamond is proportional to the magnitude of its corresponding star. All of the signs of the Zodiac are available, plus other constellations. Prices vary depending on the number of stars in each constellation and on their magnitude. For example: Libra is just $1,285 and Pisces only $1,745; while Gemini is $3,175 and Taurus is $3,320. Write to Post Office Box 401, Wiscasset, Maine 04578, or call 800-341-0788.

1310

Even though Tracey *loves* earrings, I *never* buy them for her. Why? Because her taste in earrings is *so* offbeat that I've never been able to choose a pair that she likes. Actually, it's *not* true that I never *buy* them for her— I just never *choose* them myself. What I do is pay close attention when we're out browsing together. I note what she likes, sneak back later and pick 'em up.

1311

Gold or silver? Classic or avant garde? Conservative or outrageous? Large or small? Expensive or costume? Modern or antique?

1312

Lovers can do some strange and creative things with their gifts . . . Many young women have found their diamond rings at the bottom of a glass of champagne. But here's a warning: Pearls dissolve in wine, and opals dissolve in champagne!

Chocolate

1313

Candy Bar Gazebo: The Confectionery Goodies Journal: Talk about your all-consuming passions! This quarterly newsletter is for those of you who are truly, passionately, unreasonably, insanely fond of chocolate and related candies. "But is the author really an expert on chocolate?" Glad you asked. Dr. Ray Broekel is an authority on chocolate and candy bar history; he's an historian for both the Chocolate Manufacturer's Association and the National Confectioner's Association; he's honored in the Chocolate Hall of Fame in Washington, D.C. (!); and he's authored two books on chocolate: *The Great American Candy Bar Book*, and *The Chocolate Chronicles*; and he has a collection of over 30,000 old candy bar wrappers. [Is this great or *what*?!] Anyway, you can get the newsletter for just $15. Write to Ray Broekel, Six Edge Street, Ipswich, Massachusetts 01938, or call 508-356-4191.

1314

If you're too embarrassed to go into your local chocolate shop and ask for erotic chocolates, or if you live in a town that bans pornography in all its insidious forms, this mail order catalog is for you! Erotic Chocolates, from Private Parts Adult Chocolates, 355 West Main Street, Suite 119, Norristown, Pennsylvania 19401, or call 215-627-0512.

1315

How about a dozen mixed roses—that is, six *real*, red roses mixed with six *chocolate* roses? Call ROSExpress at 800-366-6202 or 800-776-0162.

1316

[From *The Boston Globe* ... They expressed it so well, I figured I'd simply let *them* say it.] "For years, we've searched for guilt-free chocolate. In our fantasy, it would be superb chocolate—smooth, rich, its essence unobscured by excessive sugar—artfully shaped into seductive bon-bons that featured crisp, fresh, aromatic nuts. Magically, we would be Doing Good by eating these chocolates. They would have no calories. Toucan Chocolates, a new "gourmet rainforest chocolate product," comes close. Each "box" carries a mix of scrumptious light and dark chocolates—cashew caramel tortoises, nut-chocolate clusters, cashew bark... A portion of the proceeds is donated to Cultural Survival, a Cambridge-based human rights and rainforest group. The company uses no preservatives and recycled paper, vegetable-based inks, water soluble adhesives and sea grass in its appealing, unconventional package—a seagreen slipcase with jaunty, batik-like toucan seal. The calories, alas, are still with us, but we enjoyed consuming every one." To find out where to buy 'em in your local area or via catalog, call Toucan Chocolates at 617-964-8696, or write to Post Office Box 72, Waban, Massachusetts 02168.

1317

A nomination for the Best Book Title of the Year:

Death By Chocolate!

(Subtitled *The Last Word on a Consuming Passion*.) This cookbook serves up more than 80 recipes from Marcel Desaulniers, the executive chef of the Trellis Restaurant in Williamsburg, Virginia. The book itself is nearly edible! (FYI, "Death by Chocolate" is a 10-pound cake made with seven layers of chocolate!)

1318

Gourmet Magazine: "Ben Strohecker has a burning ambition to make 'the best chocolate in the world, regardless of the cost.' His unswerving pursuit of perfection has put Harbor Sweets in the 'very expensive' category, priced by the piece rather than by weight. He will not compromise on quality; he uses no artificial ingredients, no synthetic flavors, no shortcuts, and no preservatives. As further safeguards to quality, each piece is individually foil-wrapped, and the boxes are dated when they are packed so that they can be replaced if they are sold more than six weeks after they have come from Harbor Sweets." [A visitor to the Harbor Sweets kitchen described it as "...a cross between Willie Wonka's chocolate factory and Santa's workshop."]

Smithsonian Magazine: "In an informal taste test of gourmet candies by experts on one David Susskind TV show, Harbor Sweets won, hands down."

Marie & Alan Weiss, of East Greenwich, Rhode Island, who brought Harbor Sweets to my attention: "They make an unbelievable chocolate Advent Calendar! And did you know that the owner recently took a year off, letting his employees manage themselves, while he dedicated himself to increasing awareness of AIDS among top corporate honchos?"

Harbor Sweets: Visit them at Palmer Cove, 85 Leavitt Street, Salem, Massachusetts 01970-5546; or call 'em at 800-225-5669 or 508-745-7648.

1319

And this just in from Nantucket Island . . . Sweet Inspirations Chocolates offers a Year-Round Chocolate Gift Hotline. Call 508-228-2345, 9-5, EST. Proprietors/Chocolatiers Kathleen Henry and John West will handle your quality chocolate needs with award-winning sweets, including handmade chocolate truffles and chocolate bay scallop shells. Yum!

Flowers

1320

A rose is a rose is a rose—right? *Wrong!* The folks at ROSExpress specialize in especially beautiful, extra-long-stemmed roses. (They sell roses and nothing *but* roses!) Nationwide delivery is available; but if you're lucky enough to live in Boston, Washington, D.C., Philadelphia or San Francisco, you can get free delivery via tuxedo-clad driver! Call 800-366-6202 or 800-776-0162.

1321

Edible flowers! Tiger lilies, zucchini flowers, nasturtiums, calendulas, Johnny jump-ups, lemon-scented marigolds, pineapple sage and rose geraniums. [Now, do I put this item in the *Flowers* chapter or the *Food* chapter??]

1322

❖ Make your own Hawaiian lei, "the woven symbol of love" for your lover. Any kind of flowers will do, but larger ones work best.
❖ Think on *this* one: In Hawaiian, "Aloha" means "hello," "goodbye," and "love." [That's what I call an *all-purpose* word!]

1323

FTD has more than *24,000* member florists in the U.S.! With one on virtually every street corner, there's *no possible excuse* for not bringing flowers to your lover more often.

1324

Take that *extra step* and create a flower arrangement that has symbolic significance. Christa Cragg, for instance, once sent 11 red roses and one white rose. The note, of course, said, "You're one-of-a-kind!"

"It's very sensitive of you to realize that men like to get flowers!"

1325

Why, *oh why* won't you procrastinators listen to me?! *Don't wait until the last minute to order those flowers.* Especially for Valentine's Day!! [I've heard some truly pathetic stories from readers over the past year!] Do you people think your florist is sitting around waiting for you to call at 4:00 P.M. on Valentine's Day?! *Hah!* You'll be lucky to get a handful of dandelions wrapped in a rubber band by then! Call *several weeks early*! Write a note in your To-Do List. Tie a string around your finger. Do *something* to remind yourself to do it early.

1326

Preserve your bridal bouquet—or other special flowers—as a work of art. Ann Plowden is a pressed flower artist who creates truly memorable and beautiful gifts. Call for a brochure, 617-267-4705, or write to 375 Commonwealth Avenue, Boston, Massachusetts 02115.

1327

You're walking down the street, carrying a bouquet of flowers to give to your mate. *How do people look at you?*

They *smile!* They actually *look at you and smile!!* Isn't that *amazing?* Isn't that *wonderful?!* Flowers break down that impersonal barrier of anonymity that separates strangers walking down the street. When someone sees you with flowers, they *instantly* know that you're either on your way to give them to a loved-one, or that you just *received* them from a loved-one—and this makes them smile! It gives them a connection with you. Cool, huh?

Cars

1328

I've discovered a kind of passion that rivals that of Romeo for Juliet: It's the passion of a car buff for his beloved VW Bug. If your honey's hot for his Beetle, give him a gift certificate for a trip to VW Restorations & Customs in Virginia. These guys customize, re-build, re-paint and revitalize all kinds of Bugs—even those "hundred-buck junkers." If you've seen the movie *Chances Are* (with Cybill Shepherd, Robert Downey, Jr. and Ryan O'Neal), then you've seen their handiwork: A hot red 1963 VW convertible. If you want to turn *your* VW into a real Love Bug, call owner Paul Suplizio at 800-869-7543—and tell him Greg sent you.Call 800-869-7543, or write to 8223 Conner Drive, Manassas, Virginia 22111.

1329

"The one time you can let romance take a back seat in your life: When it's in the back seat of your car!" {Mrs. L. Blackstone, Kansas.}

1330

Here's a new Car Game called "Break-Down." To play it you need: 1) A car, and 2) A gullible girlfriend. Instructions: You're tooling down the road, when you suddenly swerve off the road and come to a sudden stop. Put your best "concerned" look on your face; turn to her in mock seriousness, and say, "Honey, I think it's—true love!"—and you grab her and kiss her passionately. [Corny, but very appreciated, from what I hear.] {Thanks to Tim Moody, of Salem, Massachusetts.}

1331

It seems there's just no fathoming the depths of some men's love for their. . . *cars*. If you think *your* man is car crazy, consider the case of Bob Moran, a car buff of grand proportions. He found an architect who was just as auto obsessive as he is, and they designed an entire house that's been described as "a car freak's candy store." A two-story bay window suggests a car's radiator grille; the porch railing resembles the bumper of a Ford Model A; steel pipe columns are capped with actual Volkswagen piston barrels; living room sofas are Citroen seats; and an enlarged reproduction of a 1948 DeSoto hood ornament tops the roof. If you can't beat 'em . . .

1332

❋ For owners and admirers of the Ford Mustang:
  ✳ The Mustang Club of America, Post Office Box 447, Lithonia, Georgia 30058.
  ✳ The Mustang Owners Club International, 2720 Tennessee N.E., Albuquerque, New Mexico 87110.

❋ And for those who love classic Chevys:
  ✳ Classic Chevy International, 8235 North Orange Blossom Trail, Orlando, Florida 32810; 407-299-1957.
  ✳ The Late Great Chevy Association, 2166 South Orange Blossom Trail, Apopka, Florida 32703; 407-886-1963.

1333

For the car buff in your life: The Imperial Palace Auto Collection, in Las Vegas. This huge collection includes such notable cars as Jack Benny's 1910 Maxwell, Emperor Hirohito's 1935 Packard, and Cadillacs owned by Al Capone, Herbert Hoover and Elvis Presley! Call 702-731-3311.

Sports

1334

When some people refer to the "Flame of Passion" they *mean* it—*literally!* Cynthia and Gabe Potter, of Oklahoma, were inspired by the 1980 Olympics and the "Eternal Flame" concept: "Every single day for more than a decade now, we keep a candle lit in our home whenever we're around and awake. It's our private ritual, which we've never shared with anyone—until now. We thought that other romantics would like to hear about our idea! The flame symbolizes many things for us: Love, passion, the Holy Spirit, the light we bring to each other's life, our life force, etcetera. (Yes, we spend a lot of money on candles—but not as much as some people spend on cigarettes, and this is so much healthier!) We've written each other poems about our flame, we've written special affirmations that help us stay centered, and we've found many ways of incorporating candles into other standard holidays and traditions."

1335

The way to a man's heart is through . . . his sports obsession! Stacey and Mark, of Nashua, New Hampshire, live a life that centers on baseball: On the night they met they sat on the bleachers of a local ballpark and talked; Mark proposed to her in a ballpark; and . . . they once made love on the pitcher's mound of a ballpark! Not only that—and here's the really cool part—during that particular lovemaking session they conceived their son! True to the spirit of the event, they named him Nolan Ryan, after the great pitcher for the Texas Rangers. {Stacey related this story to me, DJ Mike Morin, and thousands of Lawrence and Boston-area listeners of WCGY-radio!}

1336

(To the tune of "Take Me Out to the Ballgame" . . .)

Take him out to the ballpark,
For his birthday, let's say . . .
Put his name up on the score-board-there,
Tell him you love him and show that you care!
{Christine C., of Redding, Connecticut did this once with great effect!}

1337

Two of the most fanatical types of sportsmen are those who fish and those who golf. If your lover is among the possessed, get him one of these T-shirts, polo shirts or sweatshirts:

- ✓ "I fish, therefore I am."

- ✓ "I only play golf on days that end in Y."

- ✓ "If it goes right, it's a slice. If it goes left, it's a hook. If it goes straight, it's a miracle."

Available through the *Wireless Catalog*, call 800-669-9999.

1338

Let's look at this whole Relationship-Thing another way. You see, guys understand sports, but they don't seem to understand women. Why? Well, in the "game" of Relationships, there aren't any clear-cut rules, so how's a guy to know how to proceed? You don't get awarded points, so you don't know where you stand. And different players of the game have different goals—so it's like playing basketball, and suddenly being told that the goal is to get a touchdown! And, to make matters worse, lots of guys are confused as to whether women are their teammates or their opponents! No wonder guys have a tough time with all this romance nonsense!

1339

Chocolates in the shapes of . . . footballs, little bite-sized footballs, football players, bite-sized baseballs, baseball gloves, baseball players, golf balls, golf bags, bowling trophies, skateboards, tennis racquets and bite-sized basketballs . . . are available from The Chocolate Gallery. Call 800-426-4796 (10-6, M-S, PST), or write to 5705 Calle Real, Goleta, California 93117-2315.

The
Opposing Viewpoint

1340

Some thoughts on romance from a variety of readers, presented without editorial comment:

- ☛ "Romance is a man's sneaky way to get sex."
- ☛ "Romance is a woman's sneaky way to trap a man."
- ☛ "Romance is Nature's way of continuing the species in an animal whose brain too often gets in the way of natural physiological/sexual functioning."
- ☛ "Romance is God's way of encouraging fidelity."
- ☛ "Romance is the Devil's own special form of temptation. Shame on you!"
- ☛ "Romance is Society's way of ensuring civility between partners who might otherwise murder one another."
- ☛ "Romance is a fiction dreamed-up by Madison Avenue and Hallmark."
- ☛ "Romance is a fairy tale told to children, and practiced by overgrown adolescents."

1341

One of the "nation's leading psychiatric authorities on interpersonal skills and effective relationship communication" disagrees *heartily* with my stand on romance! Following extensive psychological counseling, I've decided that the only way for me to deal with this in a healthy way is to share some of his ideas with you, and let *you* decide who's right! [I feel better *already*!]

These excerpts are from *The Dirty Half Dozen—Six Radical Rules to Make Relationships Last:*

Rule 1: *Don't keep the romance alive.* The best way to destroy a relationship, any relationship, is to try to keep the romance alive . . . Working on making a relationship exciting is guaranteed to destroy whatever spark may be left.

Rule 2: *Don't fight fair.*

Rule 3: *Don't talk about everything.*

You'll have to discover the remaining rules for yourself, if you're interested.

1342

Happiness Through Superficiality: The War Against Meaningful Relationships, by Jerry Newmark, Ph.D. & Irving Newmark, D.D.S. is a humorous book about life's most serious aspects. Discover how to stop taking everything so seriously! [This book was a collaborative effort by a doctor of philosophy and a doctor of dentistry: How could it *not* be unusual?!]

1343

Some scientist-types have been studying love and romance (as if it were, say, a frog that one could dissect).

➦ Psychologist John Alan Lee has identified nine varieties of love, and has labeled the head-over-heels variety "mania"—as he considers it a form of madness.

➦ Behavioral scientists Stanton Peele and Archie Brodsky argue that romantic love is a form of addiction. They observe that people in love often display two major characteristics of drug abuse: Tolerance and withdrawal.

➦ Psychologist Lawrence Casler's theory is that love is a cultural invention to overcome our Puritanical guilt over sex. We pretend that lust is the by-product of love, when in reality love is the by-product of lust.

1344

Sleeping in the same bed may actually be *harmful* to some people's relationships! Some experts counsel people to sleep in separate beds—or *rooms*—when they can't resolve issues of bed-sharing, cover-stealing, and whether the window stays open or closed. [I'm gonna keep my mouth shut on this one . . .]

1345

"Jealousy, in moderation, says 'I care.'" says the headline in one magazine article, reporting on what some psychologists say on the subject. [Sorry, I just can't buy this one. I've read a *lot* about what the experts have to say about jealousy, and I *still* believe that jealousy is comprised of a lack of maturity and/or lack of self-esteem. Period.]

1346

"... I do sometimes wonder what is really being accomplished by being so virtuous. Most mammals take their pleasure where they find it, and our fellow primates are for the most part shameless libertines. Why should humans be any different? Don't get me wrong. I enjoy the security and reliability of monogamy, and I like my marriage. But might there not be someplace for the exercise of simple lust in this arrangement? A kind of escape hatch for the libido? . . . If one can take a vacation from work, why not from love? If it were up to me, I'd pattern a "love vacation" after the seventh-year sabbaticals enjoyed by college professors . . . so how about a marriage sabbatical? After seven years of marriage, each spouse would be free to spend seven weeks' vacation away from the marriage with whomever he or she chose. A sexual holiday, in short . . . but only for seven weeks after seven years. I don't think of the sabbatical plan as a license to screw around indefinitely . . . Instead of undermining a marriage, the marriage sabbatical may well serve to restore it, awakening sexual desires that may have gone dormant over the years. And spouses finally given a chance to indulge their adulterous fantasies may well discover how much they already have in their marriage. After all, it is only after traveling that one fully appreciates him." {John Sedgwick, writing in *Boston Magazine*.}

"I believe that husbands should bring home flowers even when they're not cheating on their wives!"

~ Teri Garr

Dear Mr. Romance

1347

"What's the difference between "romance" and plain old thoughtfulness and everyday considerateness?" {J.G., San Diego, California.}

Dear J.G.:

The difference is in the **nature of the relationship,** *not* in the gestures or words themselves. Sending a birthday card to your mother is considerate; sending a birthday card to your wife is romantic. Romance is "plain old thoughtfulness and everyday considerateness" toward your intimate partner. And don't forget, true romance is a *voluntary* expression of love, not an *obligatory* gesture performed out of duty or guilt.

1348

"Romance is all well and nice, but how can you spend so much time on a little dalliance when there are serious problems like world peace to worry about?" {M.R., New York City.}

Dear M.R.:

You're right—romance doesn't rank up there with Mother Teresa's work, and a little romance isn't going to bring about world peace, but there's a time and a place for everything, right? Expressing your feelings for your intimate partner through romantic gestures brings a little more light of Love into the world—and this world is certainly in need of more Love, don't you think?

You know, now that I think about it, isn't it true that one must be a loving, caring, trusting, unselfish person in order to be romantic? Well, maybe if our world leaders had truly healthy, intimate relationships with their spouses, and if they themselves were happy and fulfilled—and not so egotistical, greedy and insecure—then maybe they wouldn't be so aggressive, short-sighted and selfish. Hmm . . . As a matter of fact, M.R., perhaps Romance *is* the answer to world peace!

1349

"Isn't romance just another form of Codependency?" {S.T., Chicago.}

Dear S.T.:

No.

P.S. Here's the definition of codependency from Melody Beattie, author of the bestselling *Codependent No More*: "A codependent person is one who has let another person's behavior affect him or her, and who is obsessed with controlling that person's behavior." I believe that romance has a *lot* to do with how your lover's behavior affects you, but it has nothing whatsoever to do with controlling his or her behavior. Anyone who uses romance to manipulate another is misusing a powerful tool—It's like using a hammer to smash windows instead of build houses. The responsibility does not lie in the tool, but in he who wields it.

1350

"Who died and made you King? I'll treat my wife my own way in my own good time." {S.S., Memphis, Tennessee.}

Dear S.S.:

Anyone who interprets my books as prescriptions and rules has missed the point. I'm simply presenting 1001 options, ideas, suggestions and questions for you to consider. I have much too much respect for every person's unique Path and individual style to attempt to tell you specifically what will work for you. "King"?? Heck, I roll my eyes, too, when people refer to me as an "expert" on romance. I just happen to have a passion for this topic, I'm a magnet for romantic ideas, I save stuff, I manage to string words together in a manner that some people like (my mother, for one), and I'm not shy about standing up before audiences to share this Message.

1351

"Can you define "romance" exactly? You dance around the issue, and you seem to assume that we know what it is." {C.D., Delta, Colorado.}

Dear C.D.:

➤ Answer #1: When you define "love" *exactly*, I'll define "romance" *exactly*.

➤ Answer #2: (Ro' • mans) 1) The expression of love. 2) Love in action. 3) A state of mind, in which one's intimate partner (lover) is forefront in one's thoughts. 4) A state of being, in which one's love is continuously expressed through action. 5) A way of life, in which love is openly expressed, passion flourishes, and intimacy grows.

1352

"Don't you think romance is just looking at the world through rose colored glasses?" {S.T., Sussex, Delaware.}

Dear S.T.:

Absolutely! Romance *is* a "filter" on what is commonly referred-to as the "real world." In fact, this "filter" may help you see past the many illusions of that "real world" and help you see the Reality behind it! (Don't confuse "rose colored glasses" with "blinders"!)

1353

"Can you give someone *too much* romance? Is it possible to love someone *too much*?" {G.D., Roanoke, Virginia.}

Dear G.D.:

No.

Erotica

1354

Erotic chocolates! [Author's note to editor: Am I allowed to use the phrase *Chocolate Penis* in the book? Do you think many readers would be offended by *Milk Chocolate Breasts With Vanilla Nipples*? Please get back to me before the book goes to press.] See the "erotic chocolates" item in the *Chocolate!* chapter!

1355

FM shoes.

1356

How do *you* let your lover know you're in the mood for making love? Many readers have written to share some rather interesting, and—uh, unusual, methods for expressing their erotic desires!

- ✗ "Believe it or not, my wife can raise her right eyebrow like Mr. Spock on *Star Trek*. When she wants to make love, she gives me that expression. If I'm in the mood, I say, 'Live long and prosper.' If I'm not in the mood I say, 'Highly illogical.' (Please don't print my name—my friends would think I'm crazy!)" {A Trekker in Pennsylvania.} [Author's note: I just hope she's interested more often than once every seven years, like most Vulcans!]

- ✗ "I simply turn-down the corner of the bedspread if I'm "in the mood." If my husband is too tired, he straightens-out the bedspread; if he's "in the mood" too, he turns-down the other corner of the bed." {J.C., Washington, D.C.}

- ✗ "My wife turns on our Lava Lamp whenever she wants me to turn her on!" {F. Evans, Fort Lauderdale, Florida.}

1357

Here's how an innocent typo led to a night of intense passion: This guy—let's call him "Steve"—typed an invitation to his girlfriend—let's call her "Linda"—saying: "You are invited to my apartment for an evening of movies and popcorn, so come prepared for an entertaining evening." Innocent enough, right? Well, unknown to him, hapless Steve typed "porn" instead of "popcorn." Linda—being an adventurous, open-minded woman—figured she'd match Steve's mood, so she arrived at his door dressed in a trench coat . . . with a black garter belt and stockings on underneath. (Needless to say, they never did get around to watching *Pretty Woman*. [Just as well.])

1358-1360

✗ *Erotica*—The title of Madonna's 1992 album. This marks her return to the dance-driven numbers that first made her popular. One song is called "Deeper and Deeper." Uh-huh.

✗ *The Erotic Mind*—The title of a book on eroticism and human sexuality that emphasizes the mind/body connection. By Jack Morin, Ph.D.

✗ *Erotic Chocolates*—From Private Parts Adult Chocolates, 355 West Main Street, Suite 119, Norristown, Pennsylvania 19401, or call 215-627-0512.

1361

The Perfect Fit: How to Achieve Mutual Fulfillment and Monogamous Passion Through the New Intercourse. [I don't know about you, but *I'm* still working on the "old intercourse"! Oops! Sorry.] Seriously, now . . . This book introduces the "Coital Alignment Technique," known as CAT, which is designed to give couples more simultaneous orgasms, more frequent orgasms for women, and heightened sexual pleasure. [Worthy goals, one and all.]

1362-1364

"Choreograph" your lovemaking to your favorite music! This may sound artificial and contrived, but several people in the Romance Class have told me that they often do this, although they never thought of it as "choreography." I don't mean that you plan every movement, but rather that you match some favorite music to the general mood and pace of your lovemaking.

➤ For example, some people like to start slowly and gently, and build to a fast-paced climax. [Pun intended.] Their musical choreography could look like this: Start with a little George Winston; move to some Al Jarreau; mix-in some Benny Goodman; and finish-up with Maynard Ferguson!

➤ Others like to start-out fast and passionately, and wind-down to a gentle conclusion. Their musical choreography could look like this: Start with the sound track from *9-1/2 Weeks*; move to the sound track from *When Harry Met Sally*; and end with the sound track from *Out of Africa*.

➤ One couple from New Jersey prefers Mozart symphonies. "Beethoven is great music, but too frenetic for our lovemaking. Mozart is great—especially The Jupiter Symphony, No. 41. It has four movements, which correspond with our pattern of lovemaking. 1) The first movement, Allegro Vivace is strong and passionate, which gets us going; and it runs 11:50—good for energetic foreplay. 2) The second movement, Andante Cantabile, slows the pace, which allows us to talk a little and build the intimacy more; this runs a good 10:53. 3) The third movement, Menuetto: Allegretto, picks up the speed again, which moves us from quiet intimacy into a more intense passion; this one is quick, at 5:13. 4) The last movement, Molto Allegro, races to a roaring and passionate conclusion; and runs 8:37." {The musical lovers A. & N. Rossini, of Seattle, Washington.}

1365

Erotic fiction, humbly submitted for your perusal:

* *Tart Tales—Elegant Erotic Stories*, by Carolyn Banks
* *My Secret Garden*, by Nancy Friday
* *Forbidden Flowers*, also by Nancy Friday
* *Women On Top*, by . . . Nancy Friday
* *The Unbearable Lightness of Being*, by Milan Kundera

1366

Boudoir photography, revisited. Many people—mostly *women*—have written to me (sometimes in embarrassing detail!), explaining that a "Fantasy Photo" was the best gift they've ever given or received. Here are a few new resources, in addition to some from the first book:

* Boston: Fantasy Photography by Daphne: 617-641-2100
* Detroit: Captured Glamour, Carol Goren: 313-855-0310
* New York City: Lucienne Photography: 212-564-9670
* San Diego: Classic Cheesecake, Kimberly Bennett: 619-453-FOTO
* Santa Monica: Don Myers Photography: 213-399-4646
* Washington, D.C.: Lee's Photography: 703-237-4911

1367

Erotica, etcetera . . .

* DJ Mike Miller, at WJNO-Radio in West Palm Beach, Florida, recommends the *Emmanuel* movies—"But only the ones starring Sylvia Crystal!" he cautions.

* *Perceptions*, the quarterly newsletter of "sensual self-expression." See the listing in the *Newsletters Galore* chapter.

1368

Today's vocabulary lesson seeks to make some distinctions among some similar-yet-different words. [Mrs. Wilcox would be *scandalized*!]

- *Erotic*: "Arousing or satisfying sexual desire." Her erotic dance put him in the mood for love.

- *Sensual*: "Arousing or exciting the senses or appetites." The dinner was a sensual delight, which added to the romance of the evening.

- *Voluptuous*: "Implies the luxurious gratification of sensuous or sensual desires." She looked voluptuous in the slinky gown.

1369

Lingerie Catalog Update

These are a few of the new lingerie catalogs that I've discovered since the publication of *1001 Ways To Be Romantic*: Secret Passions, Private Pleasures, Hidden Secrets, The Red Garter, Kathleen's Collection, Aries Catalog, and Satin & Ruffles. [It's a tough job, but *someone's* got to do this research!] And the research isn't completed. You see, most of these catalogs only advertise as part of "group ads" in magazines—you can't reach them directly. Thus, many of the catalogs I've ordered [for research purposes *only*] haven't arrived here yet, so I don't have their direct numbers for you. —Here's an idea! I'll devote an *entire* issue of my *Romance Newsletter* to lingerie catalogs. Okay? —Until then, some of the above catalogs can be ordered through Intimate Treasures at 415-896-0944, and the Cosmopolitan Catalog Showcase, at 800-241-9111, extension 316.

> *"The best sexual lubricant is communication."*
>
> *~ June Reinisch, Ph.D.,*
> *Director of the Kinsey Institute of Sexual Research.*

1370

Have you ever covered a portion of your lover's body with food, and then licked it off?

1371

After years of painstaking research, the Institute for Erotic and Romantic Studies is ready to report that the most sensual fruit is *not* the banana . . . but the *persimmon!* Knowing little about this exotic fruit, your intrepid researcher sought-out self-proclaimed persimmon aficionado Robert Kaufman. Let me tell you in all honesty that I have *never* spoken with *any*one who was as *passionate* about a topic as Robert is about persimmons. And, I'll confess, I have *never* had a conversation with a *man* that was so, um . . . ah—*erotic.*

"The persimmon, you see, is a total sensory experience. It's a feast for the eyes, the fingers, the mouth." [See what I mean?] "Persimmons are not like other fruits, which you can just buy and eat, without even thinking about it. You don't just *eat* a persimmon—you have a *relationship* with it. When you first buy one, it's hard, like an apple. You put it on a window ledge and watch it. For two to four weeks. This ripening process also builds the anticipation, making the final experience all the more enjoyable!" [Sounds like foreplay to me.] "You must resist the temptation to open it too early. When a persimmon is truly ripe, it's an *incredible* thing. Hold it in your hand: It resembles a female breast in its texture, weight, fluidity and shape. Now, to eat it, you slice a section out of the top, then gently suck the fruit out. The main fruit pulp is a soft, jello-like fluid. Also, there are several 'tongues' inside; they're kind-of like orange segments. The taste— ah, the taste!—It's the most delicious taste imaginable. Any description fails to do it justice." [*Whew!*]

Exotica

1372

Africa! I'd never considered "The Dark Continent" romantic until two things coincided: I saw the movie *Out of Africa*, and I met Mark Nolting, a safari leader, tour operator, and author of the excellent book *Africa's Top Wildlife Countries*. It highlights and compares all the top wildlife countries and reserves, making it easy to plan an excellent photographic or adventure safari. His second book, *Travel Journal Africa*, is the perfect book for adventurers to take with them on safari, as it is a wildlife guide, language guide, trip organizer and diary—all in one! Write to Global Travel Publishers, 1620 South Federal Highway, Suite 900, Pompano Beach, Florida 33062; call 305-781-3933 or 800-882-9453.

1373

How about having an exotic adventure without leaving your armchair? Pick-up the book *Out-of-Body Adventures: 30 Days to the Most Exciting Experience of Your Life*, by astral travel expert and workshop leader Rick Stack.

1374

What could be cooler than working on the Love Boat? Getting a job on a cruise ship *could* be a once-in-a-lifetime opportunity! Some of those ships have crews of 1,000+ people—including shop clerks, hair stylists, photographers, entertainers and casino dealers. I hear that the pay is "Okay but not great"—but food and lodging are free! Here's the guidebook listing the organizations that staff most major cruise lines: Ticket to Adventure. It's $15.95—write to Box 41005, St. Petersburg, Florida 33743, or call 800-929-7447.

1375

If you want a cruise with a little more *adventure*, get aboard the Polaris and go on a special expedition along with Sven-Olof Lindblad's Special Expeditions. Guests of the Polaris describe her as "A happy ship," and many of them return for additional expeditions. The ship is large enough to go anywhere and be comfortable, yet small enough to allow entry to isolated areas, and also to small harbors inaccessible to larger ships. The Polaris carries 80 guests, "The ultimate luxury," according to Sven-Olof.

Here are just a few of the expeditions available:

❖ *Two Thousand Miles Up the Amazon*
❖ *Exploring the British and Irish Isles*
❖ *Rediscovering Russia and the Baltics*
❖ *Exploring Arctic Norway and Spitsbergen*

Call Special Expeditions at 800-762-0003.

1376

The Orient-Express—the world's most romantic train. Twice weekly it leaves London on its legendary journey. Paris, Zurich, Innsbruck and Venice or Salzburg, Vienna and Budapest. Just $3 for a brochure describing the adventure. Write to the Venice Simplon Orient-Express, 1155 Avenue of the Americas, 30th Floor, New York City, New York 10036, or call 800-524-2420.

Romance is creating memories.

European Romance

1377-1378
Amsterdam

* Elegant hotel: Pulitzer: Concealed gardens and covered walkways connect a complex of 24 restored townhouses and converted warehouses. Located between the Prinsengracht and the Keizersgracht canals. 315-331 Prinsengracht. Telephone: 523-5235.
* Romantic restaurant: De Goudsbloem: Gabled setting, flowered garden patio and walkway, and views along two canals. 315 Prinsengracht, in the Hotel Pulitzer complex. Telephone: 523-5235.

1379-1380
Stockholm

* Classy hotel: Hasselby Slott: Regal quarters in a castle that dates back to 1652. Located in a small park just off the shores of Lake Malaran. 1-3 Maltesholmsvagen, Vallingby. Telephone: 89-02-20.
* Romantic restaurant: Min Lilla Tradgard ("my little garden"): A tiny, lovely neighborhood restaurant. Hidden away in the basement/garden of a residential building in the most exclusive part of town. 4 Lutzengatan. Telephone 661-5117.

1381
Copenhagen

* Classic hotel: Skovshoved: A cozy inn that looks like an oversize vacation house. Every room is unique—some overlook the sea; others have views of the courtyard. 267 Strandvejen, Charlottenlund. Telephone: 31-64-00-28.

1382-1384
London

✳ Unusual hotel: Portobello: A hotel known for its bohemian qualities. Room #16 has a circular bed—and an enormous Victorian bathtub right next to the bed. Room #13 has an enormous four-poster bed complete with steps to climb into it! 22 Stanley Gardens. Telephone (071) 727-2777.

✳ Most romantic restaurant: Odette's in summer. After dinner, you can stroll to the top of Primrose Hill for the best starlit view of London. 130 Regent's Park Road. Telephone: (071) 586-8766.

✳ Shoes to die for: Lobb & Company makes custom shoes that cost $1,000 or more! They're crafted from wooden models of your feet that are kept on file for your next pair! 9 St. James's Street. Telephone: (071) 930-3664.

1385-1386
Edinburgh

✶ Romantic hotel: Prestonfield House: Setting a new standard for the word "small," the Prestonfield has only five bedrooms. It does, however, have two restaurants!—One French, one Scottish. Priestfield Road. Telephone 668-3346.

✶ Romantic Restaurant: The Waterside Bistro and Restaurant: A grand space, brimming with cut flowers, serving international food. Don't miss the romantic little bar downstairs. 1/5 Waterside, Nungate Haddington. Telephone: (062) 082-5674.

1387-1388
Zurich

✳ Romantic hotel: Ermitage: A great summer hideaway, 15-minutes outside Zurich. Private beach on Lake Zurich; lovely garden restaurant, bar and grill. 80 Seestrasse, Kusnacht am See. Telephone: 910-5222.

✳ Romantic restaurant: Tubli: Exceptional international cuisine with an Italian emphasis. Try the seven-course extravaganza; or maybe just the five-course lunch! 8 Schneggengasse. Telephone: 251-2471.

1389-1390
Vienna

◇ Romantic hotel: Romischer Kaiser: A 23-room Baroque palace. Small and centrally located, between the State Opera and St. Stephen's Cathedral. 16 Annagasse. Telephone: 51-27-75-10.
◇ Fanciest restaurant: Steirereck: New style Viennese, superb service. 2 Rasumofskygasse. Telephone: 713-3168.

1391-1392
Budapest

✳ Picturesque hotel: Gellert: The grande dame of Budapest hotels lives on in serene Habsburgian splendor. The rooms are fine, but the real draw is the Gellert's famous baths, with their magnificent Art Nouveau/neo-Romanesque decor, towering marble pillars, and intricately patterned mosaic tiles. 1 Szent Gellert Ter. Telephone: 185-2200.
✳ Romantic restaurant: Paradiso: Located in an old villa. Excellent Continental cuisine. A wonderfully romantic ambiance. 40a Istenhegyi Ut. Telephone: 156-1988.

1393-1395
Paris

✳ Small, luxurious hotel: La Tremoille: A favorite of guests who appreciate large rooms, understated atmosphere, and a great location in the golden triangle of Paris shopping, just off the Avenue Montaigne. 14 Rue de La Tremoille. Telephone: 47-23-34-20.
✳ Romantic restaurant: Au Clocher du Village: A charming old bistro on a leafy square opposite the Eglise d'Auteuil. Lovers linger long after their meals are through. 8 bis Rue Verderet. Telephone: 42-88-35-87.
✳ Best ice cream: Zagori Haute Gourmandise. 6 Rue Lafayette. Telephone 43-87-40-83.

1396-1398
Madrid

✳ Small, luxurious hotel: Santa Mauro: A restored 1894 palace. With only 36 rooms, and 70 staff members to serve guests! 36 Calle Zurbano. Telephone: 319-6900.

✳ Fine restaurant: El Amparo: One of the city's finest restaurants, known more to locals than to visitors. Don't be daunted by the narrow alleyway and the insignificant-looking black door. 8 Callejon de Puigcerda. Telephone: 431-6456.

✳ Romantic garden: El Capricho park, hidden away on Alameda de Osuna, near the Madrid airport. Fountains and numerous secret corners. Particularly luxurious in the spring, when thousands of purple lilac bushes are in bloom.

1399-1401
Rome

◆ Luxurious hotel: Sole al Pantheon: A completely restored 15th century treasure, the oldest hotel in Rome. Many rooms have fabulous views of the Pantheon. Jacuzzis, too. 63 Piazza della Rotonda. Telephone: 678-0441.

◆ Romantic restaurant: Girone VI: Romantic tables outside, weather permitting. Particularly good wine cellar. 2 Vicolo Sinibaldi. Telephone: 654-2831.

◆ Best bar for watching sunsets: The Casina Valadier on the Pincio hill in the Villa Borghese gardens. 1 Piazzale Napoleone.

1402-1403
Venice

➤ Quaint hotel: Accademia: A 28-room hotel with the feeling of a country villa, even though it's just off the Grand Canal. Many rooms overlook secluded gardens. 1058 Fondamenta Bollani, Dorsoduro. Telephone: 523-7846.

➤ Romantic restaurant: Da Fiore: An intimate rendezvous tucked away on a tiny street just off the square of San Polo. 2202 Calle del Scaleter, San Polo. Telephone: 72-13-08.

Love, American Style

1404

Autumn colors can be very romantic, but don't leave your travel plans to chance! These fall foliage hotlines give the latest reports on the leaf situation in various parts of their states:

- ❍ Vermont: 802-828-3239
- ❍ New Hampshire: 800-258-3608/3609 or 603-262-6660
- ❍ Maine: 800-533-9595
- ❍ Massachusetts: 617-727-3201; in Massachusetts, 800-632-8038; in the Northeast 800-343-9072
- ❍ Rhode Island: 800-556-2484
- ❍ Connecticut: 800-282-6863 or 203-566-5348
- ❍ New Jersey: 201-579-3933
- ❍ New York: 800-CALL-NYS
- ❍ Pennsylvania: 800-FALL-IN-PA
- ❍ Nationwide: 202-205-1780; reports on foliage in the national forests

1405

America's romantic hideaway island: Martha's Vineyard. Great for small, elegant, private affairs—whether they're affairs of the heart, or affairs like small weddings or anniversary parties. If you'd like some help in planning and implementing your romantic adventure on the island, call Romance Martha's Vineyard. Laura Joseph and James Schot, who know every little romantic spot and service on the island, will assist you in making every arrangement, with attention to detail that will astound and delight you! Call them at 508-693-5299.

Lawyers In Love

1406

The following item is reproduced without editing:

"My wife is a lovely, wonderful person except for *one* thing—she's a *lawyer*. I think it's against the ethical standards of the bar for lawyers to be romantic. I don't mean this as a *criticism*, but merely as a statement of fact. For example, my wife insisted that we sign a prenuptial agreement before we got married last year. I reluctantly agreed, but under *one* condition: That we *also* sign a 'Romance Contract' that I wrote with the help of two lawyer friends of mine. It may not sound romantic, but sometimes you've got to fight fire with fire!" [Sounds like a great plot for a sit-com!] {Name withheld to avoid any lawsuits!}

1407

If you've got three days you can go on a cruise! One long weekend will do it! There's no longer any excuse—even for busy lawyers and harried executives. Hop a plane, hop a ship, and relax. Forget about your cares for a few days. Spend some quality time with your honey. Swim. Shop. Laze. Read. Fool around. Dance. Eat. Sleep. Read. Repeat.

1408

"*Time is money.*" You've heard it a *thousand* times. A call for efficiency. A time management maxim. An excuse for workaholics. A lie! Time is **not** money! You can *save* money, but you *can't* save time—it's slipping-by all the time, regardless of what you do! See?—Look!—Aaaugh!—*There goes another minute!—Followed by a few precious seconds!—Wait!—Stop!—I'm not ready!* See what I mean? Also, you can create *more* money—by working harder or longer or smarter. But you *can't* create more time. *That's it. Sorry. Nope. No more. No—you can't live on "borrowed time"—what a ridiculous concept.* So . . . I'd suggest that you *save the money* (perhaps for a big gift or special event)—but *spend the time* now, while you still have it!

1409-1410

Do you mentally "bring your work home with you" every night? If so, you're contaminating your leisure time, harming your health, eroding your relationships and diminishing the general quality of your life. Experts advise that you need to "decompress"—you need to create a regular routine that will allow you to shift gears and clear your mind, as you make the transition between work and home. Here are some tips:

◆ On your commute home, re-orient your thoughts from the corporate to the domestic. Go through a mental rehearsal of the restful activities you'll undertake at home—instead of rehashing events at work.

◆ Symbolically change your identity—from Super Lawyer to Super Dad, or from Wonder Secretary to Wonder Wife!—by changing into a favorite outfit, going for a walk, or taking a shower.

◆ Meditate. Oooooommmmm.

◆ Listen to 20 minutes of Mozart or George Winston. *Aaaaaah!*

◆ Write in your journal.

◆ Or *calmly* read this book: *It's All In Your Head: Life-style Management Strategies for Busy People,* by psychologist Bruce Baldwin, Ph.D.

"The problem with the Rat Race is that even if you win the Race, you're still a Rat!"

~ *Lily Tomlin*

MBAs In Love

1411

Buy her one share of stock in her favorite company! Sara Lee, Gitano, Disney, McDonald's, Coca-Cola, etc.

1412

Some new line-items for your household budget: Flowers. Surprise gifts. Get-away weekends. Romantic miscellany.

1413

Trying to win her heart? Why not take a tip from some of the most savvy marketers, from American Express to Publishers Clearinghouse: Create a direct-mail campaign to convince her to "buy the product"—you! Use your imagination to create a whole campaign: A series of mailings over several weeks to get your point across. (Or, if you have more money than time or imagination, hire a freelance graphic artist to whip-up some concepts on a Macintosh!)

1414

Kaizen. Well-read businesspeople will recognize this Japanese word. The principle of Kaizen—meaning small, gradual improvements over time— has helped revolutionize Japanese business. Properly implemented, Kaizen could revolutionize your *relationship*, too! Think about it!

1415

✴ In *1001 Ways To Be Romantic* I mentioned in passing that I get romantic ideas out of *The Wall Street Journal*. Several people wrote, asking me if I was serious, or just exaggerating. [Who, *me!?!*] Actually, I was quite serious. *The Wall Street Journal* was the first publication to report on the existence of musical greeting cards—*six months* before they appeared on store shelves. And, through an ad in the *Journal* I discovered a company that makes custom chocolate bars: Miramar packs 15 tasty chocolate bars with customized wrappers in a redwood box for your chocolate-lover. (Call 800-222-1624.)

✴ Heck, I even get romantic ideas out of my accountant's newsletter! Tracey and I now celebrate a new holiday: "Tax Freedom Day." An article in the newsletter described it as that day when the average American has worked enough days to satisfy all federal, state and local tax obligations, with every cent earned from the beginning of the year going to tax collectors. It's approximately 126 days into the year—putting Tax Freedom Day around May 2nd to the 5th. This may sound depressing to you, but we believe in facing reality, and grabbing *any* excuse to celebrate! {Thanks to Forman, Itzkowitz, Berenson & LaGreca, of Newton, Massachusetts.}

1416

Budget your *time* as well as your *money*!

Has your life become your to-do list?

~ Maggie Bedrosian

1417

Do you travel on business a lot? Surprise her by returning home a day early! Declare it a "Bonus Day" and spend it together in some fun, frivolous manner!

1418

You single-minded business types may not believe this, but it's true:

The romantic/interpersonal skills you practice in your love relationship will benefit you in your business life.

Managers must communicate well with their employees. Salespeople must understand and empathize with their customers. Everyone must be attentive to details, while watching the big picture, too. The most successful businesspeople have short-term tactics and strategies that work toward long-term goals. See? Being romantic will not harm your business life. *Whew!*

1419

The Continuously Improving Self: A Personal Guide to TQM, by Jeffrey E. Lickson, Ph.D. This book will help *anyone*, but it will ring special bells with you businesspeople who are familiar with the management technique called TQM—Total Quality Management. Models and exercises built around Deming's principles have been developed to stimulate self-awareness and questioning. This book will help you learn the psychological, social and cognitive issues most likely to block self-development.

Q&A

1420

How many *minutes per day of undivided attention* do you give your lover?

1421

Have you ever interrupted a lovemaking session to answer the phone?

1422

If your relationship were a painting . . . What does it look like? How does it compare with the rough sketches of your earlier relationships? What color is it? How do you two artists share the work of creating it? Do you display your artwork for all to see, or are you waiting for a grand unveiling? How will you know when it's complete enough to show? Are you happy with the progress you're making? What *style* of artwork is it? (Are you painting an Impressionistic image over *here*, while she's painting an abstract image over *there*? That's fine—but how will you merge the two harmoniously?)

1423

Have you been receiving your M.D.R.R.? (Minimum Daily Requirement of Romance.) How much romance *do* you want and need in your life? How much do you want daily—weekly—monthly—yearly? How does this compare with your *partner's* wants and needs?

1424

A few *romantic* questions for you women to ask of your man, to get a little intimate conversation going:

- ■ "If you love someone, how often should you tell them?"
- ■ "How old would you be if you didn't know how old you were?"
- ■ "What's your favorite type of kiss?"
- ■ "When you're in love, do you *walk* differently?"
- ■ "When you're away from your lover, do you wonder if she's thinking about you?"

These questions are from the great book *237 Intimate Questions . . . Every Woman Should Ask a Man*, by Laura Corn. For a copy, call 800-547-2665.

1425

And, if you *dare* . . . a few of the sexual questions from *237 Intimate Questions*:

- ● "Would an occasional *quickie* at unexpected times and places fulfill a special sexual need?"
- ● "What do you enjoy most about kissing a woman's body?"
- ● "Should oral sex be included every time you make love or just often enough to keep it special?"
- ● "Do you feel you have a comfortable balance between your sexual urges and reality?"
- ● "What is the one fantasy, the *trigger* fantasy, that you think about most?"

1426-1437

"What Is Healthy Loving?"

1. *Healthy loving is creating opportunities to grow individually and together by making a continuing commitment to foster patience and kindness, and to make conscious choices to respond to each other as lovers.*

2. *Healthy loving is setting priorities in your life so that there is time to create a safe, intimate, and beautiful environment for the ongoing discovery of each other.*

3. *Healthy loving is appreciating, respecting, and valuing your partner's thoughts and feelings even though you may not approve or agree with each other.*

4. *Healthy loving is encouraging your partner to grow as an individual even when you may feel threatened by their new directions. It is believing in them even when they don't believe in themselves.*

5. *Healthy loving is being responsible and accountable for your own life: The degree to which you experience happiness, love, joy and growth both for yourself and for your relationship.*

6. *Healthy loving is recognizing the need for playfulness, spontaneity, and the pleasuring of each other, thus providing treasured moments that nurture, encourage, and support the relationship.*

7. *Healthy loving is choosing not to manipulate or control each other.*

8. *Healthy loving is recognizing that being open and vulnerable makes a relationship intimate and special. This requires a willingness to risk being hurt, rejected, and even feeling unloved.*

9. *Healthy loving is trusting your love for each other so you can see beyond anger, fear and disappointment, and overcome obstacles inherent in any loving relationship.*

10. *Healthy loving is recognizing that love is never enough. It is being willing to learn the skills that are necessary for nurturing and sustaining an intimate and mutually satisfying relationship.*

11. *Healthy loving is creative problem solving through negotiation which leads to a mutually acceptable agreement. It is sharing in decision making and taking equal responsibility for the results.*

12. *Healthy loving is aspiring to live in truth and harmony. It is giving freely, receiving graciously, and being thankful, day after day, for the opportunity to be together.*

{Excerpt from *Duos—Choosing to Live as Lovers,* by Jacqui Stratton & Susan Lawton. Call for a free copy of "What Is Healthy Loving?": 408-464-1780.}

1438

Who was the wise guy who named the "love seat"? He must have had either a twisted sense of humor, or a twisted marriage, which led him to call a couch-for-two with seats facing in *opposite directions* a "love seat"!

ABC

1439-1464

"Do you know your ABCs?" Ask your partner to pick a letter. Then read the list of corresponding words. He or she has 24 hours in which to get a romantic gift or perform a romantic gesture based on any one of the key words.

A is for Attitude, Available, Accept, Ardor, Accolades, Admire, Aphrodisiacs, A' La Mode, Anniversary, Ambrosia, Ardent, Athens, Australia

B is for Boudoir, B&B, B&Bs, Buttercups, Beaches, Blue, Books, Boston, Bings, Balloons, Bicycling, Broadway, Brandy, Bubblebaths, Bahamas

C is for Champagne, Creativity, Candlelight, Cunnilingus, Candy, Chocolate, Convertibles, Casablanca, Cognac, Caviar, Chivalry, Crabtree & Evelyn

D is for Diamonds, Dinner, Daffodils, Dancing, Dating, Dolls, Dirty Dancing

E is for Enthusiasm, Energy, Excitement, Emeralds, Earrings, Elvis, Erotic, Exotic, Expensive, Escapes

F is for Flirting, Fantasies, Feminine, Faithful, Fellatio, France, Flowers, Fruits, Frenching, Foreplay

G is for Garters, Gardenias, Godiva, Get-Aways, Gifts, Glenn Miller, Gourmet, Greece

H is for Hearts, Humor, Hugs, Hide-Aways, Horses, Honeymoons, Hawaii, Hershey's Kisses, Hyatt

I is for Intimacy, Intrigue, Italy, Inns, Islands, Ingenuity, Ice Cream, Ice Skating, Interdependent, Imaginative, Invitation, Incense

J is for Jewelry, Java, Jasmine, Jello, Jazz, Journey, Joyful, Jacuzzi

K is for Kissing, Kinky, Kittens, Koala Bears

L is for Love, Lingerie, Laughing, Love Letters, Lilacs, Lace, Leather, Leo Buscaglia, Lobsters, Lovemaking, Limousines, Lovesongs, London

M is for Monogamy, Marriage, Masculine, **m&m**'s, Massage, Movies, Mistletoe, Music, Mozart

N is for Negligee, Naughty, Nibble, Nighttime, Nubile, Novelty, Nurture, Nymph, Naples, Nightcap, Nape, Nepal, Necklace

O is for Orgasm, Opera, Orchid, Outrageous, Outdoors

P is for Passion, Perfume, Poppies, Poetry, Persimmons, Paris, Polkas, Panties, Pizza, Photos, Pearls, Picnics, Playfulness, Purple

Q is for Quiet, Quaint, Quality, Queen, Quebec, Question, QE2, Quiche, Quiver

R is for Rendezvous, Roses, Rubies, Red, Reading, Rome, Rituals, Riviera, Restful, Rapture, Rings, Rio, Rainbows

S is for Sex

T is for Talking, Teasing, Tulips, Titillating, Theatre, Togetherness, Tickets, Toasts, Toys, Trains, Trinidad

U is for Umbrellas, Uxorious, Undress, Undulate, Urges, Unexpected, Union, Under The Spreading Chestnut Tree

V is for Violets, Virgins, Vibrators, Venice, Venus, Valentines, Vegetables, Victoria's Secret

W is for Wine, Wisteria, Walking Hand-In-Hand, Weddings

X is for X-Rated, Xerographic, Xylophones, Xmas

Y is for Yachts, Yes, Yellow, Yin & Yang, Young-at-heart

Z is for Zany, Zanzibar, Zeal, Zings, Zodiac, Zurich

1465-1490

A little advice.

Always kiss each other upon departing. **B**e there for her. Always. **C**reate an environment of love. **D**o it. Now. **E**scape from the kids. **F**ight fair. **G**ive of your time. **H**andle with care. **I**nspire your partner with your love. **J**udge not. **K**eep your good memories alive. **L**isten to her. **M**ake love with your partner's needs foremost. **N**ever go to bed mad. **O**ffer to handle an unpleasant chore. **P**raise him. **Q**uality Time isn't just for the kids. **R**espect her feelings. **S**ay what you feel when you feel it. **T**ell her you love her every day. Every day. Every day. Every day. **U**nderstand your differences. **V**alentine's Day is every day. **W**alk together. Talk together. E**X**cite your partner as only *you* know how. **Y**ou can never say "I love you" too often. **Z**ero-in on his little passions.

1491

Chocolate letters! (And numbers!) Block letters about four inches high, weighing 1-1/4 ounces each. Great for spelling-out love messages, invitations, proposals—use your imagination! Only a buck-fifty each—and a buck-and-a-quarter for 10 or more. (Available in milk chocolate or dark chocolate, of course!) Call The Chocolate Gallery at 800-426-4796 (10-6, M-S, PST), or write to 5705 Calle Real, Goleta, California 93117-2315.

1492

Uxorious (uk-sor'-ee-es): Excessively devoted to one's wife. {Thanks to the charming Nancy Lawton, of Boston.}

The Metaphors of Love

1493

We all know that "good chemistry" is important in a relationship, but what about good *physics*? Good math? Good architecture? Good business? Good ingredients? Good colors? Good karma? Good humor? Good art?

1494

- ■ A bad relationship is like a box: Rigid, confining, unyielding, square and dark inside.
- ○ A good relationship is like a bubble: Flexible, translucent, light, magical and shining.

1495

If they gave out degrees in "Relationships," what is your current level of Relationship Education?—Elementary Level, Junior High, High School, College Level, Masters, Ph.D., Nobel Prize Winner, Guru?

1496

A "relationship" is an entity, a living, growing *thing* that is related-to, but still *separate from* the individuals involved. There's *you*, there's *me*, and there's this mysterious, indefinable, invisible-yet-very-real *us*. And just as each individual person needs time, attention and care, so does the relationship.

1497-1498

❖ If your life together were a book or a movie, what *kind* would it be? A comedy? A horror? A thriller? A mystery? A tragedy? A romantic comedy? A foreign film? A grade-B movie? An X-rated movie? An Academy Award Winner? A treasured classic? Fiction or non-fiction?
❖ What *roles* are each of you playing?—Which roles might you like to try on?? Hero? Heroine? Good guy? Bad guy? Martyr? Jester? The strong, silent type? The silently-suffering type? The temptress? The Prince? The Princess? The Wicked Witch? The breadwinner? The Mother? The bumbling idiot? The jokester? The handyman? The lover?
❖ Get the book *Illusions*, by Richard Bach. Read pages 101 to 113.

1499

My favorite message on a T-shirt: "I am a work in progress." Your *relationship* is a work in progress, too. It's a painting, a sculpture, a collage that's never finished. It's always evolving and changing. What does your relationship-artwork look like?

1500

❤ "Romance is the laughter of love." {J.D., Dallas, Texas.}
❤ "Romance is going above-and-beyond the call of duty."

1501

Create your *own* model that describes the way *you* view the workings of a relationship. This metaphor could help you get in touch with some of your unconscious beliefs about relationships that affect the way you feel, and the way you act, in relationships. It could also help your partner understand you better!

1502

Romance is like baseball: You don't have to hit home runs every time. Heck, batting .300 is *excellent*, and .200 is still respectable! If you strike out—if you lose a whole inning—don't worry about it. There are lots of innings to go. Take a seventh inning stretch.

1503

Relationships are like fine wine: They get better with age.

The Nature of Love

1504

You've heard it said that "There are no guarantees in life." Well, that's true. But you just may be able to get a *Warranty*. Here's what Bob Howell, of San Francisco, did: As a surprise, at the conclusion of his marriage ceremony, he presented his new wife Dora with a "Lifetime Relationship Warranty." [Dynamite idea!!] It was rendered in calligraphy on parchment paper.

✦ Bonus Tip from *1001 Ways To Be Romantic*: For the most awesome, unique and beautiful calligraphy you've ever seen, call Maria Thomas at Pendragon Ink, 508-234-6843. Perfect for poems, song lyrics, wedding invitations, special occasions, love letters, scrolls—you name it! [FYI, Maria painted the flowers on the covers of my books.]

1505

Romance is learned behavior. It is not an inborn quality. *Anyone* can learn it. And it's *never* too late to learn.

1506

Here's some common advice that *sounds right* at first, but may or may not be true *for you*: Your lover *must* be your best friend. Passion always fade over time. Be realistic in your expectations. Share *all* your feelings.

1507

"Lack of romance is a self-esteem issue, pure and simple," according to one psychologist.

1508

Romantic love consists of a triad of passion, commitment and intimacy. Let's take a quick look at how these ingredients combine and re-combine at different stages in a relationship. Passion usually takes the lead during dating. Commitment may be non-existent, and intimacy is just a potential. As the relationship progresses, commitment and intimacy twist and turn around one another, building a framework for further relationship growth. Spurred-on by passion, commitment often turns serious, and marriage results. Newlywed passion usually carries the relationship for a year or two, while commitment is assumed, and intimacy builds. When the inevitable challenges and temptations arise, it is hoped that the commitment is strong enough, and the intimacy deep enough, to sustain the relationship. Passion, commitment and intimacy all come under fire from a variety of outside sources: Jobs, friends, money issues, children, etc. Some of the challenges come from *internal* sources: Insecurity, lack of self-esteem, fear, immaturity, lack of experience, etc. The combined strength of the passion/commitment/intimacy will determine the fate of the relationship. If commitment is strong but passion weak, the couple will "hang in there" but will not be particularly happy. If passion and commitment are strong but intimacy weak, the couple will stay together but fail to grow. The happiest couples are able to achieve a *dynamic balance* of passion, commitment and intimacy.

1509

Passion, creativity and spontaneity—three key elements in romance—are largely uncontrollable, unpredictable and messy. They don't respect any timetable, and they're hard to schedule. They follow the whims of the heart. With so much of the rest of our lives under tight reins, I'd think more people would opt for the roller-coaster ride of romance!

1510

Relationships are cyclical. They have their ups and downs and loop-de-loops. And even though certain things in all relationships *are* predictable, *every relationship has its own unique patterns.* Learn to recognize your *own* patterns. Respect them. And don't be taken-in by some pompous "expert" with the next hot advice book! Many of these people promote "Quick-And-Easy-Rules-For-Relationship-Success!" and "The *Secrets* of Permanent Passion" [That always kills me—the "*secrets*"!] [Do you know what else bugs me? Well, I'll tell you *anyway*: Articles that claim to have THE answers: "The 7 Stages of Love," "The Sexual Turn-Ons Men Desire," and "How to Please a Man." These articles and books prey on people's wishes for quick-and-easy answers. This is a personal pet peeve of mine. I know I can't change the world, but I feel better just telling you about it. Thanks.]

The *real* secret is to find an author/counselor who respects you; guides you without forcing you; gives guidelines instead of rules; has a humble attitude, instead of an arrogant one (meddling in people's lives is not something to be done lightly); and offers advice with love.

Lovesongs II

1511

And now, some romantic R&B greats . . .

☆ Peabo Bryson	☆ Natalie Cole	☆ Anita Baker
☆ Sade	☆ Mariah Carey	☆ James Ingram
☆ Freddie Jackson	☆ Vanessa Williams	☆ Mike Howard
☆ Luther Vandross	☆ Atlantic Starr	☆ Smokey Robinson
☆ Billy Ocean	☆ Diana Ross	☆ Patti Austin

1512

Guys, take note! Is your lover already immortalized in song?

☆ *Sara Smile*, Hall & Oates
☆ *Jane*, Starship
☆ *Barbara Ann*, Beach Boys
☆ *Carol*, Neil Sedaka
☆ *My Maria*, B.W. Stevenson
☆ *Valerie*, Steve Winwood
☆ *Rosalita*, Bruce Springsteen
☆ *Roseanna*, Toto
☆ *Susan*, Buckinghams
☆ *Jennifer Juniper*, Donovan
☆ *Beth*, Kiss
☆ *Lucille*, Little Richard
☆ *Mary's Prayer*, Danny Wilson
☆ *Sheila*, Tommy Roe
☆ *Hey Paula*, Paul & Paula
☆ *Sherry*, Four Seasons

☆ *Sara*, Starship
☆ *Aubrey*, Bread
☆ *Wendy*, Beach Boys
☆ *Eleanor*, Turtles
☆ *Thinking of Laura*, Christopher Cross
☆ *Valarie*, Monkees
☆ *Rosalinda's Eyes*, Billy Joel
☆ *Amie*, Pure Prarie League
☆ *Suzanne*, Leonard Cohen
☆ *Victoria*, Kinks
☆ *Peggy Sue*, Buddy Holly
☆ *Sweet Mary*, Wadsworth Mansion
☆ *Amanda*, Boston
☆ *Oh Sheila*, Ready for the World
☆ *Angelia*, Richard Marx
☆ *Julie, Do Ya Love Me*, Bobby Sherman

These 34 name-songs are in *addition* to the 25 listed in *1001 Ways To Be Romantic*. {Thanks to the husbands and boyfriends of Sara, Carol, Valerie, Wendy, Vicky, Jane, Mary and Julie—and to Nancy Quill, that music maven at WMJX-Radio in Boston!}

1513

You want to make a tape of romantic music, but your music collection is limited to the Monkees on old 45s, and boxed sets of Mozart's symphonies. —Not to worry! Call Personics! They've got *thousands* of tunes on file: From rock to rap, classical to country, blues to disco! You can get 10 songs for just $9.95—or 20 songs for $17.95. Call 800-822-9665, or send $1 for a catalog of song titles to Personics, 981 Bing Street, San Carlos, California 94070.

1514

Some romantic albums/CDs for your consideration:

- ☆ Roberta Flack, *The Classics*
- ☆ Art Garfunkel, *Breakaway*
- ☆ Anne Murray, *Greatest Hits*
- ☆ Billy Ocean, *Suddenly*
- ☆ Teddy Pendergrass, *Love Language*
- ☆ Lionel Richie, *Lionel Richie; Can't Slow Down*
- ☆ Carly Simon, *My Romance*
- ☆ Barbra Streisand, *A Collection; Memories*
- ☆ Surface, *The Best of Surface*
- ☆ Luther Vandross, *Power of Love*
- ☆ Anita Baker, *Rapture*
- ☆ Michael Bolton, *Time, Love & Tenderness; Soul Provider*
- ☆ Peabo Bryson, *Collection*
- ☆ Linda Ronstadt, *Lush Life; What's New*

1515

And now, as a public service, I'd like to bring you *Cosmopolitan's* list of "The 12 Most Romantic Albums Ever Recorded":

- ✳ Frank Sinatra, *The Capitol Years*
- ✳ Nat "King" Cole, *The Nat "King" Cole Story*
- ✳ Stan Getz & Astrud Gilberto, *Getz & Gilberto/With Antonio Carlos Jobim*
- ✳ Willie Nelson, *Stardust*
- ✳ Patsy Cline, *Patsy Cline's Greatest Hits*
- ✳ Ella Fitzgerald, *Ella Fitzgerald Sings the George & Ira Gershwin Songbook*
- ✳ Maurice Ravel, *Bolero*
- ✳ Billie Holiday, *The Billie Holiday Story, Volume II*
- ✳ Van Morrison, *Moondance*
- ✳ George Winston, *Autumn*
- ✳ Johnny Mathis, *Johnny Mathis's Greatest Hits*
- ✳ Tony Bennett & Bill Evans, *The Tony Bennett/Bill Evans Album*

1516-1517

✓ Blasts From the Past
  - ★ Johnny Mathis
  - ★ Nat King Cole
  - ★ Roberta Flack
  - ★ Barry White
  - ★ Righteous Brothers

✓ Some Country Favorites
  - ★ Patsy Cline
  - ★ Kenny Rogers
  - ★ The Judds

New Age

1518

Music, computers, electrical engineering and meditation come together in five compositions of "meditation music" composed while in a trance by Marcey Hamm. "Perhaps I'm touching upon a common note within us all," she says. "Beneath our physical differences we all come from the same place anyway. When people hear my music on the outside, they become more aware of their own inner music. And to me—that's the true meaning of harmony." The five albums are titled *Inward Harmony, Z, Celestial Dance, Anthem To Soul,* and *Dream Partner.* Cassettes are $12.95 to $14.95, and CDs are $16.95. Write to Marcey, Box 831210, Richardson, Texas 75083, or call 800-843-3240.

Romance is expressing your feelings in your way.

1519

How about a *magical* spin on your relationship? A delightful book jumped off the shelf into my hands one day at the Boston airport: *Love Magic: The Way to Love Through Rituals, Spells, and the Magical Life,* by Laurie Cabot with Tom Cowan. It weaves a variety of traditions into a fanciful yet practical book for men and women, singles and marrieds—anyone who wishes to attract or enhance a loving relationship. The book introduces you to concepts of astrology, spells, meditations, rituals and incantations that can affect you and your loved one. You don't need to be a "believer," you just need to suspend your disbelief and have a little fun. "Magic is about shifting consciousness." Included are a "Love Dance Spell" and a "Love Growth Spell."

1520

☞ The answers you're looking for may *already* be there—in the palm of your hand! Boston palmist and psychic Judith Nadell reads "romance lines" on the palm, and combines this information with astrological readings to help you chart your relationship activities! Readings can be done via phone, if you first send a photocopy of your palm! (How's *that* for combining modern technology with ancient traditions?!) Readings are just $50. Call 617-731-2999.

☞ Or, you could read-up on the art and science of palmistry and do-it-yourself! *Romance On Your Hands—Palmistry for Lovers,* by Spencer Grenhahl.

1521

A variety of related techniques can help you attract love, enhance your relationship, and create a more fulfilling life. Creative Visualization and "magnetizing" are two techniques that I have found useful in my relationships, as well as in my writing.

↠ A book with the business-sounding title of *Creating Money* is actually a spiritual guidebook for determining just what you truly want in your life, and then drawing it to you through various "magnetizing" exercises.

↠ *Creative Visualization,* by Shakti Gawain, is the classic book on this topic.

1522

A whole new way of relating to your lover is promoted by the believers and practitioners of *out-of-body travel*. By leaving your physical body behind and exploring your mind and other dimensions with your consciousness and essence, you can achieve the ultimate spiritual experiences, they say. I haven't tried it myself, so I won't render an opinion. Sounds like fun, though!

- ◆ *Beyond the Body*, by Susan Blackmore, Ph.D.
- ◆ *Bridge Across Forever* and *One*, by Richard Bach
- ◆ "Amphibians," a short story by Kurt Vonnegut, in *Welcome to the Monkey House*

Oldies But Goodies

1523

Romantic Myth #85: Older folks lose interest in sex.

More than a third of American married men and women over age 60— and 10% of those over age 70—make love at least once a week! And, a sizeable number of seniors make love outdoors, enjoy undressing one another, taking showers and even skinny-dipping together! All this from a study by the National Opinion Research Center at the University of Chicago. "There is much more sexual activity and playfulness going on in the bedrooms of older men and women than the rest of society seems to understand or perhaps is ready to believe," said Rev. Andrew Greeley, sociologist and best-selling novelist, who wrote the report. "The empty nest may actually be a love nest!"

1524

"You want something helpful-yet-philosophical for that book of yours?—Put *this* in your next book: *Potential, unrealized, is non-existent!* How's *that*?! Remind your readers that people aren't batteries. Our potential is worthless unless we use it. Too many people in this world die without using *nearly* all of their potential, or expressing a *tiny fraction* of the love they have inside of them. But all that bottled-up 'love' isn't *really* **love**—until it comes out! So there!!" {Advice given to me on the Boston Subway—the Green Line—June 7, 1992, by a sprightly little old woman in a yellow flowered dress, who scooted off the train without leaving her name.}

1525

"The sad thing about Valentine's Day is that we assume it's the one and only day of the year on which it's okay to display our vulnerability, to indulge ourselves in romance and sentimentality. What a waste! Romance and sentiment should be part of every day. My grandfather, a man of sound, solid common sense, always brought my grandmother her breakfast in bed, with a flower on the tray. I am sure there were other factors involved, but they remained happily married for over 50 years, and it has often occurred to me that in his courtly, old-fashioned, Edwardian way, Grandfather knew something that has escaped most of us, which is that a day that begins with a touch of romance is likely to end well." (Michael Korda, *Penthouse*.)"

1526

On his 100th birthday, in 1991, Edward L. Bernays observed, "When you reach 100, don't let it throw you, because a person has five ages—and chronological is the least important." The other ages are bodily, mental, emotional and societal. [Interesting concept, eh?] What are *your* ages? How do they compare with your partner's? This could yield some interesting insights. Mr. Bernays, a nephew of Sigmund Freud, and the founder of modern public relations, put his bodily age at "between 62 and 64—the same as it was when I was 95." He said his mental age was "no different than when I was 45. My societal age is also about 45, but my emotional age is nobody's damn business!"

1527

1. Almost Like Being In Love
2. At Long Last Love
3. Can I Steal A Little Love
4. Crazy Love
5. Don't Take Your Love From Me
6. End Of A Love Affair
7. Everybody Ought To Be In Love
8. Everybody Love Somebody
9. Falling In Love With Love
10. Farewell, Farewell To Love
11. Give Her Love
12. Half As Lovely
13. Hallelujah, I Love Her So
14. Hello Young Lovers
15. Hey Jealous Lover
16. How Are You Fixed For Love
17. I Am Loved
18. I Believe I'm Gonna Love You
19. I Can't Believe That You're In Love With Me
20. I Can't Stop Falling In Love With You
21. I Fall In Love Too Easily
22. I Fall In Love With You Ev'ry Day
23. I Got A Gal I Love
24. I Love My Wife
25. I Love Paris
26. I Love You
27. I Love You (Version #1)
28. I Love You (Version #2)
29. I Loved Her
30. I Wish I Were In Love Again
31. I Wish You Love
32. I Would Be In Love Anyway
33. If I Ever Love Again
34. If I Loved You
35. It's A Lovely Day Tomorrow
36. I've Got A Love To Keep Me Warm
37. I've Never Been In Love Before
38. Just One Way To Say I Love You
39. The Last Call For Love
40. Let's Fall In Love
41. Like Someone In Love
42. Look Of Love
43. Love And Marriage
44. Love Is A Many Splendored Thing
45. Love Is Here To Stay
46. Love Is Around The Corner
47. Love Isn't Just For The Young
48. Love Lies
49. Love Locked Out
50. Love Looks So Well On You
51. Love Me
52. Love Me As I Am
53. Love Me Tender
54. Love Means Love
55. Love Walked In
56. A Lovely Moonlit Night
57. Lovely Way To Spend An Evening
58. Lover
59. Love's Been Good To Me
60. Melody Of Love
61. Mind If I Make Love To You
62. Moon Love
63. My Love For You
64. My One And Only Love
65. Once I Loved
66. Once In Love With Amy
67. The One I Love
68. One Love
69. One Love Affair
70. P: S: I Love You
71. People Will Say We're In Love
72. Prisoner Of Love
73. Secret Love
74. So In Love
75. So Long My Love
76. Somewhere My Love
77. Take My Love
78. Taking A Chance On Love
79. Tell Her You Love Her
80. Tell Her You Love Her Each Day
81. That's How Much I Love You
82. Then Suddenly Love
83. This Is My Love
84. This Love Of Mine
85. This Was My Love
86. To Love And Be Loved
87. Two In Love
88. What Is This Thing Called Love
89. What Now My Love
90. When I Stop Loving You
91. When I'm Not Near The Girl I Love
92. When Somebody Loves You
93. When Your Lover Has Gone
94. Wives and Lovers
95. You Brought A New Kind Of Love To Me
96. You My Love
97. You'd Be So Easy To Love
98. You'll Always Be The One I Love
99. Your Love For Me
100. You're Nobody 'Til Somebody Loves You

Do you know who sang and recorded *all* of these love songs? Who else but *Frank Sinatra*? On behalf of all the lovers and romantics in the world, "Thanks, Frank!" {And thanks to *Encore! Magazine* for the research, and to Dale K. for sending it!}

As Time Goes By

1528

Knowing your lover's Yearmates is a great way to spark romantic ideas. [What!? You don't know what a "Yearmate" is?] Yearmates are simply people born in the same year. FYI, here are some celebrity Yearmates:

- ✦ **1941** Ann-Margret, Joan Baez, Beau Bridges, Chubby Checker, David Crosby, Faye Dunaway, Bob Dylan.
- ✦ **1942** Barbra Streisand, Paul McCartney, Paul Simon, Aretha Franklin, Harrison Ford, Linda Evans.
- ✦ **1943** Julio Iglesias, Mick Jagger, George Harrison, Chevy Chase, Robert DeNiro, Penny Marshall, Joni Mitchell.
- ✦ **1944** Danny DeVito, Timothy Dalton, Roger Daltry, Gladys Knight, Patti LaBelle.
- ✦ **1945** Mia Farrow, Goldie Hawn, Tom Selleck, Rod Stewart, Priscilla Presley, Rob Reiner.
- ✦ **1946** Candice Bergen, Sally Field, Diane Keaton, David Lynch, Liza Minelli, Ozzy Osbourne, Dolly Parton, Linda Ronstadt, Susan Sarandon, Sylvester Stallone, Robert Urich.
- ✦ **1947** Arnold Schwarzenegger, Elton John, David Bowie, Glenn Close, Billy Crystal, Ted Danson, Farrah Fawcett, Kevin Kline, David Letterman, Olivia Newton-John, Steven Spielberg.
- ✦ **1948** Mikhail Baryshnikov, James Taylor, Barbara Hershey, Jeremy Irons, Kate Jackson, Perry King, Stevie Nicks, Donna Summer.
- ✦ **1949** Whoopi Goldberg, Billy Joel, Bruce Springsteen, Meryl Streep, Sigourney Weaver, Jeff Bridges, Richard Gere, Don Johnson, Jessica Lange.
- ☆ **1950** Stevie Wonder, Cybill Shepherd, Tony Danza, John Candy, Peter Gabriel, William Hurt, Bill Murray, Randy Quaid.
- ☆ **1951** Phil Collins, Sting, Timothy Bottoms, John Cougar Mellencamp, Elvira, Mark Hamill, Harry Hamlin, Mark Harmon, Michael Keaton, Joe Piscopo, Kurt Russell, Jane Seymour.

☆ **1952** Robin Williams, Mr. T, Dan Aykroyd, Roseanne Barr, David Byrne, Nora Dunn, Pee-Wee Herman, Grace Jones, Isabella Rossellini.

☆ **1953** Kim Basinger, Jeff Goldblum, John Goodman, Cyndi Lauper, John Malkovich, Tom Petty.

☆ **1954** Patrick Swayze, John Travolta, Ellen Barkin, Corbin Bernsen, Ron Howard, David Keith, Dennis Quaid.

☆ **1955** Kevin Costner, Kirstie Alley, Jeff Daniels, Billy Idol, David Lee Roth, Bruce Willis, Debra Winger.

☆ **1956** Mel Gibson, Tom Hanks, Larry Bird, Delta Burke, Carrie Fisher, Eric Roberts, Mickey Rourke, Joe Montana, Dale Murphy, Martina Navratilova.

☆ **1957** Michelle Pfeiffer, Theresa Russell, Vanna White, Geena Davis, Spike Lee, Donny Osmond, Melanie Griffith.

☆ **1958** Madonna, Prince, Michael Jackson, Arsenio Hall, Steve Guttenberg, Wade Boggs, Jamie Lee Curtis.

☆ **1959** Judd Nelson, Rosanna Arquette, Sheena Easton, Holly Hunter, Victoria Jackson, Marie Osmond, Martha Quinn, Randy Travis.

❦ **1960** Valerie Bertinelli, Eric Dickerson, Joan Jett, Natassia Kinski, Apollonia Kotero, Sean Penn, Tracey Ullman.

❦ **1961** Eddie Murphy, Jon Bon Jovi, Boy George, Rae Dawn Chong, Amy Grant, Wayne Gretzky, Daryl Hannah, Timothy Hutton.

❦ **1962** Tom Cruise, Matthew Broderick, Emilio Estevez, Jodie Foster, Demi Moore, Meg Ryan, Ally Sheedy.

❦ **1963** Whitney Houston, Michael Jordan, Julian Lennon, Andrew McCarthy, George Michael.

❦ **1964** Tracy Chapman, Jose Canseco, Phoebe Cates, Melissa Gilbert, Robin Givens, Rob Lowe, Matt Dillon.

❦ **1965** Brooke Shields, Nicolas Cage, Ronnie Gant, Mario Lemieux, Paulina Porizkhova, Katarina Witt.

❦ **1966** Justine Bateman, Tom Glavine, Janet Jackson, Dave Justice, Charlie Sheen, Mike Tyson.

❦ **1967** Julia Roberts, Boris Becker, Lisa Bonet, John Cusak.

❦ **1968** Mary Lou Retton, Molly Ringwald, Jonathan Knight.

❦ **1969** Andrea Elson, Steffi Graf, Donnie Wahlberg, Danny Wood.

✦ **1970** Kirk Cameron, Debbie Gibson, Jordan Knight, Emily Lloyd, Malcolm-Jamal Warner.

1529

Whenever possible, turn something *practical* into an *item with special significance* to your honey. For instance: Calendars! Wall calendars, day-at-a-glance calendars, monthly calendars, poster calendars! Choose a calendar that matches your lover's interests/hobbies/passions.

❋ What is she "into"? Whatever it is, there's probably a calendar to suit her interests: Cats, astrology, food, flowers, Chippendales, teddy bears, dolls, mountains, poetry, trivia, boys, men, models, hunks, wildlife, rain forests, whales, running, The Far Side, Cathy, Calvin & Hobbes.
❋ What is *he* "into"? Dogs, beaches, Playmates, golf, football, basketball, hockey, cities, countries, worlds, stars, lingerie, vocabulary, maps, architecture, Garfield.

1530

✳ One of *my* favorite calendars is the *Edibles* calendar, from Silver Visions. It's a monthly wall calendar with close-up photographs of various luscious colors and juicy aromas of food, you'll love this calendar! Available at gift stores everywhere, or directly, by calling 617-244-9504.
✳ Any maybe—just *maybe*—you'll see a day-at-a-glance *romance* calendar in 1994 . . . *365 Ways To Be Romantic*. Has a good ring to it, don't you think?

1531

Warning: *One* partner will remember every detail—the color shirt you wore on your first date . . . what she had for dessert during that dinner where you had that big fight. The *other* partner will be lucky to remember your name. It's a cosmic law or something.

❋ Adapt your personal romantic strategies to fit your natural inclinations.
❋ Adjust your expectations of your partner to fit reality. [I'm not saying that you can't *push* reality a bit—but still, let's live in the real world, okay?!]

{Many thanks to the well-travelled McGarrys of Atlanta.}

Yin & Yang

1532

It seems to me that a lot of problems and misunderstandings—from marital spats to world wars—are caused by people ignoring the fact that everything from people to nature seem to operate under the principles of Yin and Yang. We seem to get unbalanced and kind-of crazy when we forget that most everything has the reality and/or the potential to include good and bad, masculine and feminine, plenty and poverty, love and hate, give and take, dark and light, ebb and flow, joy and sadness, tragic and comic, life and death, strong and weak, chocolate and vanilla, black and white, loud and soft, funny and serious.

1533-1534

✪ Celebrate your differences.
✪ Take comfort in your similarities.

1535-1536

✦ Live in the present! *Now* is all there is! Free yourself from the past.
✦ Keep your memories alive. Nostalgia fuels romance.

1537-1538

✿ Read books! They contain wisdom, great ideas and inspiration!
✿ Throw the books away! Listen to your Inner Voice. Don't over-analyze!

1539-1540

➤ Say what you feel when you feel it. Be totally honest with your partner.
➤ Choose your words carefully. What you say creates your reality.

1541-1542

✳ Budget vacation tip: Save on accommodations—splurge on meals!
✳ Budget vacation tip: Sleep in luxury—avoid over-priced restaurants!

1543-1544

♥ Treat her like your *best friend* as well as lover—You'll build intimacy.
♥ Treat her like a *stranger*—It will add spice to your life!

1545-1546

♛ Throw-out your TV: It will create more time for you to share with him.
♛ Buy a *huge* large-screen TV: All the better to watch those romantic movies on.

1547-1548

♣ Lighten-up! Have more *fun* with your honey. Experience the joy of life!
♣ Get serious! Successful relationships require work!

1549-1550

✳ Romance is easy! Just express yourself! Romance is "Adult Play"!
✳ Romance is hard! Plan, shop, hide, wrap, write, surprise, deliver, drive, call, remember . . .

1551-1552

☞ Actions speak louder than words. *Do* something, don't just *talk*—Talk is cheap!

☞ Communication is the cornerstone of a good relationship. Talk. Listen.

1553-1554

♦ Travel inspires romance: Exotic locales, foreign food, high adventure!

♦ Home is where the heart is: A cozy fire, a romantic bedroom, a hot tub!

1555-1556

✱ "Shake-up" your life! Go to a Tony Robbins Seminar! Go skydiving!

✱ "Slow-down" your life. Meditate. Find your center. Listen. Shhh.

Do's & Don'ts

1557

Don't coast! Relationships in Neutral end-up in Reverse! "You start taking your mate for granted, you're coasting as a lover. You start taking your kids for granted, you're coasting as a parent. You start taking your work for granted, you're coasting as a professional. And please remember when you coast, you only coast downhill . . . Whenever you ease up, everything else goes down." {Thanks to Joe Charbonneau, a business consultant and professional speaker.}

1558

Do the opposite of what everyone else is doing. **Don't** go out on New Year's Eve—**Do** stay home and cozy-up with your lover near the fireplace. **Don't** buy roses for Valentine's Day—**Do** buy flowers that begin with the first letter of her name. **Don't** go to the beach on the crowded weekends—**Do** go mid-week. **Don't** give her a birthday present—**Do** give her seven gifts: One for each day of her birthday *week*! **Don't** go shopping for gifts during the crazed Christmas Season—**Do** shop year-round (and stash those gifts and presents in your Gift Closet). **Don't** go to popular vacation spots during their most popular seasons—**Do** go right on either edge of the hot season. **Don't** buy show tickets after they're advertised (all the best seats will already be gone)—**Do** buy a subscription series, become a theatre supporter, or join a "Show-of-the-Month" club. **Don't** watch your favorite TV shows when they're broadcast (keep control over your *own* Prime Time)—**Do** tape them and watch them later. **Don't** read the newspaper at the breakfast table—**Do** talk with one another.

1559

Learn from your "Romantic Bloopers." **Don't** beat yourself up because of your past mistakes. But **do** learn from them and grow. Change your behavior. Change your attitudes. Change your approach. Just *don't keep doing the same old thing.* Some classic Romantic Bloopers include: Being so nervous that you talk nonstop about *yourself* during an entire date. Sending two dozen *red* roses after a first date. (Yellow or pink are usually more appropriate. And a *dozen* is probably overkill.) Calling her *too often.* Pushing too fast for intimacy. Not risking intimacy at all.

> *"Say what you feel when you feel it."*
>
> ~ *Sam*

1560

More wise words from Leo: "Some of us have the mistaken notion that when we love someone we are compelled to say yes to them all the time no matter how capricious or frustrating their demands or behaviors. We feel we owe our loved ones everything in return for the love they give. In such cases it is important to understand the difference between being loved and being manipulated." Mature lovers **don't** barter, they **don't** "give-in," and they **don't** squelch their own needs and desires. They **do** give freely, they **do** love unconditionally, and they **do** sometimes say "No!" {Thanks to Leo Buscaglia and his most recent book *Born For Love*.}

1561

Luck? Fate? Serendipity? —*Hah!!* **Don't** wait around for Luck, Fate and Serendipity to bring your mate to you, or make your life more exciting. **Do** give Luck, Fate and Serendipity a hand—Take action. Take *risks!* Get *out* there! Do it *now!*

1562

Do's and Don'ts for *singles.* "When you describe yourself to a prospective partner—or you're describing the kind of person you want to meet—whether in person, over the radio, or in a personal ad—be *specific*, don't be *generic!* What makes you *different*, what are you *passionate* about?" says Boston's singles guru Dick Syatt. Dick *knows* what he's talking about, as he runs adult singles dance parties and hosts the popular "Dick Syatt's Hot-Line Radio Dating Show" on WRKO-Radio. "Here are some of the worst, most meaningless things people can say: 'I just want someone who's honest and sincere. Looks don't matter.' Yeah, right! More meaningless descriptions: 'I like movies and walks on the beach.' Who doesn't?!" Dick's advice? **Do** be *specific*: If you're a vegetarian, say so. **Do** be *straightforward*: If you love The Carpenters and hate Madonna, say so! **Do** be *honest*: If you smoke, say so! **Do** be *yourself*: **Do** be patient. **Don't** act desperate. **Don't** be too pushy, but do take some risks. **Do** reveal yourself. **Don't** do all the talking!

Isn't That *Special?!?*

1563

Buy two theatre tickets. Mail one to her anonymously, or "From Your Secret Admirer." Be in *your* seat early, waiting with a rose. {Thanks to Scott, from the July Romance Class in Boston.}

1564

Romantic readers' favorite romantic songs:

- ♥ *The Nearness of You*, Hoagy Carmichael. {Mark Strauch, San Diego, California.}
- ♥ *Rambling Rose*, Nat King Cole. {Randy & Georgia P., North Pole, Arkansas.}
- ♥ *I (Who Have Nothing)*, Tom Jones. {Sharon Smith, San Antonio, Texas.}
- ♥ *True Love*, Bing Crosby. *Suddenly*, Billy Ocean. {Mark Duemmel, Rochester, New York.}
- ♥ *In Your Eyes*. {Gloria Fisher, Camillus, New York.}
- ♥ Everything from *Phantom of the Opera*! {"The Incurable Romantic," Naperville, Illinois.}
- ♥ *Shower Me with Your Love*, Surface. {Samantha Azer.}
- ♥ *Time in a Bottle*, Jim Croce. *Dream On*, Oak Ridge Boys. {Christa Cragg.}
- ♥ *Have I Told You Lately That I Love You*, Van Morrison. {Jackie & Tim Martin, Corona, California.}
- ♥ *Everything I Do, I Do It For You*, Bryan Adams. {Sherrill Suzuki, Honolulu, Hawaii.}
- ♥ *To Be With You*, Mister Big. {Audra Lillies, Surrey, British Columbia, Canada.}
- ♥ *You're My World*, Helen Reddy. {Francine Barry, Rochester, New York.}

[This is a very small selection from the *thousands* of nominations sent by readers. I couldn't possibly fit all of them into the book. Hmmm—Maybe I'll devote an upcoming issue of my *Romance Newsletter* to *your* romantic song selections. Stay tuned!]

1565-1568

Romantic readers' favorite romantic surprises:

* Engagement ring in movie popcorn. {Francine Barry, Rochester, New York.}

* Finding one's mate in the living room, watching TV buck naked and nonchalant, as if nothing at all were unusual! {T.M., California.}

* A "secret message" word scramble puzzle with words in a dictionary. Selected words are circled in the dictionary; you give your partner a note with page numbers listed on it. She has to find each page, find each word, and build the message. [A+ for creativity, D- for defacing a dictionary, says Mrs. Wilcox!]

* A bedroom filled with helium balloons—with a message attached to *each* one! {F.B., Rochester, New York.}

1569

Romantic readers' favorite romantic movies:

☆ *Children of a Lesser God*. {Mark Strauch, San Diego, California.}
☆ *Roxanne. All of Me.* {Randy & Georgia P., North Pole, Arkansas.}
☆ *Cousins. Roman Holiday.* {Mark Suemme, Rochester, New York.}
☆ *Far and Away.* {Audra Lillies, Surrey, British Columbia, Canada.}
☆ *Falling in Love.* {Tracy, Rochester, New York.}
☆ *Ghost. Pretty Woman* {Many, many, many, many, many, many readers.}

[Again, these are just a few of the thousands of responses that people sent to me. Thanks to everyone. Look for a special "Movie" issue of my *Romance Newsletter!*]

1570

One advantage of being a couple comprised of one right-hander and one left-hander is that you can sit very close to one another at dinner without bumping elbows! Sign-up your Southpaw in Lefthanders International, a company that "serves the needs and rights of lefthanded people, who are somewhat discriminated against because they are perceived as having a handicap." You can receive the bi-monthly Lefthander Magazine and the Lefthanders Catalog for just $15. Write to Box 8249, Topeka, Kansas 66608.

1571

Some people have the ability to take the commonplace and make it *special*. Take your average year, for instance. Most of us wait around for outside events to lend significance to certain years: 1976, 1984, 2001. But what's special about *this* year, or *next* year? The Hollys, of Geneva, New York offer an answer. They've been creating "themes" for every year since 1960. Their method is to "Let inspiration strike us sometime between Christmas and New Year, to name the upcoming year. It's usually a joint decision." Here are a few of their themes: Getting to Know You • Flowers• Wife Appreciation Year • Sex, Sex, Sex! • New York, New York • The Year of the Baby • The Year of Getting Out of Debt • The Year of the Big Vacation • The Year of Many Small Vacations • Scratching the Seven-Year Itch • Rededication Year • Appreciation• Memories• Getting Serious • Getting Back in Shape • Golf! • Bingo!

Happy Anniversary

1572

I posed this rhetorical question in #597 of *1001 Ways To Be Romantic*, which listed the traditional and modern gifts for wedding anniversaries: "Just who made up this list, anyway??" No one has been able to answer the question, so I figure *my* list is *just as good* as anybody else's! [Now, if I could just get somebody to print up zillions of those little plastic cards with this list on them, I'd *really* be able to get things rolling!]

Year	Traditional	*Modern*	Godek's
1	Paper	Clocks	Lingerie
2	Cotton	China	Lingerie
3	Leather	Crystal/glass	Software
4	Fruit/flowers	Appliances	Lingerie
5	Wood	Silver/silverware	Books
6	Candy/iron	Wood	Lingerie
7	Wood/copper	Desksets	Wine
8	Bronze/pottery	Linens/laces	Cameras
9	Pottery/willow	Leather	CDs
10	Tin/aluminum	Diamond jewelry	Jewelry
11	Steel	Fashion jewelry	Silk
12	Silk/linen	Pearls	Perfume
13	Lace	Textiles/furs	Umbrellas
14	Ivory	Gold jewelry	Lingerie
15	Crystal	Watches	Computers
20	China	Platinum	Champagne
25	Silver	Silver	Jacuzzis
30	Pearl	Diamond/pearl	Canoes
35	Coral	Jade	Sculpture
40	Ruby	Ruby	Stocks & bonds
45	Sapphire	Sapphire	Lingerie
50	Gold	Gold	Rolls Royce
55	Emerald	Emerald	Gold
60	Diamond	Diamond	Vacations

1573

Have a wedding cake made for your anniversary!!

1574

Make a giant banner celebrating your anniversary. Hang it over a bridge that he passes on his way to work. Grab an old sheet and a can of spray paint!

1575

Get a vintage wine from the year of your anniversary. (Or, if your budget can stand it, you might search for a vintage bottle from the year of his birth!) Either way, *cheers!*

1576

Here's how one husband fanned the flames of passion in his 10-year marriage: For their 10th wedding anniversary, he created a theme of mystery and intrigue using Incognito Perfume. Starting two weeks before their anniversary date, he began sending his wife little love notes in the mail. Each note was perfumed with Incognito. His anniversary gift of elegant lingerie was likewise mysteriously scented. And finally, his written invitation to dinner was ribboned to a bottle of Incognito.

P.S. His wife, being rather clever herself, showed up at the restaurant *incognito*—wearing a wig and dark glasses! [Some people are *shamelessly* romantic!]

1577

How many people do you know who've celebrated *288* anniversaries? Well, meet the Claytons, of Nebraska. "We've celebrated our wedding anniversary *every month* for 24 years now. We don't buy gifts every month (we'd be more broke than we are now) but we *do* recognize it somehow: With a kiss, a flower, or a short note."

Travel Tips

1578

Books for honeymooners (and other lovers!)

➤ *Frommer's Honeymoon Destinations*, by Risa Weinreb. Covers the U.S., Mexico, the Caribbean, the Bahamas and Bermuda.
➤ *Honeymoons—A Romantic Travel Guide*, by Elizabeth Harryman and Paul Lasley. Presents 60 gorgeous escapes in the U.S., Hawaii, Mexico, Canada, the Caribbean, Europe, Asia and the South Pacific.
➤ *Romantic Weekend Getaways—The Mid-Atlantic States*, by Larry Fox and Barbara Radin-Fox. Short but romantic escapes in the Northeast.

1579

Passport—The quintessential newsletter about interesting places that have yet to be "discovered." London's intimate (yet affordable) hotels near the best shops and theatres. The best little bistros in Paris. The San Francisco most people never see. Call for a free preview issue: 800-999-9006, or write to 350 West Hubbard, Suite 440, Chicago, Illinois 60610.

1580

You'd like to rent a tropical villa on a tranquil island, but you don't know how to find one, right? Well, you came to the right place! Hideaways International publishes a semi-annual guide and a quarterly newsletter that profiles intimate unspoiled resorts, luxury condos, yacht charters and tropical villas. Hundreds of romantic hideaways in the Caribbean, Mexico, U.S. and Europe are detailed. Most are for rent from the owners at very reasonable prices. A one-year membership is $79, and a four-month trial membership is $27.50. Write to Post Office Box 1270, Littleton, Massachusetts 01460, or call 800-843-4433 (in Massachusetts, 508-486-8955).

1581-1583

If you like walking hand-in-hand—with an emphasis on the *walking*—then you oughta consider a walking/hiking vacation. They range from Vermont to the Himalayas, and from easy, to moderate to difficult.

Easy/Walking

* Alternative Travel Group Ltd. will take you on easy walks through Italy, France, Portugal and Spain. Call 800-527-5997.

* Country Walkers specializes in inn-to-inn nature walks in Vermont and Maine. Call 603-356-9696.

Moderate/Hiking

* Journeys East specializes in Japan. Hike Mount Fuji, the Japan Alps and Kyoto. Call 510-601-1677.

* Above the Clouds Trekking specializes in Nepal and the Himalayas, and other exotic spots around the world. Call 800-233-4499.

Difficult/Backpacking

* ABEC offers backpacking treks to the interior of Alaska. River-rafting too! Call 907-457-8907.

* Himalayan Travel also arranges trips to Corsica, Crete, Iceland and Morocco. Call 800-225-2380.

1584

Charter your own yacht and set your own itinerary for a truly incredible vacation! Professional crews and gourmet cooks! Staterooms with private baths! Yachts from 50 to 100 feet. Many islands stops are accessible only via yacht. Set sail for the Bahamas, Virgin Islands, French Antilles, St. Lucia, Grenada, Tonga, Tahiti, French Riviera, Corsica or Spain! Call The Moorings at 800-437-7880.

1585

If you'd like to combine a little physical conditioning with your romantic vacation, try a spa!

❖ Saybrook Point Inn is a luxurious waterfront resort on Long Island Sound, in Connecticut. Elegant over-sized rooms—many with balconies and fireplaces. Call 800-243-0212 (in Connecticut, 203-395-2000).

❖ The Spa at Cordillera is located atop the Rocky Mountains overlooking the Vail Valley in Colorado. Hydrotherapy, mountain biking and more. Call 800-548-2721.

❖ The Regency Health Resort & Spa is the only health resort in South Florida directly on the ocean. A holistic approach to wellness. Call 305-454-2220.

1586

How about a few travel magazines? (A *few?!?*)

+ *Just Go!*—415-255-5951
+ *Asia Pacific Travel*—415-697-8038
+ *Leisure Ways*—416-595-5007
+ *Adventure Road*—212-673-8930
+ *Arizona Highways*—602-258-6641
+ *California Highways*—213-935-3107
+ *Expedition World*—203-967-2900
+ *Endless Vacation*—317-871-9504

+ *Romantic Traveling*—415-731-8239
+ *The Discerning Traveler*—215-247-5578
+ *Conde Nast Traveler*—212-880-2102
+ *TravelTips*—718-939-2400
+ *Relax*—708-940-8333
+ *Travel & Leisure*—212-382-5600
+ *Railways*—818-500-0542
+ *National Geographic Traveler*—202-828-5484

1587

And now, the Top 10 Underwater Wonders of the World in range of snorkelers:

1. Crystal River, Florida: Swim side-by-side with manatees (!)
2. The North Shore of Providenciales Island in the Turks and Caicos chain of the Caribbean: Reefs like bonsai gardens, exotic fans and sponges usually found at much greater depths.
3. Heron Island, Australia: A microcosm of the Great Barrier Reef.
4. Sting Ray City, on Grand Cayman: Swim with sting rays (!)
5. The Red Sea's Gulf of Aqaba: Incredibly colorful coral reefs.
6. Qamea Island, in Fiji: Some of the world's best soft corals.
7. Madang in Papua New Guinea: Vibrant with oceanic activity.
8. Yap, in Micronesia: If you like manta rays!
9. Delos, Greece: Sunken ruins: Temple columns and mosiacs!
10. La Paz, Mexico, in the Sea of Cortez: Consort with playful sea lions.

{Thanks to *Rodale's Scuba Diving Magazine*.}

1588

What makes a *great* beach? It all depends on what you're "into."

❂ Great beaches for lazing:
  ➠ Molokai, Hawaii. Dozens of isolated, idyllic sandy beaches.
  ➠ North Island, New Zealand. A geothermal wonderland of hotsprings.
  ➠ Isla de Cozumel, Mexico. Miles and miles of undeveloped beaches.

❂ Great beaches for beachcombing:
  ➠ Sanibel Island, Florida. Great beachcombing, but lots of people.
  ➠ Pamana, Indonesia. Home to many chambered nautiluses.
  ➠ Mindoro, Philippines: The shell capital of the world!

❂ Great unspoiled beaches:
  ➠ Kea, in the Greek islands. Quiet ambience. Sandy coves off clifftop paths.
  ➠ Barbuda, West Indies. Picture-perfect. 17 miles of perfect pink sand.
  ➠ Mustique, West Indies. Jetsetters abound nearby, but the beach is *incredible*.

{Thanks to *Islands Magazine*.}

Love in the Nineties

1589

The 50th space shuttle mission, that of Endeavor in September of 1992, was noted for a number of "firsts"—among them was the first married couple in space: Jan Davis and Mark Lee. NASA was skittish, and the media had a heyday, over the issue of sex in space. The official word is that "Nothing happened." [Yeah, *right*!] I don't know about *you*, but if *I* had an opportunity like *that* to make history . . . There's no *way* I would pass it up! I can see the immortal words in future history books: "That's one erotic step for man—one orgasmic leap for womankind!"

1590

One of the lessons of the 1980s was that *We* is more important than *Me*. After a decade unparalled in its greed, irresponsibility and narrow-minded thinking (The Reagan Era), many in our society emerged into the Nineties with a re-awakened appreciation for the values of monogamy, individual and global responsibility, and genuine spirituality. I, for one, am glad it's *Now*, and not Then!

1591

Most relationships now and then enter "Danger Zones"—times of difficult transitions or intense challenges. There's the famous "Seven-Year Itch" and the well-known "Mid-Life Crisis." Some observers are also seeing a "12-Year Danger Zone" during which a disproportionate number of divorces seem to occur. These Danger Zones do not, of course, apply to everyone. However—every couple has its own patterns, cycles and unique Danger Zones. Watch for them; talk about them; love one another; don't let them get to you! {Thanks to Valla Fotiades, TV host and professional speaker.}

1592

Quality Time and **Quantity Time**: Do you utilize *both*? Yes, yes—I *know* you're busy—but you've *still* got to spend some serious time together. But that's not *all*.—You've got to spend *quality* time together, too. Do you give one another your undivided attention?—At least a little bit each day?— And twice on Sundays?

1593

It's much easier to be romantic when your life is simpler. Two threats to romance that are inherent parts of our modern world and our American society are Information Overload and Responsibility Overload. Just think of the time you'd free-up if you cut your TV viewing by 50%, and your club/committee/activity responsibilities by 25%!

1594

Marianne Williamson (author of the bestselling *A Return to Love*) on modern romance: "The Nineties will be interesting. Although we no longer want to jump into bed with a stranger, the air's beginning to crackle with genuine romantic energy. So everything will be fine." {Psychology Today.}

1595

I used to feel sorry for people in long-distance relationships. But I don't anymore. A letter from Peter C. changed my mind. He's in a long-distance relationship with Renee (San Diego-to-Akron!). Here's part of what he wrote: "You can see that because this is a long-distance relationship, it takes time to maintain the bridge of communication. And in so doing, it gives each of us innumerable opportunities to express our creativity and our caring for one another." Peter and Renee are being *forced* to work hard at their relationship. If they become a committed couple, I'm sure they'll be stronger for having endured this long-distance relationship. Best of luck!

Romance Despite the Kids

1596

Travel With Your Children—the newsletter! Help for the harried! Tips on where to go, where to get help, and how to combine parental responsibilities with adult fun! For a sample issue send $1 to TWYC, 80 Eighth Avenue, New York City, New York 10011.

1597

More than a few parents have written to me saying that Summer Camp has saved their marriages! "For as lovable as all these angelic children can be, it's still nice to get the little monsters out of our hair for a few weeks!" {Jan T., Manchester, New Hampshire.} "Summer camp allows us to re-claim our house. It's so nice to have loud orgasms for two weeks out of the year!" {M.J.}

(*Hello Mudduh, Hello Fadduh!*)

1598

Dick and Jane (not their real names) were a young couple with kids, who treasured their intimate times as well as their family times. While summering at their cabin on Lake Wenatchee, in Washington (their real cabin), they came up with all kinds of places to escape the kids for a few minutes of lovemaking: In the woods, on the mountain, in the canoe. Years later, with the kids grown, the whole family often got together at the cabin. Well, sure enough, Jane and Dick kept their tradition alive, and periodically snuck off. When confronted by their adult children, they confessed. The kids exclaimed, "We always wondered why you wouldn't take us with you! We should have known!"

1599-1600

Let me state this right up front: Tracey and I do *not* have children (yet). [We're on the Five-Year Plan.] My suggestions for how to keep the romance alive with kids around come mostly from parents in my Romance Classes. While we all know that children have a dramatic (usually negative) effect on a couple's romance, there *are* couples who manage to keep their relationships alive and passionate despite the rug rats. How do they do it? Here are a few things my research has turned up:

➢ First, it appears that the children are getting an unfair share of the blame for their parents' distress. Extensive 15-year studies have shown that "the seeds of new parents' individual and marital problems are sown long before baby arrives. Becoming parents does not so much raise new problems as bring old unresolved issues to the surface." {*Psychology Today.*}

➢ Couples who suffer the most tend to be those who don't know what to expect, or those who have unrealistic expectations about what family life will be like.

➢ Time is a big issue. Plan more. Schedule-in time for each other.

➢ Talk more. Listen better. Miscommunication—and outright *non*communication—is common during the first two years with children.

➢ Adopt an *experimental attitude* in place of a *judgmental attitude*. Nobody knows how to be a perfect parent. Give yourselves a break! Experiment with various methods of dealing with the kids, and dealing with each other.

1601

Is it *really* a paradox that parents who keep their love for *each other* at the center of their lives are also the most loving and caring parents? Parents who martyr themselves for their children are *not* doing them any favors.

1602

♦ *How to Stay Lovers While Raising Your Children*, by Anne Mayer.
♦ *When Partners Become Parents: The Big Life Change for Couples*, by Carolyn Pape Cowan, Ph. D. and Philip A. Cowan, Ph.D.

Engaging Ideas

1603

After you've popped the question—or had it popped *on* you—it's time to get down to business. How about a seminar called "How to Plan Your Wedding—What the Vendors Won't Tell You"?! It's taught by Debbie Ludovico, Executive Director of the American Society of Wedding Professionals. She's also authored *The Complete Wedding Organizer*. For a *free* Wedding Planner call 800-7WED-PRO, or 508-368-7055, or write to 87 Old County Road, Suite B, Lancaster, Massachusetts 01523.

1604

Joan almost missed Harold's proposal amid the many political bumper stickers during a recent election year. You see, Harold had a bunch of custom bumper stickers made-up that read "Joan: Vote YES to Marrying Harold". He then put them on both their cars, plus the cars of all Joan's neighbors! It took a month, but Joan finally noticed one of the bumper stickers on a neighbor's car while driving through town. ("Nearly caused an accident—but the surprise was worth it!" Harold reports.) The wedding is set for next June.

1605

For your wedding library:*Weddings from the Heart—Ceremonies for an Unforgettable Wedding*. For those of you who don't want a traditional ceremony. This book offers five complete ceremonies: One on the psychological dimensions of love; one for the previously married and blended family; one celebrating the unmatched joy of finding the love of your life; a ceremony for people in recovery; and a ceremony for people who wish to emphasize the spiritual quality of their commitment.

1606

Coincidences abound in the world of romance. There I was in the studio at KISS-108, WXKS-FM radio in Boston, just before Valentine's Day, talking about (what else?) romance with DJ Matt Siegel, when he took a call from Christine Crowley, of Hanover, Massachusetts. She began telling us how her boyfriend had proposed marriage just the previous weekend, by posting a sign on a ski lift at Bretton Woods Ski Area in New Hampshire. Matt nearly jumped out of his seat—"I was *there!* I *saw* that sign! Was that *you? Congratulations!*"

Here's the behind-the-scenes story from the perpetrator, Edward "Vin" McDonald: He'd prepared the sign ahead-of-time, and got the help of the resort's lift crew. Christine didn't suspect a thing Friday night, when Vin drove off for a pizza and called to say he'd had car trouble. Nor did she suspect anything Saturday when the ski lift suddenly shut down. But Vin was ready: The sign was posted on a nearby pole, and the diamond ring was in his pocket. He pointed to the sign. She cried. She said yes. He had a dozen long-stemmed red roses waiting in her room. The rest, as they say, is history.

1607

If she's *really* set on a fairy tale wedding, head for Disney World, in Orlando, Florida. You can now hold a "dream-come-true wedding with Disney's whimsical touch." The Disney folks have spent millions to create romantic settings for story-book weddings. (And no, Mickey can't be your best man: The 'toons can't stand up for you. But you *can* request their presence.) Prices start around $17,500 for a 100-guest event. Call for more info! 407-363-6333.

1608

Guys: Are you ready to toss that *Little Black Book* and commit yourself to that one special woman? To dramatize your decision, you could do what Howard Beal, of Los Angeles, did: He bought a *Little Black Book* and filled *every page* with his fiance's name! He then giftwrapped it and gave it to her.

1609

During your engagement, sign all your letters

"Mr. & Mrs. (Name)-To-Be."

{Thanks, Beth Elliott!}

1610

For the sound track to your wedding:

❦ *Everybody's Favorite Wedding Music*, CD for $12.98, cassette for $8.98. Call 800-262-6604.

❦ *The Wedding Album*, CD for $13.99, LP for $7.98. Call 800-221-8180.

1611

"Tradition" takes on a whole new meaning for those who long for the Good Old Days!

- You could hold a *Colonial Wedding*—at Old Sturbridge Village, a 19th Century community in Sturbridge, Massachusetts. There's no electricity, but there *are* horse-drawn carriages, candlelit ceremonies and an antique pipe organ! Call 508-347-3362.

- Or, you could stage an *Olde West Wedding*—in Central City, an early mining town in Central City, Colorado. Invitations are sent on parchment, and wedding parties dress in Victorian styles. Call The Teller House at 303-279-8306.

- Or, how about a wedding straight out of the Old South—in colonial Williamsburg, Virginia. Picture the bride in hoop skirts, and an elegant affair in a grand plantation. Call The Colonial Williamsburg Foundation at 804-220-7460.

Kitchen Romance

1612

Call his mother. Find out what his favorite childhood dessert was. Then, prepare it for him as a surprise—even if it's cherry Jello with shredded carrots on top!

1613

How many pies have you baked in your life? How many times have you poked holes in the crust with a fork? How many times have you spelled-out "Kiss me" with fork-holes?? Terry Barber, of Ashford, Connecticut, thought to do this—to the *delight* of her husband! (She also thought to bake a *second* pie with a *different* message . . . one we can't print here!)

1614

Fresh-squeezed orange juice! (You only get *half* as many Romance Points if you use a juicer machine.)

1615

Make bread together. The yeast you can do is knead one another! [Editor's note: Greg, you don't *really* want to leave these puns in the book, do you??]

1616

If your mother told you not to play with your food, then your mother wasn't much of a romantic. Here's a little romantic favorite of Tracey's: Make some toast. Carefully carve-out a heart in the middle. Set the toast in a frying pan. Fry an egg in the heart-shaped hole. Serve to your lover. *Voila!*—A romantic breakfast!

1617

A very, *very* cool little book: *The Foods of Love—Containing the DELIGHTS, Vertues, Magickal Properties & SECRET Recipes for All Manner of Exquisite LOVE POTIONS & Proven Aphrodisiacs* [*Whew!*], by Max de Roche. A thousand years of aphrodisiacs and secret potions are distilled within this volume of delights. The book itself is a sensual delight. It's elegantly printed on rich paper, with color photos and illustrations throughout. It was printed in Italy, and may be hard to locate. If so, call the publisher, Arcade Publishing, a subsidiary of Little, Brown and Company, in New York City.

1618

A Recipe for Romance: Bake a homemade loaf of bread—and just before you stick it in the oven, insert a handwritten note to your lover. (Wrap the note in foil, then wrap it with plastic wrap. Insert it into the loaf so that your lover will discover it no matter where he or she cuts into the bread!) {Thanks to Victoria Copson—a wildly creative romantic—of Encino, California!}

Bedroom Romance

1619

✦ The scene: An average, suburban home in Cleveland.
✦ The situation: Husband home alone; wife's gone visiting relatives for two weeks.
✦ The Romantic Surprise of the Decade: Husband throws-out all bedroom furniture. Wallpapers and re-furnishes room. Classic four-poster bed. Antiques.
✦ The result: Wife nearly drops dead of heart attack. Then they try-out the classic four-poster bed. All weekend. {J.M.—"Please don't use my name—the guys would never let me hear the end of it!"}

1620

Pillowtalk: I

Your bed is a great place to have intimate conversations. Do you give yourselves enough time to lounge, laugh, love and talk in bed?

1621

Pillowtalk: II

Books about bedrooms: Great ideas for creating a cozy, romantic atmosphere.

❤ *Beds*, by fashion designer Diane Von Furstenberg: Provides a peek at the bedrooms of the rich & famous. Includes some bedtime rituals and superstitions—"The head should face north, and the foot south."
❤ *The French Woman's Bedroom*, by journalist Mary-Sargent Ladd: Takes you on a tour of the boudoirs of 31 fashionable Gallic aristocrats, designers, etc.
❤ *The Bed*, by Alecia Beldegreen: Full of inventive design ideas and practical advice on choosing and caring for beds and bedrooms.

1622

Canopy beds.

1623

And then there was the Massachusetts woman who wrapped herself in the new bed, and waited for her husband to discover her.

1624

Feather beds! Turn your ordinary bed into a luxurious, billowy cloud! [One of our favorite wedding gifts was a feather bed from John and Amy. Thanks!]

1625

If you were going to spend an entire Sunday in bed with your lover, what supplies would you need in order to make your bedroom a self-sufficient oasis?

1626

Have you always wanted to mirror your bedroom ceiling, but were afraid that it would come crashing down on you in the middle of the night? Well, space age technology comes to the rescue! You can now get a lightweight mirror-like material that attaches to ceilings or walls with simple tabs. The 60x40-inch surface comes rolled, and it can be removed and reattached—without any tools—in seconds! Just $29.95, from Image Tech, 163 Denton Avenue, Lynbrook, New York 11563.

Romantic Getaways

1627

Some summertime favorites, from coast-to-coast:

- New York: Mohonk Mountain House, a rambling, 276-room Victorian resort festooned with balconies and filled with fireplaces. Call 800-772-6646 or 914-255-4500.
- Los Angeles: Ritz-Carlton Laguna Niguel, an "English country manse" on the cliffs of the Pacific Ocean! Call 800-241-3333.
- Denver: The Lodge at Cordillera, a mountain-top, European-style chateau with *huge* rooms and a complete spa. Call 800-548-2721.
- Baltimore/Washington: The Inn at Perry Cabin—for lovers of Laura Ashley decor! Call 800-722-2949.

1628

Did you know that there's a Yellow Pages of travel resources? All of the listings have toll-free 800 numbers. Most of the listings are for organizations in the U.S. of A., but there are *some* international listings. Sample categories include "Hotels, Motels & Resorts" (by state), "Rafts & River Trips," "Bed & Breakfasts" and "Campgrounds." More than 6,000 listings are included! *The AT&T 800 Travel Directory* is just $4.99! Call 800-426-8686.

1629

There's just something enchanting about waterfalls, isn't there? The Bakers, of Atlanta, Georgia, plan their vacations around falling water. Some of their favorite "smaller" falls:

- ✦ Chute Vaureal, on the island of Anticosti, in the St. Lawrence River, Canada.
- ✦ DeSoto Falls, in DeSoto State Park, in Alabama: 205-845-0051.
- ✦ Amicalola Falls State Park, Georgia: 404-265-8888.
- ✦ Cumberland Falls State Resort Park, Kentucky: 800-325-0063.
- ✦ Linville Falls, on the Blue Ridge Parkway, North Carolina: 704-259-0701.
- ✦ Turner Falls Park, Oklahoma: 405-369-2917.
- ✦ Issaqueena Falls, in Stumphouse Tunnel Park, South Carolina: 803-646-3782.
- ✦ Gorman Falls, in Colorado Bend State Park, Texas: 915-628-3240.
- ✦ The Kaanapali area on Maui, Hawaii.

1630

- ❋ Montego Bay, "Arguably the most romantic spot on the face of the earth," according to *Los Angeles Magazine*.
- ❋ Vermont, "Leaf-peeper heaven," says Autumn afficionado J.L.B.
- ❋ Heron Island, Australia, "Coral reef heaven," according to M.I.
- ❋ Mindoro, Philippines: "The shell capital of the world," according to *Islands Magazine*.

1631

Some of my readers' favorite charming inns:

★ Vermont: The Old Tavern, a beautifully restored 18th Century inn set in the Green Mountains. Grafton, Vermont 05146, 802-843-2231.
★ Pennsylvania: Historic Smithton Country Inn, with canopy beds and handmade Pennsylvania Dutch quilts. 900 West Main Street, Ephrata, Pennsylvania 17522, 717-733-6094.
★ Michigan: Crane House, a homey farmhouse with antiques, potbelly stove, and an apple orchard next door. 6051 124th Avenue, Fennville, Michigan 49408, 616-561-6931.

Romantic Exercises

1632

Try this little exercise and see if it doesn't affect the way you view the world. Don't read today's newspaper. Stick in a box, along with the next issues of *Time, Newsweek, The Wall Street Journal,* and one or two other periodicals that you read regularly. Stick the box under your bed. Six months later, pull out the box and read everything. You'll see that most of the "important news" and screaming headlines of yesterday are foolish and either humorously irrelevant or tragically transitory. Yesterday's "facts" are today's lies. *I've* always found that the most worthwhile, helpful, and Truthful parts of the media are those articles that deal with interpersonal relationships, or those that report on *factual* things, like gift ideas, interesting ideas, or fascinating places to visit and unusual things to experience.

I've never quite understood people's perverse fascination in the "news." Guess I'm just strange.

1633

Grab your partner. Grab two pads and pens. Title a page: "Reasons I'm Not More Romantic." And list as many reasons as you possibly can. Your reasons can be logical, emotional, factual or financial. Don't stop until you list at least a dozen reasons. Trade lists. Categorize your partner's list into three categories: 1) We can work on this, 2) Insurmountable, and 3) *Bullshit!* Discuss strategies for overcoming obstacles, facing some stark realities of life, and admitting to some of the flimsy excuses we all use.

1634

D.B.S.M.

"What do you want more of in this relationship?" Each of you writes a list of the four things you want more of. The goal is to identify four *very specific* things. Now, trade lists. Talk about them. Write reminder notes to each other, using only the first initial of each item.

"D.B.S.M.—Dancing, Bridge, Sex, Money." From a Valentine's Day card to professional speaker Glenna Salsbury from her husband Jim. Thanks, Glenna!

1635

Here's a twist on the above item. Each of you titles a page "Things I Want You to Do For Me & With Me." The goal here is to create as long a list as possible—at *least* 25 items long. The lists can cover anything and everything! Now, trade lists. Talk about them. What's realistic? What's *un*realistic? How important are certain items? Now, take back your own list and prioritize the top 20 items. (This may take a while!) Then, trade lists again. Cross-out the five items you care least about. Take your own list back. You cross-out five more items—the things you want to do least. You each now have a list of 10 things that you want from your partner, and that your partner is likely to act-on. Tack both lists to the refrigerator, and work toward fulfilling your partner's desires!

1636-1637

Here are two exercises that will expand your thinking, and lead to two (or more!) great custom gifts for your lover:

* Number a sheet of paper from 1 to 100, and title it "100 Reasons Why I Love You." Complete the list over the next week.
* *Another* list: "100 Places Where I'd Like to Make Love With You/ French Kiss You/(___) With You"
* This type of idea lends itself beautifully to a rolled scroll or a framed presentation, rendered—of course—in calligraphy.

1638

Gary G. gets *his* romantic exercise by stealing street signs that contain his wife's name! He says he has quite a collection from cities and villages across the U.S.A. [I'm not *endorsing* this kind of heinous behavior, of course. But it *is* a pretty cool idea, don't you think?!]

1639

Here's one that's *sure* to threaten a few of you . . . First, you should only do this in the context of a loving, committed, long-term relationship. This is not to be attempted on a first date. [If you do so, the management takes no responsibility for broken hearts or bruised egos.]

★ You and your partner each create a "List of Fears"—things that you're scared-of about love, romance and relationships. For example: Fear of embarassment; fear of rejection; fear of divorce; fear of losing my individuality to you—or to the relationship. Trade lists and discuss. Quietly. Sensitively. Open-mindedly. Lovingly.

1640

Here's an exercise for you to do by yourself and *not* share with your partner. Draw a vertical line down the center of a sheet of paper. Title one side "My Life Priorities"; title the other side "How I *Actually* Spend My Time." The Priorities side is about your goals, your wishes, your Vision for your life. The other side is about your actual day-to-day activities. Compare your two lists—and be prepared for some major discrepancies! Don't try to change things overnight, but keep this list around as a tool to help you as you attempt to bring your life into line with your Vision.

1641-1644

Create four lists:
+ A "Wish List"—for *things* you want.
+ A "Fantasy List" for sensual and sexual activities you desire.
+ A "Couple's To-Do List"—for activities/restaurants/movies.
+ A "Dream List"—for travel and vacations.

Romantic Strategies

1645

Turn romance into a habit—a *good* habit. It may feel awkward, unnatural or contrived at first, but keep at it! Research has shown that it takes about three weeks to form new habits. [This is true—not just made-up by me.] If you repeat an activity or thought pattern several times a day over three weeks, you'll get it ingrained into that stubborn brain of yours! Go for it!

1646

"The mailbox—*not* the telephone—is the god of the long-distance relationship, for women. They like to have something tangible—like a card or letter," according to L-D veteran Jeff Place. "And for *men*, it's reversed: Guys like the phone. They like to hear their woman's voice—I guess it's reassuring to us." And Jeff knows what he's talking about, as he's the male half of a relationship that's spanned five years and two continents!

1647

Be 1% better at a thousand different things.

You don't need to be 50% more romantic. You don't need to make *major* changes in your life. You just have to do lots of little things. Little, thoughtful, loving, caring gestures. This "1% Mindset" has helped many of the reluctant to overcome their resistance and give romance a try. {Adapted from a presentation by consultant/speaker Lou Heckler.}

1648

If you're simply *not* a planner, if you always do things last-minute—fine! Don't worry about it; you don't need to change! But it might help to join the "Short Notice Cruise Club." They'll let you know about last-minute deals. Save money, be spontaneous, and be more romantic—all at the same time . . . sounds like the perfect combo to me! Call 800-432-3491 or 714-545-3737.

1649

One way to generate romantic ideas is to *focus* on your partner. If you focus your attention on her—just *think* about her a little more often—then romantic ideas will simply *pop-up* all around you! I *guarantee* it. Romantic gifts will jump off store shelves into your hands, and romantic opportunities will present themselves to you unbidden.

1650

Do you want your partner to be more romantic? Set high standards for him to live up to! People usually rise or fall to the level of our expectations of them; many psychological studies affirm this phenomenon. It's the old "self-fulfilling prophecy" thing: If you're always nagging him and complaining that he's a no-good romantic bonehead, chances *are* that he'll remain so. Change your tactic!—Accentuate the positive, and let him know that you *know* he loves you and that you *know* he'll find fun ways of expressing his affection. View it as a little psychological experiment.

1651

Here's how I gather a lot of romantic ideas. It's really the secret of an "information junkie" I know quite well, who uses this technique to stay on top of hundreds of magazines and newspapers every month (which gives her a competitive edge over her business colleagues): It's called "Scan-and-Rip." You don't "read," you literally scan publications for key words, phrases and topics; you then rip-out any articles or ads that might in any way be of interest to you. You stack 'em up and read 'em later. Sort them and organize them if you want, or just toss 'em in a shoebox. Many of these items will be valuable resources for you later. [Look what it's done for me!] {Thanks to C.C., PR maven of Boston, Massachusetts.}

1652

The different types of romantic surprises: 1) Total surprises, 2) Unfolding surprises, 3) Bait-and-switch surprises, 4) Mystery Event surprises, 5) Big surprises, 6) Little surprises, 7) *Totally unexpected* surprises, 8) Expected but-not-right-*now* surprises, 9) Group surprises, 10) Surprise vacations, 11) Surprises in public, 12) Surprises in private, and 13) Surprises involving one or more collaborators.

1653

Some relationships are based on good "chemistry." Others are based on good "physics"!

▲ *Quantum* Romance: "A sudden and significant change in state"—A dramatic change in your mindset—Turning over a new leaf—Taking a Tony Robbins seminar—Realizing the error of your ways!

▲ *Process* Romance: "Slow change over time"—A gradual shifting of your mindset—Small changes over time—Reading *You Just Don't Understand*, by Barbara Tannen—Subtle shifts in your behavior.

Romantic Memories

1654

"Give memories as gifts." {From a Toastmasters talk given by business consultant, professional speaker, and friend Paul Burke, of Mansfield, Massachusetts.}

1655-1656

- ❤ "The French Rabbit"—A Treasure Hunt Leading to a Rendezvous. Send your honey on a treasure hunt that leads to a rendezvous with you—the "treasure"—at your favorite romantic location. The stops along the way will generate excitement and anticipation, and set the stage for a very romantic evening. The French Rabbit kit includes: Seven cards and envelopes; a small rabbit (stuffed); a rabbit cookie cutter; rabbit ears and bow tie (!); a booklet with step-by-step instructions; location suggestions and recipes!
- ❤ "A Formal Affair"—An Imtimate Dinner Party for Two. Whether you dine in the privacy of your own home, at sunset in a park, or in an elegant hotel suite, A Formal Affair will create a memory that lasts a lifetime. The Formal Affair kit includes: Five cards and envelopes; a handpainted penguin (!?); a cassette tape of romantic music; two pillowcases (!!) and a step-by-step guidebook with recipes.
- ❤ Either kit is just $29.95, plus $5 for shipping, from the Latty Marketing Group, 5199 East Pacific Coast Highway, Suite 303-A, Long Beach, California 90804; or call 800-368-7978, or 310-597-5755.

1657

Wrap yourself up and wait for your lover underneath the Christmas tree! {M.M., in Ashland, Wisconsin, did this last year. Ho-ho-ho!}

Romantic Mischief

1658

Does his favorite radio station have a "Listener Request Line"? Heck, even if they *don't*—why not call 'em and ask for a special dedication to your honey? [Tell them it's a Romantic Emergency: Tell them it's your 50th anniversary, or that she's about to leave on the next Space Shuttle mission.] Ask them to play "Your Song." (If you think she'll miss it, *tape it for her!*) {Thanks to Bruce Cartier, Valley Cottage, New York.}

1659

A delightfully mischievous collection of potions, herbs, prescriptions and recipes, *A Dictionary of Aphrodisiacs* reveals many intriguing ways for lovers to enrich their relationships. Included are quotations from classical writers and famous love manuals; many folk traditions; and the lore of love—all of which gives amusing insight into the superstitions and wishful thoughts people have had about love throughout the ages. Seven delicious recipes are offered for gourmet lovers.

1660

Does he read his horoscope every day in the newspaper?

✱ Get the paper before he does. Write a custom horoscope and paste it over his real one.

✱ If you really want to go all-out: Match the newspaper's typeface with a computer font. Write your custom horoscope, then print it on blank newsprint paper! Carefully paste it in the newspaper. The possibilities for romantic mischief are endless!

1661

I laughed out loud at the cleverness of this idea when I read the letter sent to me by Mark Duemmel, of Rochester, New York: If you can't find a local drive-in movie, create your own! *Set-up your TV and VCR in your garage!* Add to the experience by having popcorn and soda in the kitchen, which you run-for during an "Intermission." (Or go *upscale* with wine and cheese!) Another creative twist is to pre-tape a personal message to your lover on the videotape!—And arrange for it to play while you're running to the "refreshment stand."

1662

Take all the furniture out of your dining room. Roll up the rug. Move your stereo speakers into the room. Dig-out your favorite dance tunes. Greet him at the door dressed in your finest . . . and dance the night away!

Romantic Resources

1663

If you're into costumes, fantasies, movie stars—or if you're just looking for something truly different to do this week—head for your nearest theatre company's costume shop. Many of them rent wonderful, outlandish, and elegant costumes.

✷ My personal favorite is the Center Theatre Group's Costume Shop in Los Angeles. In addition to *40,000* costumes that are available for rent year-round, they have many costumes that were designed for movie and theatre stars. Call and ask for Corky or Lady Jane: 213-267-1230, or write to 3301 East 14th Street, at Lorena Street, Los Angeles, California 90023.

✷ On the opposite coast, drop-in to the Boston Costume Company at 69 Kneeland Street, Boston, Massachusetts, or call 617-482-1632. (Owner David Bertolino is known as "Mr. Halloween" in the costume industry.)

1664

Looking for a unique location for a surprise party, second wedding (or first!), or other event? Call "Locations," a revolutionary computerized site selection service. Their database has *thousands* of entries that would take you *years* to research! You give 'em your specifications, and they give you a detailed, customized report. The cost is just $25—not much for saving you hours of time and frustration! Call 800-827-2562, or write to Three Lincoln Street, Wakefield, Massachusetts 01880.

1665

The International Association du Romance offers a wide variety of romantic activities, services and products. Among them are . . .

→ Romance TRAINing: Romantic train trips that include hand-picked guest speakers who will "train" you in the various romantic arts!

→ DWHIMing Lessons: Combining your DREAMS with your WHIMS results in DWHIMs! [Bet you didn't know that, did you??] Making your DWHIMs come true is accomplished through custom-designed romantic excursions—around the country or around the world!

→ *Romancipation*: "Emancipate" your heart to "participate" more in the joy of romance! How? Through a special publication called the "Menu du Romancipation," which provides you with an easily accessible menu of romantic services.

Call the International Association du Romance at 800-967-6368, or write to 1998 San Remo Drive, Laguna Beach, California 92651.

1666

Tools for long-distance lovers.

☎ Western Union: 800-325-6000
☎ FTD's toll-free line: 800-SEND-FTD
☎ Portable computers with modems
☎ The best Frequent Flyer program you can find
☎ Money. Lots of money!
☎ Stamps. Lots of stamps!
☎ Cards. Lots of cards!
☎ MCI/Sprint/AT&T Frequent Caller programs
☎ Faxes
☎ Walkmans & custom tapes

Romantic Evenings

1667

Romantic Evening #1: "An Evening of Romance"

- 🐚 *Music*: Glenn Miller, George Benson, George Winston, Al Jarreau
- 🐚 *Movies*: *Casablanca*, *Ghost*, any Fred Astaire movie, *West Side Story*
- 🐚 *Food*: French bread & cheese
- 🐚 *Drink*: The most expensive champagne you can afford
- 🐚 *Dress*: Tuxedos & evening gowns
- 🐚 *Props*: Candles, red roses, crystal champagne flutes

{Thanks to Josephine & Fabian Douglas.}

1668

Romantic Evening #2: "Beach Party"

- ✛ *Music*: Beach Boys, Monkees
- ✛ *Movies*: *Beach Blanket Bingo*
- ✛ *Food*: Grilled burgers, chips
- ✛ *Drink*: Beer
- ✛ *Dress*: Swimming trunks & bikinis
- ✛ *Props*: Cool sunglasses, sand, beach balls, Coppertone

1669

Romantic Evening #3: "Sex, Sex, Sex!"

- ➤ *Music*: Eurhythmics, *9-1/2 Weeks* soundtrack, Sade
- ➤ *Movies*: *9-1/2 Weeks*, *Body Heat*, *Emmanuel*
- ➤ *Food*: Smoked oysters, Godiva Chocolates
- ➤ *Drink*: Champagne
- ➤ *Dress*: Optional
- ➤ *Props*: According to your particular liking or fetish!

{Thanks to Roy Anderson, of New York City.}

1670

Romantic Evening #4: "1950s Nostalgia"

☆ *Music*: Elvis, The Four Freshmen, Buddy Holly
☆ *Movies*: Elvis movies, *Picnic*, Doris Day & Rock Hudson movies, *Grease*
☆ *Food*: Burgers, onion rings, diner food, Jello
☆ *Drink*: Moxie, milk shakes
☆ *Dress*: Bobbie sox & saddle shoes, poodle skirts, Varsity sweaters
☆ *Props*: A '57 Chevy, Horn rimmed glasses

1671

Romantic Evening #5: "1960s Nostalgia":

🦋 *Music*: Beatles, Rolling Stones, Bob Dylan, Janis Joplin
🦋 *Movies*: *Goldfinger, Yellow Submarine*
🦋 *Food*: Granola
🦋 *Drink*: Electric Kool-Aid
🦋 *Dress*: Hip-hugger jeans, tie-dyed T-shirts, love beads, head bands
🦋 *Props*: Peace signs, happy face pins, Lava Lamps, black light posters

1672

Romantic Evening # 6: "High School Reunion"

✧ *Music*: Top hits from when you were a teenager
✧ *Movies*: Some of your drive-in favorites
✧ *Food*: The junk food of your adolesence
✧ *Drink*: Coca-Cola
✧ *Dress*: Whatever you wore in high school
✧ *Props*: Stuff from that old musty chest in your attic

Bonus Chapter: Highlights from *1001 Ways To Be Romantic*

1673

#1 Romance is a state of mind.

#2 Romance is about the little things.

#20 "The Romantic Law of Inverse Proportions": *The more you need romance in your life, the less likely you are to do it; the less you need it, the more likely you are to do it.*

#22 Remember—Romance isn't barter! You'll lose every time if you use romantic gestures to barter for favors or forgiveness.

#31 Go out this weekend and buy $50 worth of greeting cards. Just do it!

#69 "The Perpetual Bouquet": Bring home one flower a day. You'll build a wonderfully diverse bouquet day-by-day.

#70 Place a flower under the windshield wiper of his car.

#114 Send a taxi to pick him up after work; pre-pay the cab fare (including tip!) and instruct the driver to take him to your favorite restaurant, where you'll be waiting for him!

#161 Use sparklers instead of candles on his birthday cake.

#167 Get her an actual newspaper from the day she was born! Call The Historic Newspaper Archives at 800-221-3221.

#170 Send him one birthday card for each year of his age—one-a-day for as long as it takes. *Or* . . . send him one birthday card for each year of his age—all at one time!

#195 Brush her hair for her.

#217 Put a written message inside a ballon, then attach a pin to the string.

#228 Get the pizza chef to arrange the pepperoni in the shape of a heart.

#231 Gourmet popcorn, anyone? More than 30 amazing flavors are available from the Popcorn Parade at 508-745-1040.

#245 "Christen" every room in your house by making love in it!

#310 A wintertime bath suggestion. Warm her towel in the dryer!

#316 Write "I love you" on the bathroom mirror with a piece of soap.

#318 Hide 25 little love notes all over the house.

#328 How about a batch of *custom made* Chinese fortune cookies?! Call Lucky Duck Fortune Cookies at 617-389-3583.

#329 The most *unbelievably* beautiful calligraphy flows from the pen of Maria Thomas, who runs Pendragon, Ink. Call 508-234-6843.

#336 Have a custom perfume created for your one-of-a-kind woman. Contact Ralph Taylor, Caswell-Massey at 212-755-2254.

#363 Long-stemmed chocolate chip cookies! Call 800-843-9315.

#390 GIANT BANNERS, from Supergram, at 800-3-BANNER.

#396 Custom-made jigsaw puzzles from Bits & Pieces: 800- JIGSAWS.

#515 Romantics live in the moment. "Carpe diem"—*Seize the day!*

#524 Try "Couple-Thinking"—viewing yourself *first* as a member of a couple, and second as an independent individual.

#542 Join the "Panty-of-the-Month Club"! Call 718-PANTIES.

#660 Have his favorite song—or "Your Song"—playing on the stereo when he returns home from work.

#699 Tie a piece of string to the inside doorknob of your front door. String it throughout the house, tracing a path that leads to the bathtub; be in it waiting for your lover.

#723 Pick wildflowers—from a field or from the side of the road.

#756 "Choice seats on short notice"—great tickets for Broadway shows, sports events and concerts. Call Tickets On Request at 212-967-5600.

#767 800-284-JAVA . . . will get you coffee delivered to your doorstep.

#783 Relationships aren't 50/50! They're 100/100.

#906 Give him a custom-made tape in a Walkman just before he goes on a business trip. Tell him he can't play it until the plane is airborne.

#932 Join the Mile High Club!

Communicate

1674

You've heard the phrase "read between the lines." Well, you'll improve the effectiveness of your communication 100% if you *listen* between the lines. How do you "listen between the lines"? *You listen with love.*

1675

Leave messages for each other on a Scrabble board. Sally and Howard Beemis, of New York City—self-described word puzzle aficionados— started leaving short "love messages" for each other soon after their 20th wedding anniversary. "It sounds silly, but it's really spiced up our lives! We love each other, and we love word games and puzzles. Combining the two, we're now constantly challenging ourselves to express our love in short, clever phrases."

1676

Do you ever wonder why you don't connect well with your partner? Give this book a try. *The Art of the Possible: A Compassionate Approach to Understanding the Way People Think, Learn, and Communicate*, by Dawna Markova, Ph.D. We have been mis-educated into believing that all human beings use the same processes for thinking since we all have the same basic equipment. The truth is, however, that there are six unique patterns of perception, each with its own way of learning, organizing, remembering and expressing experience. This book shows you how to communicate with others of different patterns, thereby improving understanding in relationships. This could be especially helpful in your intimate relationship.

1677

Here's a great little "Relationship Rule" that helps keep communication flowing: Neither partner is allowed to say "Nothing" when the other asks "What's wrong?" Your two choices are to 1) Explain what's wrong, or 2) Request that you discuss it later. ("Later" must be within a week.) {Thanks to Gregory Lund, of Auburn, New York.}

1678-1679

Sometimes, a very functional household item can become a medium for communicating your romantic impulses.

➤ Many refrigerators across America are the one point of consistent contact between busy two-career couples. My mail indicates that Post-It Notes are the Number One communication tool, followed closely by comics held up by magnets. {Special thanks to T.J. in Cleveland, Ohio; Nancy & Jim B. in Rochester, New York; and "Stinky & Binky" in Burlington, Vermont.}

➤ And what about a good old-fashioned chalkboard? Artist/framer Bruce Thomas has turned this American basic into an elegant-yet-functional wall hanging. He frames slate chalkboards in styles ranging from baroque to contemporary. {Bruce and his wife Maria leave "all kinds of interesting messages for each other" on their own chalkboard in the kitchen.} Bruce's shop is at 102 Grove Street, Worcester, Massachusetts 01605; you can call him at 508-755-1064.

1680

"There are two extremely critical times for communication between a husband and wife. Both times involve only four minutes!" [Can you guess when these two critical times are?] "They are the first four minutes upon awakening in the morning and the first four minutes when you're reunited at the end of the day. These eight minutes can set the tone for the day and evening." There's a lot more wisdom like this in the book *So You're Getting Married*, by H. Norman Wright.

1681

Ho'oponopono

Ho'oponopono—an ancient Hawaiian method for improving interpersonal relations—is attracting the attention of modern experts. In the Hawaiian language, Ho'oponopono means "setting to right" the problems and conflicts one experiences so as not to carry around that burden of discord which spoils the good aspects of life. Ho'oponopono requires participants to face their problems with honesty and humility, to talk openly, and to forgive and be forgiven. (There's a lot more to it than that, of course. If you're interested in the return to spirituality and traditional healing that seems to be taking root across the nation, you may want to contact Sonny Kinney, who directs Alu Kike's Ho'oponopono Project on the island of Hawaii. Two video introductions of Ho'oponopono are available at the University of Hawaii's School of Social Work at the Manoa campus.

1682-1683

Some specific strategies to help you *listen* better.

- ↔ Give your undivided attention.
- ↔ Put yourself in your lover's place.
- ↔ Listen between the lines.
- ↔ Listen with love.
- ↔ Don't jump to conclusions.
- ↔ Evaluate the message—don't judge your partner.
- ↔ Remember that men and women often have different communication styles.

1684

Here's how Ginny M., of St. Paul, Minnesota, lets her hubby know that she's "in the mood." She's made a special "outgoing message" tape for their telephone answering machine: It's the same as their regular message, except that Glenn Miller's *In the Mood* is playing in the background. When her husband Jim calls home before he leaves work, he definitely "gets the message!"

1685-1687

✦ *How* do you connect? Through words, actions, music, gestures, gifts, written messages, spoken messages, touch?

✦ *When* do you connect? Morning, afternoon, evening, after meals, after sex, before sex, while gardening, during TV commercials??

✦ *Where* do you connect? At home, on vacation, on walks, during talks, in a favorite room, in a favorite restaurant?

1688

Don't just give her another bunch of flowers . . . Give her a bouquet with a message. Use the flowers as symbols of your love and affection. Attach a note . . .

✦ "These white roses symbolize the light you've brought into my life".
✦ "Forget-Me-Not while I'm away! I'll be home soon."
✦ "The red rose is my passion for you. The pink rose is my tender thoughts of you. The yellow rose is the sunshine you've given me."
✦ "One flower for each day I'll be away from you. I'm glad the bouquet is small."

1689

Yes, you can often "let other things speak for you"—like songs, poems, gestures and gifts—but you still must *talk* with your partner. This may sound incredibly obvious, and it *is*!—But don't deceive yourself: It's *obvious*, but it's not *easy*! Talking from your heart is a skill that does *not* come naturally and easily to many of us. We need to work at it. I know *I* do! I'm emphasizing this point because I don't want the importance of *talking* to get lost amid all the symbols, tokens and gestures that I present in these books. There *are* 1001 ways to express love, but none is simpler or more effective than a heartfelt "I love you." Don't let your love become the victim of verbal neglect!

Celebrate!

1690

Have a romantic rendezvous with *Rendezvous—A Celebration of Light*. It's a wonderful game/experience/kit. "Rendezvous can help you create a sacred space where intimacy and new discoveries are inspired." Inside a very romantically wrapped box you'll find an invitation, guide book, three floating candles, rose essence and petals, an elegant bowl, chocolates, Kindle Cards for inspiration, intriguing dialog suggestions, a bookmark for remembrance, and more. A lot of stuff for just $32.50! Call 408-464-1780.

1691

I'm not the *only* one who feels the need to add more rituals, ceremonies and traditions in our lives. The following is from an essay by columnist Beverly Beckham, writing in the *Boston Herald*:

Today is rabbit day.
"Rabbit," I say to my husband before getting out of bed.
"Rabbit," he answers automatically.
"Rabbit," I whisper to my 15-year-old before I go downstairs.
"Rabbit," she mumbles, and returns to sleep.
"Rabbit," I repeat to the 20-year-old asleep on the family room couch. She groans, mutters "rabbit," and puts a pillow over her head.
It's silly, this "rabbit" game, but it's a tradition in our house. If on the first day of every month, "rabbit" is the first word you utter, then the rest of the month will be blessed with good fortune. If you forget, however . . . Well there's no telling what terrible things might happen.

1692

You can get congratulatory notes sent from the White House for 80th and 100th birthdays and for 50th wedding anniversaries! [Your tax dollars hard at work.] Send your request to: The White House, Greetings Office, Old Executive Office Building, Room 39, Washington, D.C. 20500. Requests must be in writing (no telephone calls or faxes) and include the names of the honorees, the type and date of the celebration, and their complete mailing address.

1693

Several Romance Class participants report that they're sick and tired of America's lack of tradition and ceremony. {Among them Sam & Paula B., of Denver, and B.&T., of Boston.} It's interesting that two very different cultures have important rituals that involve tea.

* The English tradition of afternoon tea is perhaps the most civilized development of Western culture. While in London, many Americans have been introduced to afternoon tea, which is usually held in hotels or elegant stores. There's now a service that offers Americans the opportunity to join an English family in their home for tea. Contact Home Hosting (GB), 754 The Square, Cattistock, Dorchester, dorset DT2 OJD, England, or call 011-44-300-20671.

* Several people have written to describe how they became captivated with the Japanese tea ceremony. "It's mysterious—but not really; and it's not religious or philosophical—but it *is* deep and meaningful. That's not a very helpful description, is it? It's a way of life, really," says B. Beemis, of Pittsburgh. The Japanese tea ceremony is essentially a private act between friends. "Tea is about company and guests and human relationships," according to Allan Palmer (or Sohei, his "tea name"), who is writing a book on the way of tea.

1694

Hey, gang, let's start a petition to make Valentine's Day a *national holiday*! I'm *serious*, here. We've got holidays that glorify war (Memorial Day), gluttony (Thanksgiving), consumerism (Christmas), and hangovers (New Year's Day)—don't you think it's about time we had a *real* holiday celebrating *love*?!

Send me a signed note saying you support this idea (or make a copy of this page and sign it), and I'll pass them on to the appropriate people in Washington, D.C. [I'll report back to you in future issues of the Romance Newsletter.]

Cool Stuff

1695

Custom valentines of ribbon and lace, tubes filled with heart-shaped confetti or chocolate hearts, heart-shaped baskets filled with hand-painted notes, and anything else you can think of! Call Ann Fiedler Creations at 310-838-1857, or write to 10544 West Pico Boulevard, West Los Angeles, California 90064.

1696-1698

✤ And then there was the romantic electrician who installed dimmer switches on *every light in the whole house!* {Howard Z., of Ashland, Kansas.}

✤ And then there was the romantic plumber who installed the dual shower head in the shower. {Robert M., of Franklin, Kentucky.}

✤ And then there was the romantic farmer who planted a *whole field* full of roses for his wife. {Jon R., of Blue Springs, Missouri.}

✤ And then there was the romantic chef who not only created a gourmet entree to suit his wife's tastes, he named it after her and added it to his restaurant's menu! {S.M.B., of Chicago, Illinois.}

1699

❤ *A heart-shaped whirlpool bath* in your room—at the Penn Hills Resort in the Poconos. Call 800-233-8240.

❤ *A champagne-glass whirlpool bath* in your room—at Caesars Pocono Resorts. Call 800-233-4141.

❤ *A private swimming pool* in your room—at The Summit, in the Poconos. Call 800-233-8250.

❤ *Five different herbal baths* in the exotic Terme Wailea Hydrotherapy Circuit—at the Spa Grande at the Grand Hyatt Wailea, on Maui, Hawaii. Call 800-233-1234.

1700

This idea is for couples who like the outdoors, the unusual, and the chance to hit it rich. It's also for very cheap guys looking for engagement rings. You can actually go *prospecting for diamonds* at Crater of Diamonds State Park in Murfreesboro, Arkansas. For just $3.50 a day, you can work a furrowed, 35-acre field with shovels, hoes, screens, sifters or your bare hands. Although most hunters find only bits of quartz, calcite, jasper and barite, the mine has yielded tens of thousands of diamonds, with about 20% of them gem quality. In 1990, one visitor found a four-carat diamond! It was later cut into a flawless gem worth $38,000. The park, actually the crater of an extinct volcano, is located about halfway between Texarkana and Hot Springs. For more info call 501-285-3113.

1701

If you've never seen a "Love Meter," you've *got* to get one for your lover. It's a classic "Trinket Gift." It's a blown glass gauge that measures how fast your passion boils. You hold it in the palm of your hand, and watch the colored fluid inside as it boils through twists and turns in the glass. Hard to describe, but take my word for it—very, very cool. A mere $4.50 for an 8-inch Love Meter, and $5.75 for an 11-incher. Call Stratton & Company at 408-464-1780, or write to 3125 North Main Street, Soquel, California 95073.

1702

The surprise weekend trip to Paris is, of course, one of the coolest romantic surprises imaginable. But not everyone has the ability to pull off the stunt with the creativity, the flair for the dramatic, and the downright *sneakiness* that George Slowik brought to the adventure. Here's the set-up: George told his partner that his upcoming birthday celebration would consist of a small party at home with friends; to be followed by an "outlaw party" at the airport to welcome Madonna's entourage returning from Europe. (An "outlaw party" is a New York City phenomenon, in which impromptu parties are organized in unusual places at unusual times.) [The small party at home was real; the outlaw party was the clever excuse for going to the airport.] George told his partner that the outlaw party required them to pose as airline passengers (thus making it logical for George to have luggage and airline tickets). A limo took them to the airport. They looked all around the terminal for the party, which was nowhere to be found. In mock exasperation, George finally said, "Maybe the party's on the plane!" It wasn't until they were actually boarding that his partner said, "We're *really* going to Paris, aren't we?!" The surprises continued in Paris, where they attended the *Ballade de l'amour*— "The Love Ball"—a high society fashion ball.

1703

Here's a very *different* kind of "Love Ball": It's a fun and wacky way of wrapping a bunch of "Trinket Gifts." You start with one small gift item, and wrap it in crepe paper. Create a loose ball. Add a second item, and keep wrapping the crepe paper around and around. Keep adding more items, and make the Love Ball as big as you like! "It's a *blast* to unwrap/unroll!" says M.B.S., of Lowell, Massachusetts.

1704

"Falling Rain Nature Chimes." They're like delicate wind chimes, only you don't need wind! [This ingenious device is hard to describe . . .] It's a solid maple box with hand-tuned chimes, plus hundreds of tiny metal beads, inside. You turn the box upside-down until the beads cling to the underside of the lid; you set it on its feet, and the beads slowly start to fall in random, melodic patterns. (You can watch them through windows.) They never fall in the same sequence twice, and the soft, subtle sounds can last for *hours*! For my second wedding anniversary with Tracey, I gave her the Rain Chimes along with a note that said something like "Every note is a loving thought of you." It's now one of our favorite items. Call the *Signals Catalog*. They carry two sizes of Rain Chimes (decisions, decisions!): The Large Chime (about the size of a small shoebox), with a rich, mellow tone, is $89; the Small Chime, with a sweet, bright tone, is $69. Call the Signals Catalog: 800-669-9696.

Romantic Close-Call #201:
In the romantic movie classic Casablanca,
Humphrey Bogart's character Rick was nearly played by
Ronald Reagan!

Guy Stuff

1705

- ✦ "We men are not the enemy."
- ✦ "We lie to the women we love about what we want from them, and we do it on a daily basis—because what we want from the women in our lives is *everything,* and we want it now!"
- ✦ "What we want from women is no mystery. We want salvation and succor, unconditional love and elegant eroticism. We want five-sided women with all the qualities we cherish. God, we're only asking them to be gods."

From a book of thought-provoking and controversial essays, *Naked at Gender Gap—A Man's View of the War Between the Sexes,* by Asa Baber, the "Men's" columnist for *Playboy.*

1706

Guys get a bad rap. The stereotype of men not being romantic is widespread in American culture. But the *truth* is that *lots* of men are romantic—they just don't go around writing books about it and teaching seminars . . . like *some* crazy fanatics out there! I *know* that there are lots of "Closet Romantics" out there: Because I meet them, because their wives and girlfriends tell me stories about them, and because many of them write to me. (Even *I* was surprised to discover that out of the thousands of requests for my Romance Newsletter, 40% of the requests are from men!) Guys simply don't talk about this stuff as much as women do. And while I *do* think that most of us guys would benefit from learning to communicate more (and more often), I *also* think that we don't need to turn ourselves inside-out over this thing.

1707

Even the Romantically Impaired know that they need to do *something* on major holidays like Valentine's Day and Christmas/Hanukkah . . . But what about the "minor" holidays like Halloween, May Day, Ground Hog's Day, Rock 'n Roll Day (January 8), or Flying Saucer Day (June 24)?? Howard Baker's wife Jill *loves* Halloween. This inspired him to buy 100 pumpkins for her last year. He covered their front porch with them, hid some in the bed, and sent one to her at work in the mail! *Go, Howard!*

1708

For *single* guys: If you're more likely to watch a video than read a book, here's one for you: "How To Meet Women Easily." It's a step-by-step program that deals with the art of meeting women. The tape includes: Conversation tips, interviews with women, how to increase your self-confidence. Just $29.95. Call 800-736-3361, or write to Clearpoint Productions, 520 Washington Boulevard, Suite 362, Los Angeles, California 90292.

1709

Guys are often more motivated by competition than by cooperation, right? Right. So, how do you get these guys to be more romantic? You turn it into a friendly competition! Who can find the best/funniest/sexiest greeting card this month? Who can be the most thoughtful without being a martyr this week? Who can find the best Trinket Gift? (On your mark, get set . . .)

The Psychology of Romance

1710

Every human psyche contains both masculine *and* feminine components. The sooner we realize this, explore it, come to terms with it, accept it and actively work with it, the healthier and better-balanced we'll be. (Not to mention, *more romantic!*)

1711

"We have a built-in drive for romance," says Stan Charnofsky, Ph.D., a psychologist at California State University at Northridge. "We all want to belong, to have our needs met, to be happy." The pursuit of relationship is one way we seek those things. Other people's romantic bonds offer inspiration, even instruction.

"Romantic voyeurism goes awry," says Dr. Charnofsky, when we hold our own relationships up to Hollywood or Harlequin standards." {Thanks to *Glamour Magazine*.}

1712

One excellent way to get your partner to be more romantic is simply to raise your expectations of him or her. Psychologists have shown that people tend to rise or fall to the level of our expectations of them. So... don't give up on him; don't resign yourself to being "the sole romantic in this couple"; don't settle for less!

1713

"Everyone seems to believe they know what love is. It rarely occurs to people that the reason they are *failing* in love is because what they believe is love, is not love at all." This is the kind of wisdom you'll find in John Bradshaw's wonderful book *Creating Love*. According to Bradshaw, the reclaiming of the inner child that he explored in *Homecoming* is just the beginning of learning to love. In *Creating Love*, Bradshaw takes you through the next step in learning how to have a healthy, loving relationship with another person—by finishing the past, grieving your lost childhood, understanding your own rejected and disowned feelings, needs and wants, and becoming ready to accept yourself fully. The book provides a workshop-like exploration—complete with self-inventories, practical steps and exercises—of learning how to understand and create healthy, loving relationships.

1714

"The only way that change happens is through a movement toward better connection . . .This is very different from dependence." This sums-up a relatively new psychological theory that stresses *inter*dependence rather than *independence*, as many other psychological theories do. Relationships with "Mutual Empathy"—in which people are able to feel deeply for each other—are defined as being the healthiest state. This differs from traditional teachings which say that separating from relationships and achieving autonomous selfhood is the pinnacle of development. Interested in learning more? Read *Women's Growth In Connection*, by Jean Baker Miller, et. al.

1715

Positive reinforcement works—negative reinforcement doesn't. Study after study confirms this, and yet most of us ignore it! Here's the simple rule:

Reward behavior that you want repeated.

That's it! If you want him to be more romantic, lavish attention on him every time he's the *least* bit considerate or loving. DO NOT punish him for not being romantic: Nagging doesn't work! You see, positive reinforcement is sometimes a longer, slower process—but its effects are more long-term. Negative reinforcement, on the other hand, usually works immediately, but resentment soon builds-up, and the effects don't last long-term.

1716

Charting the course of love. Some serious research conducted at Yale University focused on the major components of love: Intimacy, passion and commitment. Psychologist Robert Sternberg believes that the fullest love requires all three. He notes, however, that *each blossoms at its own pace,* and follows its own distinct course. "Passion is the quickest to develop, and the quickest to fade," he says. "Intimacy develops more slowly, and commitment more gradually still. All of this means that no relationship is stable, because the basic components change at different rates."

1717

Most everyone has a "public persona" and a "private persona." There are parts of your personality, and parts of your life, that needn't be shared with the whole world. I think that more men would be more romantic if they didn't feel the pressure to be romantic in a public sort of way. {"I got no problem running a bubble bath for my wife, but I'll be *damned* if I'm going to tell the guys down at the bar about it!" says M.C. Don't worry M.C., your secret is safe.}

1718

"If you change attitudes you *always* influence behavior; and if you change behavior you *sometimes* change attitudes." {Thanks to Bob Pike, a business consultant and professional speaker.}

The Name Game

1719

Write a phrase, sentence or poem using her name and words beginning with the first letter of her name. *Little Lola—Listen and Learn, Luscious Lady. Live and Love Luxuriously! Lately, Lovely Lambchop, Larks Laud Loudly your Lascivious Lusciousness! Love, (Your Name Here).*

1720

Sometimes romance requires the help of three burly men and a pick-up truck. Seems that B.T., in Maine, came across a department store that was going out of business. Instead of stocking up on discount merchandise, he walked off with the store's outdoor signage—which included a 12-foot tall letter "D" which he presented to his wife *Dee* for her birthday!

1721

Here's a way to help you loosen up and get those creative juices flowing, for writing outrageous love letters: Take on a pen name and/or an alter ego. Playing a role can help you tap into the creative, crazy, wild, passionate side of yourself. Some members of the Romance Class have written elaborate fantasies, others have penned intensely personal and passionate letters. {Thanks to Christa C.}

1722

Have you visited the city or town that's named after your lover?!

ALABAMA
Dora
Gordon
Kent
Kimberly
Vincent
Theodore
Margaret

ARIZONA
Florence
Gilbert

ARKANSAS
Ashley
Humphrey
Marion
Scott

CALIFORNIA
Chester
Tracey

COLORADO
Dillon
Florence
Frederick

CONNECT-ICUT
Chester

DELAWARE
Clayton

FLORIDA
Brandon
Martin
Leon
Stuart

GEORGIA
Gordon
Warren
Stewart

IDAHO
Jerome
Paul
Shelley

ILLINOIS
Christian
Christopher
Barry
Henry
Jerome
Scott
Will

INDIANA
Alexandria
Ashley
Austin
Jay
Spencer
Wayne

IOWA
Henry
Howard
Sidney
Victor

KANSAS
Allen
Edna
Thomas

KENTUCKY
Allen
Christian
Harold
Henry
Leslie
Nicholas
Owen
Wayne

LOUISIANA
Elizabeth
Vivian

MAINE
Alfred
Raymond

MARYLAND
Caroline
Kent
Howard

MASSACHU-SETTS
Douglas
Shirley
Beverly

MICHIGAN
Adrian
Barry
Wayne

MINNESOTA
Gilbert
Martin
Todd
Tracy

MISSISSIPPI
Louise
Terry

MISSOURI
Adrian
Lewis

MONTANA
Kevin

NEBRASKA
Arnold
Edgar
Gordon
Keith

NEVADA
Douglas

NEW HAMPSHIRE
Carroll
Meredith
Raymond

NEW JERSEY
Elizabeth
Florence

NEW MEXICO
Dona Ana
Eddy

NEW YORK
Alfred
Chester
Clarence
Eden
LeRoy
Lyndon
Shirley
Sherrill
Whitney
Victor
Theresa

NORTH CAROLINA
Lee
Martin
Stanley
Wayne

NORTH DAKOTA
Arthur
Ashley
Eddy

OHIO
Carroll
Lindsay
Ross
Wayne

OKLAHOMA
Alex
Craig
Jay
Kay
Luther

OREGON
Douglas
Joseph

PENNSYLVANIA
Arnold
Chester
Christiana
Jeannette
Allison

RHODE ISLAND
Anthony
Kent

SOUTH CAROLINA
Chester
Dillon
Duncan
Florence
Jasper
Joanna
Lamar
Lee
Marietta
Marion

SOUTH DAKOTA
Aurora
Brandon
Clark
Kay
Douglas
Ethan
Faith
Frederick
Grant
Gregory
Howard
Irene
Isabel
Lawrence
Martin
Mitchell
Philip
Stanley
Todd

TENNESSEE
Bradley
Chester
Charlotte
Warren
Henry
Lewis
Scott
Sharon
Stewart

TEXAS
Anna
Boyd
Claude
Clyde
Donna
Edna
Elsa
Floyd
Howard
Katy
Terry
Victoria
Whitney

UTAH
Mona
Murray
Rich

VERMONT
Chelsea
Franklin
Lyndon

VIRGINIA
Amelia
Craig
Louisa
Patrick

WASHINGTON
Juanita
Raymond

WEST VIRGINIA
Brooke
Davy
Jeffrey
Junior

WISCONSIN
Bruce
Elroy
Florence

WYOMING
Byron
Hanna

1723

You might consider visiting one of *these* romantic towns! {Thanks to J.W., of Falls Church, Virginia, and to AAA.}

ALABAMA
Angel
Love Hills

ARIZONA
Dateland
Darling
Date
Love

ARKANSAS
Eros
Heart
Romance
Hon

CALIFORNIA
Newlove
Paradise
Harmony

COLORADO
Loveland
Climax
Goodnight
Mutual

CONNECT-ICUT
Pleasure Beach

DELAWARE
Green Acres
Harmony Hills

FLORIDA
Lovedale
Romeo
Kissimmee
Venus

GEORGIA
Lovejoy
Ideal

IDAHO
Sweet
Bliss

ILLINOIS
Love
Joy
Lovejoy
Fidelity

INDIANA
Valentine
Advance
Hope

IOWA
Loveland
Jewell
Lovington

KANSAS
Lovewell
Joy
Climax
Eureka
Bloom
Protection

KENTUCKY
Lovely
Ogle
Number One
Beauty
Goody

LOUISIANA
Eros
Valentine
Sunset

MAINE
Harmony
Union
Friendship

MARYLAND
Darlington
Golden Beach
Love Point
Halfway

MASSACHU-SETTS
Hopedale
Silver Lake

MICHIGAN
Paradise
Bliss
Romeo
Climax

MINNESOTA
Darling
Climax
Harmony

MISSISSIPPI
Love
Bond
Darling

MISSOURI
Paradise
Bliss
Neck
Eureka

MONTANA
Valentine
Eureka
Paradise
Bond

NEBRASKA
Sparks
Valentine

NEVADA
Contact
Sparks

NEW HAMPSHIRE
Coos

NEW JERSEY
Loveladies
Fellowship

NEW MEXICO
Loving
Climax

NEW YORK
Bliss
Climax
Swan Lake

NORTH CAROLINA
Delight
Lovejoy
Climax

NORTH DAKOTA
Union
Bloom

OHIO
Charm
Climax
Loveland

OKLAHOMA
Loyal
Loveland
Loving
Sparks

OREGON
Diamond
Bridal Veil

PENNSYLVA-NIA
Venus
Intercourse
Climax
Lovejoy
Lover
Harmony
Paradise
Paris

RHODE ISLAND
Harmony
Hope Valley
Diamond Hill

SOUTH CAROLINA
Union
Eureka
Darlington

SOUTH DAKOTA
Ideal
Date
Eureka

TENNESSEE
Sweet Lips
Lovetown
Love Joy
Bride

TEXAS
Groom
Happy
Loving
Venus
Climax
Eureka
Lovelady
Beaukiss
Valentine
Comfort
Poetry

UTAH
Paradise
Eureka

VERMONT
Blissville

VIRGINIA
Casanova
Love
Rose Hill
Verona

WASHINGTON
Union
Eureka
Loveland

WEST VIRGINIA
Tango
Romance

WISCONSIN
Moon
Romance
French Island
Friendship

WYOMING
Diamondville
Old Faithful
Reliance

_____

CANADA

Sexsmith,
Alberta

Hope,
British Columbia

Belle River,
Ontario

Rosetown,
Saskatchewan

1724-1725

❖ "It's Miller time!" (A banner unfurled at the conclusion of Howard and Betty Miller's wedding ceremony!)

❖ "Have you driven a Ford lately?" (Part of a very provocative note sent by Carolyn Ford to her fiance!)

❖ "Heinz has 57 varieties!" (Part of a very provocative note sent by B. Heinz to his girlfriend T.Z.)

❖ "I♥NY" (A banner made by Nat Yardley's wife. Also, part of a Personal Ad for Norman Yankelovich, from his girlfriend.)

❖ For Jacks: Notes incorporating the "Jack" playing card. Also, a box full of "Jacks"—the children's game! {Thanks, B.Y., of Natick, Massachusetts.}

❖ For folks with the last names King and Queen, Ace, Club, Heart, etc: Again, use the appropriate cards from a deck of playing cards as part of notes, certificates and coupons!

❖ For most everyone: Watch for hurricane names. A great resource for intriguing newspaper headlines.

1726

☎ "E.T. phone home!" (A message from the wife of Ed Treber—"E.T.")

✳ "When you care enough to send the very best—FTD!" (Frederick Theodore Davis—F.T.D.—had note pads printed-up with this line across the top!)

The Gospel According to Godek

1727

The strongest—and happiest—couples build their relationships equally on passion, commitment and intimacy.

- ☞ Passion alone is just a fling.
- ☞ Commitment alone is a hopeless, aching relationship.
- ☞ Intimacy alone is too fragile to last long.
- ☞ Passion and commitment without intimacy is a shallow relationship.
- ☞ Commitment and intimacy without passion is flat and unexciting.
- ☞ Passion and intimacy without commitment is short-lived.

1728

Enhancing your self-esteem *always* enhances your relationship. Most *anything* will do. Choose something that fits your needs, your style. (Or, choose something that is "not like you at all." Surprise yourself—surprise your partner! A Tony Robbins Seminar. A Dale Carnegie Course. The Forum. Avatar. Outward Bound.

1729

You're never too old . . . You're never too sophisticated . . . You're never too independent . . . You're never too cool . . . You've never had so much therapy . . . that you won't benefit from a little romance.

1730

↦ The challenge of a *bad* relationship **is to determine whether or not it is salvageable, and then to either get out or work on it.**

↦ The challenge of a *good* relationship—one that is comfortable, safe and nurturing—**is to prevent the** *comfort* **from turning into** *boredom.*

↦ The challenge of a *great* relationship **is to be modest about it.**

1731

Be yourself—*intensely!*

1732

Do you know what I *really* hate? I hate all those articles that claim to have THE answers: "What Real Men of the Nineties Want," Who *are* these people who have the chutzpah to define what a "Real Man" is and is not? I don't mind people kidding around about serious topics, or saying things tongue-in-cheek—but it sure looks to me like most of them take themselves Very Seriously. Another thing I hate is when so-called experts get on TV and radio and spout-off with such conviction that their *opinions* are FACTS, and that *their* way is THE Way. I also hate any reference to the "Battle of the Sexes." It's just a cheap, provocative method for grabbing attention, with little relation to any reality. It belongs in advertising headlines, not in journalistic articles or serious discussions. As I've said before, *there's no such thing as the Battle of the Sexes.* (If one side won this so-called "battle," just what is it we would be winning??)

---

*I vow to support and nurture this relationship through its growth and changes.
I promise to be there for you always.*

~ *T.E.G.*

1733

When it comes to romance, willpower or guilt will get you through a few days or a couple of weeks—but it's your *beliefs* and *attitudes* that will carry you through your life.

1734

Everything works. It doesn't matter which Path you choose. It doesn't matter which method of communicating your feelings you choose. It doesn't matter which seminar you sign-up for. It doesn't matter which self-help book you read. Even if the methods and suggestions are totally opposite from one another. All that matters is that you 1) Do *something,* 2) Do it consistently, 3) Do it with love in your heart, and 4) Believe that it will work. *Everything works!*

* To say "I am a romantic" is to refer to a conscious, active "state of mind."

* To say "I am romantic" is to refer to an ongoing, dynamic "state of being."

Romance is a *process,* not an achievement. In order to be described as a "romantic person," one must be romantic on an *ongoing* basis. Meeting the Minimum Yearly Dosage of Romance, through a recognition of just the Obligatory Romance Days, just doesn't make it!

1735

Romance is about *you expressing the feelings that are already there.* It's not about me telling you what to do. It's not even about your wife telling you what to do—or how to do it.

> *I promise to accept you as you are.*
> *I vow my faith, love and passion for you*
> *in good times and in bad.*
>
> *~ G.J.P.G.*

For Men Only

1736

Many men view romance as "giving in" to a woman. It makes perfect sense to me that you'd resist being romantic if you see it that way. It's natural for people to resist what they view as coercion. Here's a suggestion: Don't give-in. Don't do what she expects. Don't do what society expects. Don't try to live-up to some fairy tale of what the perfect man should be. Don't follow some soap opera stereotype of a great guy. Don't do what I suggest in this book! I mean it. Here's what you could do instead: Express your own feelings in your own way. That's all there is to it. It is possible to retain your individuality, express your own feelings, do it your own way, and please her—all at the same time!

1737

Relationship intimacy does not automatically equal great sex. If you really want to get specific, pick-up a copy of the million-copy bestseller *How to Give a Woman an Orgasm Every Time*, by Naura Hayden.

1738

Romance is like working out—it's like exercising: You know it's good for you, but its difficult—sometimes actually painful!—at first. But, as any coach will tell you, the benefits will keep building if you'll just keep up the effort. And after a while, this "chore" will become a habit, and you'll be healthier and happier. A lot of guys who are He-Men in the Muscle Department, and Supermen in the Boardroom, are 90-Pound Weaklings when in comes to intimacy and love. C'mon, guys, don't let the women kick sand in your face! They tend to be better than we are at this "communication-stuff" and "connection-making"; instead of feeling threatened and running off to the gym, try learning something from the Fairer Sex. They're stronger and smarter than you may think!

1739

Here's some advice for you guys from a woman who used to work in a Victoria's Secret shop: "*Please* tell men to know their lady's bra size! Bras do not come in small, medium and large! I can't tell you how many men answer the question 'What bra size does she wear?' with 'About average,' or 'Like that—' as they point to a woman in the store, or they cup their hand in what they approximate to be the woman's size . . ." "Women will be very appreciative to have *some* bedclothes that are a little more practical . . ." "Pregnant women (and larger women) really need to feel pretty and romantic and sexy. Flowing gowns and button-up shirts are great . . ." "Most of all, tell men not to be bashful about shopping for lingerie—or shy about telling the saleslady what they're looking for: Something *sexy*? Something *cute*? Something *practical*?" {On behalf of men everywhere, I'd like to thank S.A.C., of Oklahoma City, Oklahoma!}

1740

John Goodman is not only a great plumber, he's a great chef! For the past eight years, every time he comes over to fix a pipe or replace a toilet, he regales me with stories of dinners he's prepared and recipes he's created or discovered. Really! [This one's actually true—unlike a lot of the other stuff in this book that I just make up.] I'm a pretty romantic guy, but my wife sure wishes I'd cook something besides a boil-in-the-pouch dinner. Maybe I'll pick-up this book: *How To Satisfy Your Woman In The Kitchen Every Time: The Kitchen Casanova*, by D.L. Wilson. It provides complete dinner menus along with chronological instructions and timetables for preparing each recipe to perfection.

1741

Find this book, quick! *What She's Really Thinking . . . And Why You Need to Know!* by Elayne Kahn, Ph.D. and David A. Rudnitsky. It's a guide to relationships for men who want to know what they'll be getting into before they set foot in the bedroom or into the bridal shop. "Readers will find the answers in this practical guide to the most complicated puzzle a man must confront—women!"

1742

Do you view romance as a "chore"? Well, you're in good company. [I suppose I shouldn't say "good" company—rather, "numerous" company!] As long as you view it this way, you'll make yourself miserable, and you'll probably end-up chasing your partner away. You do have a choice. You can choose to view this romance-stuff as "fun" instead of as a chore. The first step is to realize that romance ain't "giving-in" to her. It's expressing your feelings in your way. The second step is to be willing to put your fears of self-disclosure aside and take a risk. The third step is to take action. The fourth through tenth steps are to repeat the third step again and again and again and again. If it's not fun by then, here are your options: 1) Do her a favor and end the relationship, 2) Get a dog, 3) Become a monk.

1743

If you're married with children, here's a great gift to give your wife: Two days away from it all—a weekend of self-indulgence. Guaranteed, she'll return to you a new woman.

✱ Club Mom creates get-away weekends for frazzled mothers, whisking them away to a hotel in Newport, Rhode Island, where they're entertained and pampered. Massages, manicures and meals are included. For more info, write to Jean Paulantonio, Post Office Box 1485, Newport, Rhode Island 02840.

For Women Only

1744

[*Psst! Ladies!* Here's the worst-kept secret in the world: Guys *do* want and need romance. I don't know why we play this Game around it, but most men do. Just play along—okay?] And here, believe-it-or-not, from *Penthouse*:

"Men crave sentimentality as much as women, with the difference—an important one—that most of them can't admit it. The tougher they are, the more they crave for a woman to find their soft spot." (Michael Korda.)

1745

Wear less make-up! It will make you more approachable, more touchable and more *kissable.*   Nine out of ten men say they *detest* the "heavy make-up look." [P.S. Why can't the cosmetic companies create a lipstick that's more like a dry stain, and less like moist goop? Guys *love* the way lipstick looks, but we can't kiss you because it comes off on us. *And,* it's no fun when you ladies turn your heads aside so we don't smudge your lipstick.]

You can receive romantic ideas and other crazy stuff on a regular basis by sending for the "Romance Newsletter"!

See page 295!

1746

Here's a *great* way to initiate some intimate conversations with your guy: Get the book *237 Intimate Questions . . . Every Woman Should Ask a Man*, by Laura Corn. This is one *hot* book! It's a numbered listing of questions that touch on romance, sex and values. 121 romantic questions, ranging from playful to passionate, were all inspired by great song lyrics. 73 sexual questions, each following a key excerpt from a bestselling sexual book, help couples overcome natural inhibitions about sharing their fantasies and desires. 43 mind questions, evoked by great thinkers and philosophers, were selected to challenge and stimulate you intellectually. Some sample questions? . . . Okay—you asked for it!

* ✳ "What are three objects that, when looked at, arouse erotic desire in you?"
* ✳ "What would you like to do sexually that you never have? "
* ✳ "Are silent orgasms as exciting as verbal orgasms?"
* ✳ "If *you* were a woman, what occupation would you be in?"
* ✳ "How many tears have you shed in your beer over a woman?"

For a copy of *237 Intimate Questions*, call 800-547-2665.

1747

Madelline E., of Montreal, wrote to me, saying, "You've *got* to tell your readers about this *treasure* of a book. It's helped me regain control of my life, which has, in turn, allowed me to give more to my husband. And he, in turn, has begun giving more to me!"

Okay, Madelline, I'm telling them. [And thanks for writing.] *Finding Time: Breathing Space for Women Who Do Too Much*, by Paula Peisner.

1748

This has happened to me so often in the past 10 years that it's occurred to me that it must be quite prevalent. If you recognize yourself here, please *listen*:

A woman will say to me: "My husband/boyfriend just *isn't* romantic!" I nod my head understandingly and roll my eyes appreciatively, and ask her to explain. After a few minutes of sometimes-funny, sometimes-sad stories about missed birthdays, forgotten anniversaries, workaholic hubbies and sports-fanatic boyfriends, the woman will say something like, "But you know, he really *does* love me. He always fills my car with gas . . . He takes the kids when I'm frazzled . . . He fixes things and works on the house a lot . . ." *My* belief is that the husband/boyfriend on trial here probably thinks that he *is* being romantic—he's simply not measuring up to the Romantic Standard that she's created. It's not fair—and, in fact, you're discouraging him from being more romantic!—to say "He just *isn't* romantic!"

Some suggestions: Take him as he is. Appreciate his strengths. Accept his weaknesses. Love him like crazy. Use lots of positive reinforcement.

Teach Your Children

1749

Perhaps the most important legacy you can leave your children is your living example of being a loving, expressive, romantic, caring couple. Teach your children. {Thanks to Crosby, Stills, Nash & Young, for the song *Teach Your Children*.}

1750

Perhaps the most lasting impressions you can leave on the world are your loving acts. Perhaps your peace and happiness lie in your love relationship. Perhaps.

1751

Some insights from a first grade teacher in Omaha, Nebraska: There's a four-step process that repeats itself all throughout our lives: 1) Understanding ourselves, 2) Understanding others, 3) Improving ourselves, and 4) Improving our relationships. As soon as we've learned one lesson, or mastered one set of skills, there's always a related lesson or skill to be learned in one of the other areas.

1752

A children's book that every adult should own: *The Missing Piece*, by Shel Silverstein.

1753

What's the difference between *daily* romance, *weekly* romance, *monthly* romance, *yearly* romance, *once-a-decade* romance and *once-in-a-lifetime* romance? I don't know either, but it's worth thinking about, don't you think?

1754

Weekdays are for working, and weekends are for relaxing. *Sez who??* Even though Saturdays and Sundays are great days for romance, so are Monday, Tuesday, Wednesday, Thursday and Friday! While "Weekend Romance" can be leisurely and event-filled, "Weekday Romance" can be spontaneous, quick and fun! Think about it. (Also, think about the lessons you're teaching your children by your behavior: Do you really want them to grow-up believing that What Life Is All About is slaving for five days so they can rest for two?)

1755

Love doesn't teach, it shows the way. Love doesn't nag, it models loving behavior. Love doesn't lecture, it just loves! Isn't it interesting that those with the healthiest intimate relationships also tend to raise the healthiest, best-adjusted children?

1756

Rituals—both traditional rituals and personal rituals—can be a great way to add specialness to your relationship. And now, an added bonus! Researchers are discovering that family rituals—things as simple as gathering for meals—are a hidden source of family strength. "The family rituals that provide psychological sustenance range from daily routines like reading children a book at bedtime, to traditions like going to the same place for a vacation every year, to celebrations like Thanksgiving and graduations, to going to church or synagogue regularly. Some families have offbeat rituals, like an 'unbirthday party,' celebrated at a time of year when no family member has a birthday." If you're interested in pursuing this further, look for Rituals for Our Time, by family therapist Dr. Janine Roberts. "People are returning to family rituals because the world is losing a sense of what's important, offering instead shallow beliefs and sound-bite values," she says. "Family rituals help people affirm what their beliefs really are." {*The New York Times*.}

Mark Your Calendar

1757

✗ Be his "Calendar Girl": Get several photos of yourself blown-up. Then buy a wall calendar for him—replacing some of the calendar photos with *your* photos! Some suggestions: Any swimsuit calendar, Playboy's Lingerie Calendar, or a Snap-On Tools calendar!

✗ Be her "Calendar Boy": Put your face and your bod on these calendars: The Chippendales Calendar, or any calendar featuring male models!

1758

November 7: Sadie Hawkins Day. Cartoonist Al Capp's creation: The annual race in Dogpatch when the women chase the men, and then get to marry them. [See what you *miss* if you don't read the comics?!] Think-up a unique way to celebrate!

1759-1765

A romantic's weekly calendar.

Sunday—Reading the Sunday newspapers in bed. Breakfast-in-bed. Sunday brunch.

Monday—Monday—*Aaauuugh!* Monday Blues. "Monday, Monday" (by the Mamas and Papas). Back-to-work. More heart attacks happen on Monday mornings than at any other time. The Titanic sank on a Monday. Therefore . . . be *extra* romantic in order to compensate for all this misery!

Tuesday—Get the Moody Blues' first album *Days of Future Passed*. Play the song "Tuesday Afternoon." Then, schedule-in a little afternoon delight with your honey.

Wednesday—Commonly known as "Hump Day" because it's in the middle of the week . . . could be interpreted in another fashion, too!

Thursday—Pick-up some videos for the weekend—beat the weekend crowds.

Friday—TGIF! Call-in sick to work. Book a bed & breakfast.

Saturday—Sleep-in late. Weekend get-aways. Saturday Night at the Movies.

1766

Mark your calendars . . . for the *best* fall foliage.

- Vermont's Green Mountains: Peak—October 3-17
- New Hampshire's White Mountains: Peak—October 4-20
- Virginia's Shenandoah National Park: Peak—November 1-15
- Tennessee's Great Smoky Mountains: Peak—October 6-19
- Arkansas' Ozark Mountains: Peak—October 22-November 5
- Arizona's Coconino National Forest: Peak—October 1-15
- California's Yosemite National Park: Peak—October 22-November 5
- Pennsylvania's Pocono Mountains: Peak—October 6-20
- New York's Adirondack Mountains: Peak—September 29-October 2
- Wisconsin's Wisconsin Dells: Peak—October 6-20

1767-1778

A romantic's yearly calendar:

January— Make reservations at a bed & breakfast for Valentine's Day.

February—Plan your summer vacation.

March—Begin your Christmas shopping.

April—Plan a "Springtime Get-Away"—as a *surprise*.

May—Meet with your travel agent. Plan a major exotic vacation for sometime *next year*.

June—Begin looking for next year's Valentine gift.

July—Plan a way to make your *own* "fireworks."

August—August is "Romance Awareness Month." Call 800-368-7978 for some romantic ideas and a free "Romantic Idea Tip Sheet."

September—Plan a leaf-peeping excursion.

October—Plan a ski weekend for the upcoming winter.

November—Call local theatres, symphonies and ticket agencies to get their upcoming schedules.

December—Plan next year.

1779-1783

If your lover is a list-person, create a DWMQY List to help him keep romance on his schedule. (DWMQY stands for "Daily-Weekly-Monthly-Quarterly-Yearly.")

✓ Daily: Call home twice a day. Kiss before parting.
✓ Weekly: A dinner or movie date. One "Trinket Gift."
✓ Monthly: Flowers would be nice.
✓ Quarterly: A weekend escape. Champagne for no specific reason.
✓ Yearly: A major surprise gift.

1784

Weekend Romance

Re-capture your weekends! They're precious, valuable, irreplaceable times that you could be using to build intimacy with your lover—instead of using them to run errands and cut the lawn. Think about it: A summer only has 12 weekends in it!! Why squander them on mundane tasks? Here's another way to look at weekends: Even though weekends seem short when compared to the five-day workweek, a year has 102 days of Saturdays and Sundays! That's a *lot* of time!

You may want to pick-up this book: *Waiting for the Weekend*, by Witold Rybczynski. It offers a lot of fascinating facts and commentary on the state of our weekends (how we've turned fun sports into intense competition; how we've turned free time into scheduled-time, etc.)

1785

Weekday Romance

By now, I certainly hope that you no longer believe that romance is only for Valentine's Day, or for Saturday nights, or for Singles Only!

Make sure your weekdays (and nights!) include a little romance. Not a lot—just a *little*. I'm not asking much here. Really. Just try it. C'mon. Don't put it off until next week. Do it this week. It won't hurt. I promise. And it won't cost a lot. Really! You watch too much TV anyway. It'll do ya good. Your partner will appreciate it. Hey, are you listening to me??

1786

Tom and Julie P., of Santa Fe, New Mexico, have taken Sunday—often referred-to as the "Lord's Day"—and renamed it "Lover's Day." Here's their rationale: "Even though we attend church every Sunday, we found that we had difficulty in really understanding the lofty goal of 'loving God'; and we struggled for years to find a way to live our beliefs, and 'keep the Sabbath holy.' We finally realized that our salvation resides in one another—that by loving each other we were loving God. Isn't it amazing how the simplest Truths are often so hard to find?" *Amen!*

1787-1798

January—is National Hobby Month. It's also National Prune Breakfast Month. The 16th is National Nothing Day. The 28th is National Kazoo Day.

February—is National Snack Food Month. It's also Creative Romance Month. The 14th is World Marriage Day. The 19th is Temporary Insanity Day.

March—is Poetry Month, National Welding Month, and National Peanut Month. The 9th is Panic Day. The 22nd is National Goof-Off Day.

April—is National Anxiety Month and National Humor Month. The 8th is Buddha's birthday. The 29th is the day the zipper was patented.

May—is American Bike Month, Better Sleep Month, and National Barbecue Month. The 3rd is Relationship Renewal Day.

June—is National Rose Month, and National Adopt-A-Cat Month. The 19th is Garfield—the cartoon cat's—birthday. 24th is Flying Saucer Day.

July—is National Picnic Month, and National Baked Bean Month. The 13th is National Puzzle Day. The 28th is Hamburger Day.

August—is Romance Awareness Month, and National Parks Month. The 13th is International Lefthanders Day. The 25th is Kiss And Make-Up Day.

September—is Jazz Month, and National Piano Month. The 22nd is Hobbit Day. The 28th is Teacher's Day.

October—is Country Music Month, and National Adopt-A-Dog Month. The 2nd is Snoopy's birthday. The 16th is Sweetest Day.

November—is National Stamp Collecting Month, and International Drum Month. The 6th is Saxophone Day. The 18th is Mickey Mouse's birthday.

December—is Made in America Month, and Read a New Book Month. The 12th is National Ding-A-Ling Day. The 26th is National Whiner's Day.

The Voices of Experience

1799

"A marriage license is not a license to change the other person."

{A philosophy—and a lesson learned—by a friend and psychiatrist Steve Howard.}

1800

Here's one for you to think about: You've been married 10 or 20 years. You think you know each other pretty well. You've been through a lot. You've learned a lot of lessons. Here's a question for you:

"Do you have 20 years of experience—
or one year of experience repeated 20 times?"

{Adapted from a speech by professional speaker and business consultant Stan Billue, of De Bary, Florida.}

1801

Why do so many of us go about life upside-down and backwards? It's common knowledge that after many years of marriage, each partner knows the other's "Hot Buttons"—those little things you can do or say that will send your partner through the roof! Why don't many of us realize that the reverse is true, too? That after many years of marriage, each partner also knows the other's "Love Buttons"—those little, special, charming, sentimental things you can do that will bring a smile, or even a tear, to your partner.

1802

Romance is all well and fine, but there's a time to cool it, too. You simply can't stay "hot" all the time! And even if you *could*, your partner would come to take it for granted, or you would eventually burn-out. Recognize the cyclical nature of your relationship.

1803

Here's a wonderful, thought-provoking excerpt from Robert Fulghum's book *Uh-Oh*:

"How will I know when to get married or even if I should get married?"

A question asked of me by a former student who has been living with a man for three years. Their romance began in college and kept right on going through graduate school and into the "real" world of jobs and setting up housekeeping. Marriage was not in their plans because as long as things worked out just living together and taking life one day at a time, why should they mess with a good thing? But she's 27 now. "And . . . well . . . you know . . ." she says, shrugging, with eyebrows raised in that gesture people use when words can't get at exactly what's on their minds.

Here's Fulghum's Formula for Marriage Testing, as passed on to my young friend:

"Heather, give me your first gut reaction to three questions." She's ready.

"First, if I asked you to take me and introduce me to the person you've known at least five years and think of as your closest friend in all the world, who would it be?"

Her eyes answer. "Him."

"Second, if I asked you to take me to where 'home' is for you, where would it be?"

Her eyes answer. "Wherever he is."

"Third, do you ever lie in bed at night with him, cuddled up spoon-fashion, your back side to his front side and his arms around you, and neither one of you is thinking of sex—instead you are thinking how content you are just being there like that—at home with your closest friend who just happens to be the man you love?"

Quiet. She was in tears. "How did you know?"

Well, for one thing, I have a home of my own.

And I told her that if he feels the same way, they're married and just don't know it yet."

Robert Fulghum is also the author of the wonderful book *All I Really Need to Know I Learned in Kindergarten.*

1804

"Infatuation" has gotten a bad name over the years. It's become associated with adolescent crushes, immature yearnings, and even sick obsessions, as in the movie *Fatal Attraction*. Infatuation doesn't have to be any of those things. Infatuation can be a helpful tool in your relationship. In fact, you can re-create and enhance a healthy infatuation in any relationship—even in marriages of 50 years or more! Several older couples in the Romance Class have talked about how to keep passion alive through infatuation. I've distilled their experiences into the following concepts for your consideration: Remember that infatuation is comprised of uninhibited enthusiasm and intense focus. These are exuberant, childlike qualities that often get suppressed as we grow up. Infatuation can have more than one source: It can come from novelty, or a heady mix of fantasy and sexual tension (which is typical of new relationships). Another source of infatuation is an intimate connection with your lover; age and familiarity are not barriers to re-igniting the fascination and appreciation of one person for another. (This is a more mature type of infatuation.) {A nod to J&M, R&S, G&B, S&V, B&F.}

1805

✦ "Every day together is a gift. Cherish it."
  {Jenny & Milt R., Toledo, Ohio.}
✦ "The minutes you share are miracles."
  {Betty & Ralph J., Syracuse, New York.}
✦ "Today's experiences are tomorrow's memories. Live what you'd like to remember!" {Wendy & Jon B., Sacramento, California.}

1806

The enemies of romance:

- ❑ Poor timing
- ❑ Poor time management
- ❑ Children
- ❑ Too many responsibilities
- ❑ Cynicism
- ❑ Immaturity
- ❑ Stinginess
- ❑ Short-term thinking
- ❑ Lack of understanding
- ❑ Lack of awareness
- ❑ Lack of respect
- ❑ Lack of creativity
- ❑ Lack of commitment
- ❑ Lack of communication
- ❑ Stereotyped thinking
- ❑ Rigid attitudes
- ❑ Lack of patience
- ❑ Lack of empathy
- ❑ Mis-matched partners
- ❑ Fear of intimacy
- ❑ Stinginess with time
- ❑ Stinginess with money

- ❑ Macho attitudes
- ❑ Lack of self-esteem
- ❑ Feelings of powerlessness
- ❑ Lack of self-knowledge
- ❑ Resentment
- ❑ Jealousy
- ❑ Apathy
- ❑ Overly-practical attitudes
- ❑ Lack of time
- ❑ Laziness
- ❑ Lack of role models
- ❑ Generic gestures
- ❑ Repetition
- ❑ Condescending attitudes
- ❑ Boredom
- ❑ Prudishness
- ❑ Shyness
- ❑ Inattentiveness
- ❑ Unresolved resentments
- ❑ Stress
- ❑ Television

1807

"Familiarity breeds contempt"—right? *Wrong!!* It's *lack of respect* that breeds contempt! Actually, familiarity is a necessary tool for creating romantic gestures that build long-term relationships. Newspaper advice columnist Dr. Jane Shaw says: "Boredom is often a symptom, not of familiarity, but of unresolved problems in the relationship."

1808

➤ "Keep your wedding photos—or negatives—in a safe place!" advises M. Butler, of Cleveland, Ohio. "We lost all our photos in a fire years ago, and we miss those wedding pictures desperately. And, to our dismay, it was impossible to locate our wedding photographer from 24 years ago. Let this be a lesson to your readers!"

➤ The Kellys, of Bridgeport, Connecticut, had a similar experience . . . and they turned the disaster into a "Romantic Springboard": They got married *again*! Complete with a new wedding gown, complete church wedding, family and friends and a big reception. And, of course, with a photographer!

Here's Looking at You, Kid!

1809

Did you know that back in the early 1950s, the romantic movie classic *Casablanca* underwent a great wave of popularity, sparked partly by Cambridge, Massachusetts' Brattle Theatre, which ran Bogart festivals during pre-exam time at Harvard University. Just as audiences did with *The Rocky Horror Picture Show* in the 1970s and 80s, *Casablanca* fans dressed like the characters, recited lines out loud, and joined the freedom fighters at Rick's in singing "La Marseillaise." Some romantic moviegoers even popped their own champagne when they did so in the movie.

1810

Several serious movie lovers wrote to say they plan their vacations around their favorite film festivals. One couple takes in the Cannes Film Festival in France *every* May! The rest of you stay closer to home, attending these American film festivals:

- ✶ Chicago International Film Festival: Mid October. 100+ movies; 80,000+ people. Inexpensive. Call 312-644-FILM.
- ✶ Hawaii International Film Festival. Early December. Movies shown at 25+ locations in Honolulu, Maui, Kauai and the big Island. Free! Call 808-944-7007.
- ✶ New York Film Festival: Late September. Sophisticated, inexpensive. Call 212-362-1911.
- ✶ Seattle International Film Festival: Early June. Inexpensive yet well-respected festival. Call 206-324-9996.
- ✶ Telluride Film Festival: Late August. Prestigious, intimate, exclusive, expensive: $250-$1,000+. Call 603-643-1255
- ✶ Wine Valley Film Festival: Mid-July. Fine wines and fine films! Inexpensive. Call 707-935-FILM.

1811

From the wife of a movie buff, who wishes to remain anonymous: "My husband's a movie *addict*. Old movies, new movies, silent movies— you name it! It's sometimes hard to get his attention. But I finally *did* get his attention with his Christmas gift last year. It took me six months of secretive taping and editing, but it was worth it! I taped a series of great romantic (and sexy) scenes from great movies (*Ghost, Flashdance, 9-1/2 Weeks, Risky Business, Casablanca, Annie Hall*, etc.). But the grand finale was the very last scene, starring—me!! (As they say, if you can't beat 'em, join 'em!) I wrote a script, and worked with an acting coach for the romantic dialogue part; and I worked with a choreographer and a "wardrobe consultant" at Victoria's Secret for the concluding "dance" segment. (You'll just have to use your imagination!) Needless to say, this became my husband's all-time favorite gift, because it combines the two loves of his life: movies and me!"

1812

Favorite movie couples:

- 💜 Deborah Kerr & Burt Lancaster in *From Here to Eternity*
- 💜 Humphrey Bogart & Ingrid Bergman in *Casablanca*
- 💜 Patrick Swayze & Jennifer Grey in *Dirty Dancing*
- 💜 Bette Davis & Henry Fonda in *Jezebel*
- 💜 Richard Gere & Debra Winger in *An Officer and a Gentleman*

1813

Favorite romantic movies:

- ★ *When Harry Met Sally*
- ★ *Flashdance*
- ★ *Gone With The Wind*
- ★ *To Have and Have Not*
- ★ *Suddenly Last Summer*
- ★ *Splendor in the Grass*
- ★ *Frankie and Johnny*
- ★ *Bull Durham*
- ★ *Ghost*
- ★ *All About Eve*
- ★ *A Place in the Sun*
- ★ *Raintree County*
- ★ *Brief Encounter*

1814-1815

☆ Looking for books on movies and show business? Hollywood's oldest and most revered bookstore specializing in show business is Larry Edmund's Cinema and Theatre Book Shop. Drop-in at 6644 Hollywood Boulevard, or call 213-463-3273.

☆ And here are two books that will interest you lovers of movie lovers:

    ☆ *Lovers*, by Linda Sunshine. With 200 black & white photos, $27.50.

    ☆ *Love Stories*, by Daniel Kimmel & Nat Segaloff. A compilation of 82 of Hollywood's most romantic movies.

1816

Is your lover an old movie fan? [That is, a fan of old movies—not an old fan of movies ... oh, nevermind.] If so, you'll want to take him to visit the place where the first silent movies were made. The Hollywood Studio Museum has lots of the old classics, and many talkies, too. Movie memorabilia, including the chariot from Ben Hur, is also on display. Drop in at 2100 North Highland Avenue, Hollywood, California, or call 213-874-2276.

Help for the Hopeless

1817

What holds you back from seeking more love and intimacy? This is *not* a frivolous question. Everyone wants to be loved, cared-for, known and appreciated—so why do so many of us suffer in silence for so long?— Sometimes alone, and sometimes even within the framework of a relationship! Why?—Fear! Fear of rejection; fear of ridicule; fear of exposure; fear of ... whatever. Fear keeps us alone. Fear blocks love. Fear drowns the sound of your Inner Voice. And fear prevents you from reaching out and asking for help.

Fear also twists your thinking around. It has many of us believing that we are *strong* if we are alone and independent, and *weak* if we ask for help. Actually, it is a sign of emotional strength to ask for help. Asking for help from a loved-one allows you to connect, to end the loneliness, to banish the fear.

1818

We've got Frequent Flyer programs . . . We've got Frequent Caller programs ... We've got Frequent Buyer programs. Now, let's see ... There *must* be some way I can use this concept for romantic purposes. Think. *Think!*

1819

Romantic Strategy #1 For Dealing With a Couch Potato/TV-aholic:
Create little labels and attach them to the remote control: Replace PLAY,
PAUSE and REWIND with KISS, HUG and TALK-TO-ME! {Thanks to
Randy Harris Glasbergen and his comic strip *The Better Half.*}

1820-1821

Perhaps your lack of romance is a larger life issue. Maybe you need to
work on your *life* a bit, before you can really work on your relationship.
These books should help.

- *Absolutely—You Can Create Positive Life Changes*, by Charlene Shea. A
  very helpful quick-read with chapters like "The Secret of Self-Love,"
  "From Visualization to Goal Setting," and "Managing Uncertainty."
- *The Power of Positive Doing*, by Ivan Burnell, presents 12 strategies for
  taking control of your life. This book builds on the concepts of *positive thinking* and *positive talking* (self-affirmation), and takes them the
  next step.

---

*Intimacy is **not** required 24 hours a day—*
*but it is required **some time** during*
the 24-hour period.

~ Sam

Hope for the Helpless

1822

Are you married to a Couch Potato (or, if you're Republican, "Potatoe")? "There's nothing worse than knowing *Northern Exposure* beats you out," according to Elaine, in St. Charles, Missouri. Here, then, are some strategies for dealing:

> ➤ Tape: Set the VCR to record *every* episode of his favorite show. First, he'll appreciate it. Second, he won't have the excuse of having to watch all the re-runs to catch that one episode he missed last season!
> ➤ Surrender: If you can't beat 'em, join 'em! Grab the Smart Food and *sit*.
> ➤ Patience: You'll have him back when the re-runs begin.
> ➤ Violence: Shoot the TV.

1823

How about *subliminal romance tapes*?! A very desperate—and very creative—woman in Cedar Rapids, Iowa, wrote to explain that she's created her *own* subliminal romance tapes for her hopelessly practical husband. She's recorded several pieces of instrumental music, and she very quietly added her voice saying things like "I enjoy being romantic," and "I'm comfortable talking about my feelings." [I'm waiting anxiously to hear the results of her little experiment!] (She says she's not at all concerned that her husband will see this item in the book: "He thinks that everything a person should ever need to know is contained in either *The Wall Street Journal* or *Sports Illustrated*."

He Said/She Said

1824-1826

* What are the first words out of your mouth in the morning? Do you grunt and swear, "*Damn*, another day to plow through"? Or do you turn to your lover and say, "I'm sure glad I have another day with you!"?
* What are the first words out of your mouth when you return home from work? Do you plop down in front of the TV (to watch the uplifting news) and shout, "What's for dinner?"? Or do you take your partner in your arms and say, "I'm so glad to be back home with you!"?
* What are the last words out of your mouth at night? Is it a fearful, "I dread everything I have to do tomorrow"? Or do you wrap yourself around your lover like a pretzel and whisper, "I love you, I cherish you, I wish you sweet dreams"?

1827

"Happy 100th Anniversary—99 years in advance!" {A card from newlywed Suzie B. to very surprised husband David.}

1828

* Why is it that men, who understand the importance of *practicing* in sports, have such a hard time practicing relationship skills?
* Why is it that women, who understand the importance of *patience* in needlepoint, have such a hard time being patient with men, as they slowly learn intimacy?

[I *don't* have an answer to *this* one—I thought perhaps one of *you* might.]

1829

And the winner of the Best Book Title of the Year Award is . . .

Men Are From Mars, Women Are From Venus, by John Gray, Ph.D. Here's the book's metaphor: "Once upon a time Martians and Venusians met, fell in love, and had happy relationships together because they respected and accepted their differences. Then they came to Earth and amnesia set in: They forgot they were from different planets." This is a *great* book. Serious but not ponderous, enlightening but not preachy. Well-written, specific, and witty. Here are a few choice quotes:

- ● "On Venus, it is considered a loving gesture to offer advice. But on Mars it is not. Women need to remember that Martians do not offer advice unless it is directly requested. A way of showing love is to trust another Martian to solve his problems on his own."
- ▲ "Just as men want to explain why women shouldn't be upset, women want to explain why men shouldn't behave the way they do. Just as men mistakenly want to 'fix' women, women mistakenly try to 'improve' men."
- ■ "A man automatically alternates between needing intimacy and autonomy."
- ▼ "If a woman is not asking for support, a man assumes he is giving enough."

{This item is dedicated to Courtney McGlynn, a guy who knew all along that women were from Venus—or Pluto, or the Twilight Zone.}

1830

One of the best books on the different communication styles of men and women is *He Says, She Says: Closing the Communication Gap Between the Sexes*, by Lillian Glass. The book first talks about the gender differences in body language, facial expression, and speech, voice and behavior patterns. It then goes into great detail, giving many ideas and strategies for improving communication in intimate relationships.

1831

Here are some conclusions from recent research about men's and women's attitudes about one another, conducted by the Roper Organization. [Just tryin' to be helpful!]

☛ Men's self-image: Men seem to be *trying* to be more sensitive and caring without completely giving-up the "Man Thing"—which is basically characterized by interest in sports, women and sex.

☛ What women want: When given a choice between "the sensitive man" and "the macho man," women overwhelmingly choose the sensitive guy. (Further questioning shows that women want men to retain their masculine characteristics.)

☛ Men's complaints about women: They give mixed signals, they're too sensitive, and they're quick to blame men.

☛ What men believe constitutes a good relationship: Being in love, a good sexual relationship, sexual fidelity, the ability to talk about feelings.

☛ Sexual satisfaction: About 80% of both men and women said that they were satisfied with their sex lives.

{From Man Track II, commissioned by *Playboy*.}

1832

The folks at Harlequin Enterprises do more than just publish romance fiction—they also do a great job of taking the romantic pulse of the public! Here are some findings from their research among men in North America: Nearly half of the men surveyed say that a great personality is the most important attribute they look for in a woman. Eight out of 10 say that if they were getting married tomorrow, they'd choose the women they're with today. Nearly a third of them rate their mates' kisses a perfect "10". And nearly a third of them also rate their love lives as "great"—and another 36% describe them as "pretty darn good"!

☞ How would *you* answer each of these questions?

1-800-ROM-ANCE

1833-1835

☎ 800-972-JOCK . . . It was only a matter of time! First it was the "Panty-of-the-Month" and now it's the "Jock-of-the-Month"—for you ladies who want to send sexy briefs to him through the mail.

☎ 800-292-GROW . . . Is the place to call if you love to garden as much as you love roses. The Jackson & Perkins Roses and Gardens catalog offers a truly amazing variety of flowers, with a special, loving focus on roses.

☎ 800-USA-24HR . . . Will put you in touch with Black Tie Roses, a rose delivery service out of Beverly Hills that sends long-stem roses packaged in a classy box that looks like a tuxedo. Very cool.

1836

☎ 800-36-TRYST . . . Is a Romantic Hotline, sponsored by Celebrate Romance, an organization dedicated to assisting couples keep the sizzle in their relationships. Romance consultants manning the line will provide suggestions for personalizing a variety of themes. Free "Romance Tip Sheets" are available, too!

1837-1839

☎ 800-AH-KAUAI . . . All of Hawaii is wonderful, but several couples in the Romance Class have described Kauai as "breathtaking." Must be something to it!

☎ 800-84-LEX-KY . . . For Southern hospitality, antiquing, golfing, horse racing, enjoying—in Lexington, Kentucky.

☎ 800-FLA-KEYS . . . For a honeymoon, second honeymoon, third honeymoon, or . . .

1840-1842

☎ 800-34-SPRINGS . . . Will get you to "America's Desert Playground," Palm Springs.

☎ 800-8888-TEX . . . Big enough to be its own country, Texas boasts enough attractions to fill a book [Hmm . . . 1001 Ways To Vacation in Texas?!]—Country music and two-steppin', the NASA Space Center, golfing, shopping and professional sports.

☎ 800-LOVEBOAT . . . Puts you in touch with Princess Cruises. [Yes, I know this number appeared in the first book, too—but it's such a great number that I had to repeat it. But here's something *new*: I recently found out that Princess offers Fall foliage cruises along the New England shore. A great change-of-pace!]

1843-1845

Here are some European connections for you . . .

☎ Russian Travel Bureau: 800-847-1800

☎ Spain: 800-992-3976

☎ The Irish Tourist Board: 800-SHAMROCK

1846-1847

☎ Toronto, Canada's liveliest city: 800-363-1990

☎ Kissimmee Visitors Bureau: 800-327-9159 [I was heartbroken when I recently found out that Kissimmee is not pronounced KISS-ah-me, but rather kis-SIM-ee.]

1848

☎ 800-SEND-FTD . . . I *hope* I don't need to explain this one! [Service begins early in 1993.]

☆ 800-528-STAR . . . For you starry-eyed lovers: Name a *star* after your lover! The Ministry of Federal Star Registration will name the star, send you a great 11 x 17 full-color certificate listing the new name, the date of your special occasion, and the star's coordinates; plus star charts! Shipped in a decorative box, too. Just $52.90 for a *stellar* gift!

Secret Messages

1849

Even though I truly believe that nearly *anything* can inspire romance, some of my readers are truly off-the-wall! Melanie and Frank P., fans of the TV show *Get Smart*, got their inspiration from the silly "code phrases" that Maxwell and the other spies used. Melanie and Frank have developed their own code phrases that they insert into messages that they write to each other, or that they leave with each other's secretaries. They enjoy the puzzled looks, and they *never* explain what their messages mean! Here's just a sampling of the 100+ phrases they've devised:

➤ "The igloo is burning"..........means.........."I want to make love tonight."
➤ "The dog howls at midnight"..........means.........."I love you!"
➤ Any phrase using "fried clams"..........means.........."Bring home some milk."
➤ "The tire is flat but I'm still hungry".......means.......[An X-Rated phrase!]
➤ Any phrase using "Tanzania".......means......."Dinner tonight—on me!"

1850

S.O.S.—"Sex On Saturday"! Leave this "distress" message on her answering machine; mark it in his calendar; mail her S.O.S. notes; create a banner; make a "doorknob sign." {Thanks to Barbara Brewer, of Petaluma, California; formerly of Fairport, New York.}

1851

★ Create your own constellation! Jim and Julia B., of Tolland, Connecticut, have identified a "Double-J" formation in the heavens that they've claimed for their own.

★ By the way, why are there no "official" constellations in the shape of a heart? If there are any amateur astronomers who'd like to take up the challenge, I'd love to hear from you.

1852

If you look at the messages engraved on the inside surface of some of my readers' wedding rings you'll find . . .

- ○ GMFL (Which stands for "Geese Mate For Life," which, they tell me, is true.) {T. & J., of Burlington, Vermont.}

- ○ TLYTIETTLYM ("The Love You Take Is Equal To The Love You Make"—Lyrics from "The End," from the Beatles' *Abbey Road*.) {Tricia Gilpatric, of Acton, Massachusetts.}

1853

Buy a bag of walnuts. Open one walnut very carefully. Scrape it out. Insert little teeny-tiny love note. Glue the walnut back together. Wait for your lover to discover it. {Thanks to Tom Blazej, of Boston, Massachusetts.}

1854

- ✳ Is there a secret message hidden in your phone number? I LOVE YOU is hidden in the number 458-8968. WILD SEX is in 945-3739. ROMANCE is in 766-2623. PASSION is in 727-7466. MARRY ME is in 627-7963. LOVEBUG is in 568-3284. MY HONEY is in 694-6639. PANTIES is in 726-8437. SWEETIE is in 793-3843.
- ✳ Is your lover's *name* hidden in your phone number?? KRISTIN is in 574-7846. MICHAEL is in 642-4235. BARBARA is in 227-2272. GREGORY is in 473-4679. LINDSEY is in 546-3739. DEBORAH is in 332-6724. JERROLD is in 537-7654. JEAN-ANN is in 532-6266.

Romantic Roadblocks

1855

♥ Forgive him. Forgive him for forgetting your birthday last year... for being insensitive to your needs . . . for not listening to you . . . for...

♥ Forgive her. Forgive her for those unkind remarks she made during your last fight . . . for not being there for you during that rough time last year . . . for...

Unresolved problems, long-held grievance and simmering resentments may be preventing your relationship from moving forward. If any of these issues are bubbling beneath the surface, a few flowers and a couple of cards ain't gonna make much difference! Forgive one another. Then move on.

1856

The Copycat Syndrome. This guy's never had an original thought in his life. And what's more, he's proud of it! This strategy will carry you for a while—a couple of years, maybe—in a relationship, but it eventually fizzles-out. Beware if your partner's romantic gestures show no sign of creativity or personalization.

❏ Recommendation: Look elsewhere.

1857

The Identical Twin Syndrome. This gal can't figure-out why the rest of the world doesn't think exactly like she does. And to make matters worse, she usually tries to convert the rest of us. Yeech!

➢ Recommendation: A little education and a lot of patience.

1858

The Navy Syndrome. Have you ever heard the phrase, "There's the Right Way, the Wrong Way, and the Navy Way"? Members of this fanatical cult believe that there is One Right Way to do Everything. Heaven help you if you fall into his clutches. The Chosen Few are firm in their righteousness, but lonely in their relationships.

✪ Recommendation: Run for your life.

1859

The Steve Howard Syndrome. "I have to do it all myself." This poor guy has his heart in the right place, but he's so overwhelmed by work and Life and everything—believing that he's got to do it all himself—that he rarely gets around to making romantic gestures.

✱ Recommendation: Find him a book on delegating responsibilities at work.

1860

The Once Is Enough Syndrome. Have you ever heard him say, "Honey, you *know* I love you!—Why do you need to keep hearing it/Why do you need flowers?"

➺ Recommendation: Say to him, "Honey, I just made dinner for you last night!—Why do you need to eat again?!"

1861

Taking care of some "Old Business": Choose one unresolved issue between you and your partner (there must be *one* . . . maybe *two*). Something that you both keep getting "stuck" on. Make a focused effort to deal with this issue; view it in a new way; discuss it without blaming; own-up to your role in the problem; each of you take full responsibility. It will change your whole outlook on life.

1862

Help me to love again
  To open up, to give, to share

  Help me to see again
    Another love, who's deep and rare

    Help me to live again
      In quest of love, do I even dare

      Help me to believe again
        Without faith, I cannot care

With feeling and healing words such as these, poet and professional speaker Terry Lubotsky helps readers with her new book *Expressions of the Heart—A Healing Process for Love Loss*. The book is one of a new genre of books called "Self-Help/Poetry" books. I'll let Terry explain, as her words are so accurate and heartfelt. "After experiencing *so* many heart breaks, I became adept at healing from them. The process was always extremely painful, but a "system" emerged in what I went through in the process. Hence, I decided to share this with others, as a way to help them overcome love loss." Terry's book identifies 11 emotions that one progresses through when a love loss occurs. Each emotion is defined, illustrated, explained, and then expressed through poetry. Readers are invited to relate their own feelings and experiences—with space provided right in the book. If your bookstore doesn't have the book, call 305-458-3350 to order a copy!

Mindset of a Romantic

1863

"Reflexive Giving"—Giving without being asked. Blessed are those who give automatically. Lucky are those who are married to them!

1864

Right-brained vs. left-brained romance. Which is your style? Right-brainers are emotional, creative, intuitive. Left-brainers are logical, detail-oriented, organized. Everyone's "natural abilities," strengths and preferences tend to lean one way or the other. If you understand your own thought-processes, you'll be able to go with your strengths when generating romantic ideas. You'll also be able to get help from a friend who compliments your left or right brain dominance. If you're the logical-type, you may want to enlist the help of a particularly creative friend. If you're the creative-type, you may want one of your logical friends to help you organize and plan your romantic escapades. (This right-brain/left-brain description is, of course, vastly oversimplified here. But the concept can still help you identify your natural strengths.)

1865

Be careful of what you put into your head! Your mood, your attitudes, your emotional wellbeing, your entire mental health are all affected by what you think about. So why in the world do so many of us start our days by poisoning our minds with the news on TV, radio and newspapers? Why not try an alternate routine: Start your day by talking with your lover in bed for 15 minutes; showering together; then eating breakfast together. Read the damn newspaper later. [And yes, I do practice what I preach. And no, I don't live in an Ivory Tower. I read five newspapers every day, and about 100 magazines every month.]

1866

Have you ever noticed that people's experiences tend to reflect their beliefs? Do you believe in abundance or scarcity? Do you believe that the world is a harsh, cruel place, or a wondrous, giving place? Do you believe that life is to be enjoyed or endured? Do you believe that people are good or bad? Do you believe that relationships are lasting or destined to fail? Do you believe that the opposite sex is friend or foe?

Many of the happier people I know believe that their beliefs, thoughts and actions shape their world. Many of the frustrated, bitter people feel that they are helpless victims of the world.

1867-1868

Here are some different ways of viewing romance.

Micro vs. Macro

Public vs. Private

Obligatory vs. Optional

Weekday vs. Weekend

Time Spent vs. Money Spent

Little Passions vs. Big Passions

Past-Oriented vs. Now-Oriented vs. Future-Oriented

Spontaneous vs. Planned

Simple & Quick vs. Complicated & Time-Consuming

Practical vs. Frivolous

Rituals vs. One-Time Events

Gifts vs. Gestures

1869

Okay, I'll admit it: Romantics are pleasure-oriented. That's not to say we're *hedonists*. (But it's hard to picture a romantic Puritan, isn't it?) Romantics combine and balance their *own* pleasure with their *partner's*.

1870

Each month, *subtly* focus on a different part of her body. Give her massages; stroke her; buy her little gifts for that part of her body. See how long it takes her to notice! (No, you *can't* start with her breasts. *Geez*, you guys—show a little *class*—exercise a little restraint!). Hands, feet, face, hair, back, legs, shoulders, breasts, neck, etc.

Spontaneity

1871

One way to generate spontaneity is to "break the pattern" of your daily lives. Changing any one thing, or a combination of them, has the potential for creating new and exciting opportunities in your lives. What are your patterns? What time do you wake up in the morning? What do you eat for breakfast? Where do you eat? How do you dress? How long do you work? Where do you drive? What do you do with the kids? What do you watch on TV? How often do you talk by phone with each other? . . .

1872

You do, of course, have a picnic basket (full of food, of course) in your car trunk at all times, don't you?!

1873

She was all dressed-up and waiting for him to pick her up for a fancy dinner date. He was on his way, fretting because he was a little short on cash—when inspiration struck! "Are you game for a little adventure and a change of plans?" he asked. How could she say no? He pulled into a liquor store and picked-up a cold bottle of champagne. He then made a quick stop at a Kentucky Fried Chicken. He headed for a nearby park, and they had "the most wonderful, romantic and magical time you can imagine! And to this day, she doesn't know that a little fiscal crisis was really behind my romantic brainstorm." [Until she reads this, Joe. Readers will be glad to know that Mr. McBride, of Spokane, Washington, is now a successful professional speaker, who now can afford the fanciest of restaurants.]

1874

Go on a last-minute vacation. *Don't even pack any clothes—buy them there!*

1875

And then there are some romantic situations that are *impossible* to plan. Seeing a falling star streak across the sky—and making a romantic wish on it together. Finding beautiful wildflowers while on a walk. Catching a rainbow. Stumbling upon a great little romantic restaurant. Finding a secluded spot to make love in. Discovering a great little bed-and-breakfast while traveling. Tips for fostering spontaneity: Keep your eyes open. Be flexible. Keep your ears open. Banish your inhibitions.

Sex, Sex, Sex!

1876

Guess what message was communicated by all of these different items, sent one-a-week to Ginny, from her husband Tony?—A pack of matches, a wall thermometer, a bottle of tobasco sauce, a weather report, postcards from the Caribbean, a medical thermometer, a lingerie outfit, a photo of the sun, chili peppers, candles, and candy "Fireballs." If you didn't guess "I'm hot for you!" you do not pass "Go" and you do not collect $200.

1877

Erotic artwork—original drawings and paintings—by Stephen Hamilton. All subjects, sizes and mediums for the discriminating collector. Private commissions are welcome. Send $4 for a brochure: 1239 Shermer Road, Northbrook, Illinois 60062-4540, or call 708-291-9023.

1878

✗ "Discovering Your Whole Body as One Big Sex Organ"
✗ "Intimate Connection—The Ultimate Aphrodisiac"

Sound interesting?? These are just two chapters from a very helpful and sensitive book called *More Than Just Sex—A Committed Couples Guide to Keeping Relationships Lively, Intimate & Gratifying,* by Daniel Beaver, M.S., M.F.C.C. As a relationship counselor for more than 18 years, his conclusion is that the sexual revolution has failed. Western culture is fixated on the *quantity* of sex, and is ignoring the *quality* of sex. The book is a clear and authoritative guide to such topics as:

✧ Subconscious Victorian and Puritan attitudes that still sabotage us.
✧ The hidden secrets of sexual arousal.
✧ Different codes men and women use for sex—and the trouble they cause.
✧ How to have a great sex life together after having children.

1879

Yellow Silk—Journal of Erotic Arts. One reviewer described this quarterly publication thus: "Extraordinary work by people who take their craft as seriously as their passion. Nothing in the field (if there can be considered one) approaches *YS* for sheer quality—or stunning erotic intensity." A subscription is $30. Write to YS, Post Office Box 6374, Albany, California 94706.

> *"Everyone probably thinks that . . . I have an insatiable sexual appetite, when the truth is, I'd rather read a book."*
>
> ~ *Madonna*

1880

Here's a new word that we did *not* learn in Mrs. Wilcox's English Class: "Teledildonics"—defined as "simulated sex via Virtual Reality." It's not available *yet*, but those computer nerds *are* a dedicated lot! "Just what," you may ask, "is Virtual Reality?" VR (as it's called) makes use of the computer to create a simulated three-dimensional environment—one you experience as though it were *absolutely real*. (Fans of *Star Trek, The Next Generation* will recognize this concept in the "Holo-Deck.") The following "science fiction fantasies" may be closer than we think: A computer-generated "perfect partner"; the creation of wild sexual escapades that would make Madonna blush; long-distance sex via phone lines. The possibilities—not to mention the psychological effects and moral implications—are staggering! Scotty, beam me up!

1881

Are you a sexual gourmet or a glutton? "A good lover is like a gourmet," says author and therapist Barbara De Angelis, Ph.D. "He or she takes the time to seduce not only the body but also the heart and soul. This allows for sexual energy to build up slowly. And the longer you allow sexual energy to circulate in your body, the more powerful its effects." Some people erroneously believe that the only goal of lovemaking is to climax. De Angelis calls this "greedy sex." The goal of true lovemaking (as opposed to simply "having sex"—which is certainly okay sometimes) is to become emotionally intimate as well as physically intimate. The goal is *connection*, not merely satisfaction.

1882

If you think you've experienced *every* variety of sex with *every* type of partner in every *conceivable* position in every *exotic* location, you may be ready to try *astral sex*. Believers and practitioners of out-of-body experiences claim that it's deeper, more fulfilling, and more erotic than physical sex! The favorite guidebook seems to be *Out-of-Body Adventures: 30 Days to the Most Exciting Experience of Your Life*, by Rick Stack.

Miscellany

1883

If your lover loves a good mystery, secretly sign him up in the Sherlock Holmes fan club, called The Friends of Irene Adler. Write to Daniel Posnansky at Post Office Box 768, Cambridge, Massachusetts 02138. (And then, ask him if he knows the significance of Irene Adler.—The character Irene Adler is from the Sherlock Holmes story *A Scandal in Bohemia*. Irene Adler is the only character in the stories by Sir Arthur Conan Doyle *ever to outwit Holmes!*)

1884

Just thought you might like to know . . . the proper way to kiss a woman's hand. Most men—even in the movies—do it incorrectly. You're supposed to hold her hand (gently but firmly) in a comfortable position (comfortable for her, that is), and lower your lips to her hand. DO NOT raise her hand to your lips.

1885

For those of you who love to shower together, but hate to be the one not standing under the spray, here's the perfect solution: Install a dual shower head! Recently developed by David Black at Hydrokinetic Designs, this unique device is easy to install, and it's not too expensive, either. It's just $99.95 in brass or chrome, or $129.95 in gold. Call 800-225-5800.

1886

The most romantic show on radio: "Lights Out Tonight" with David Allan Boucher, on WMJX-Radio, 106.7-FM in Boston, Massachusetts. Every weekday evening.

1887

Will your love withstand the ravages of time? (Of course it will!) But will the memorabilia of your life together fare as well? Why not take some of this stuff—love letters, matchbooks, photos, newspaper clippings, ticket stubs—and bury it for posterity in your very own Time Capsule?! You can either create your own waterproof container as Lori and Eric Malcolm did (as a joint Valentine's Day project last year), or buy a sturdy, well-designed and guaranteed time capsule . . . by calling Time Capsules for a catalog: 800-468-4630.

1888

- ➤ **Most romantic recent movie:** *Ghost*
- ➤ **Least romantic recent movie:** *Alien³*
- ➤ **Most romantic comic strip couple:** Rose & Jimbo, of "Rose Is Rose"
- ➤ **Most romantic TV couple:** Clair & Cliff Huxtable
- ➤ **Least romantic TV couple:** A 2-way tie: The Simpsons & Bundys
- ➤ **Least romantic TV character:** Roseanne
- ➤ **Most romantic dinner:** Lobster & champagne
- ➤ **Least romantic dinner:** Any boil-in-the-bag frozen dinner
- ➤ **Least romantic sport:** Tennis. (Where else does Love mean "nothing"?!)

1889

A great little shop in Boston called Fine Time restores, appraises and sells unusual vintage wristwatches distinguished by the originality and beauty of their designs. The shop displays a wide variety of watches: You'll find Cartiers and Rolexes next to Ritz Cracker watches and early Mickey Mouse models, plus other quirky wristwatches dating from about 1915 to the 1950s. Prices start around $265. Stop in at 279 Newbury Street, Boston, or call 617-536-5858.

1890

From what everbody tells me, having a baby is a an *incredible* experience, but it's about as *far* from being romantic as an experience can be. (This from both mothers *and* fathers.) Here are two *exceptions* to the rule.

♥ Following the birth of their child, husband David shows up in the hospital room in a tuxedo, delivering dinner and chocolates to his wife!

♥ New-mother Valerie, realizing that new fathers often feel left-out, had a special gift for him packed in her hospital bag.

1891

One of the most novel, fun, charming and helpful books I've stumbled upon lately has the intriguing title *How To Use Poetry To Get Better Results In Your Life*. Author/poet/speaker Sidney Madwed presents a fresh approach to many important issues including love, relationships, work and success. *HTUPTGBRIYR* is a great little book to keep by your bedside. Just $11.95 for a lot of wit and wisdom! Call 203-372-6484 to order a copy.

1892

A great little catalog of hand-picked romantic gifts: *Marketplace*. Everything from Love Meters to The Loving Game, and romantic fortune cookies to massage oils. Call Stratton & Company at 408-464-1780, or write to 3125 North Main Street, Soquel, California 95073.

1893

Each month, *subtly* focus on a different part of her body. Give her massages; stroke her; buy her little gifts for that part of her body. See how long it takes her to notice! (No, you *can't* start with her breasts. *Geez*, you guys—show a little *class*—exercise a little restraint!). Hands, feet, face, hair, back, legs, shoulders, breasts, neck, etc.

1894

What are the issues and topics of most importance to married couples in America? *Marriage Magazine* conducted a survey among its readers, and here, in order, are the topics of most interest:

1. *Intimacy*
2. *Communication*
3. *Spirituality*
4. *Sexuality & sensuality*
5. *Dealing with adversity*
6. *Leisure/humor/play*
7. *Self-empowerment*
8. *Family*
9. *Romance*
10. *Rituals & celebrations*

1895-1896

Games people play!

✳ *The Loving Game*: This simple board game can enhance communication by giving partners the opportunity to ask intimate (though not necessarily sexual) questions of each other. The success of the game depends on how honest each partner is willing to be. $14.95

✳ *Getting to Know You . . . Better*. A fun game for two players to spend time together sharing preferences, experiences, desires and accomplishments. $24.95

✳ *Romantic Journey*. A sexy and daring game—for fun-loving couples with an adventurous spirit! $19.95

✳ Call Stratton & Company at 408-464-1780, or write to 3125 North Main Street, Soquel, California 95073.

1897

You can buy confetti in the shape of hearts, dollar signs, dogs, cats, pigs, stars, moons, etc. Cool, huh?

1898

One day Cindy B. awoke to the majestic (and loud) music *Fanfare for the Common Man* and her husband reading a scroll. It read, in part, "Hear, ye! Hear, ye! By royal proclamation, today my wife shall be Queen For A Day!" There followed a morning massage; breakfast in bed; a morning movie on video; a brief shopping spree at her favorite dress shop (pre-arranged with the owner); a picnic lunch in the park; an afternoon nap; a limousine tour of the city; dinner at the best restaurant in town; a theatre show. {Thanks to Jon B., of Toronto, Canada.}

1899

Knowing your odds just might help.

♥ How likely is it that a professional woman will find romance on the job? Very likely. The odds are about 55%.

♦ What are the chances of a marriage ending in divorce? 28%. [But this is among people who've never read *1001 Ways To Be Romantic*.]

✗ How likely is it that a woman between the ages of 40 and 44 will have sex more than twice a week? More than 1 in 3 women do.

{From *What Are the Chances? Risks and Odds in Everyday Life*, a fascinating book by James Burke.}

1900

There sure are a lot of crossword fanatics out there! I know because more than a few of them wrote to tell me about their favorite crossword puzzle clubs. If your lover loves puzzles or crosswords, sign 'em up! (Both clubs send five new puzzles per month; they're original, full-size puzzles of the same caliber as those in the *Sunday New York Times*.)

→ Crossword Puzzles of the Month Club: $29.95 per year. 5311 Fleming Court, Department 285, Austin, Texas 78744, or call 800-433-4386.

→ The Crosswords Club: $30 per year. Department 21219, 123 Elm Street, Post Office Box 635, Old Saybrook, Connecticut 06475.

→ (#58 from *1001 Ways To Be Romantic*): Create a *custom* crossword puzzle. Make the clues reminiscent of your life together; include private jokes, funny phrases and names of favorite songs.

The Way Men Think

1901

For many men, the "chase" is the most exciting part of a relationship . . . The challenge, the uncertainty, the seduction, the passion! And after they've "settled-down," even if they're happy, they sometimes feel "tamed," and they quietly fantasize about the Good Old Days (even if they really weren't that good!) What's a woman to do? Well, first, you'd better realize that you ain't gonna change him. It's one of those "guy-things" that's genetically programmed into us. And second, you could re-introduce a little challenge into your relationship: Play a little "hard-to-get." Add a little coyness to your manner. Try a little teasing. I'm *not* advocating a return to the submissive female roles of the 1950s—but rather a creative 1990s approach to reviving the interest of that man 'o yours. The specific method is up to you!

1902

A guy who will spend hundreds of dollars on management seminars and sales training tapes won't spend a dime on his relationship. No *wonder* he's a success in business and a failure in relationships!

1903

Hard to motivate your guy? Is he a sports nut? *Great!* Do something he'll understand: Put him on a "Point System"—Turn romance into a "game." Write your own rules, post them on the refrigerator door, create score sheets, and keep statistics. Award him points for various romantic activities. When he racks-up 100 points, he wins something that *truly* motivates him—You decide what: Anything from sex to pizza, or from backrubs to doing his most hated chore for him!

1904

"Most men's primary fantasy is still, unfortunately, access to a number of beautiful women. For a man, commitment means giving up this fantasy. Most women's primary fantasy is a relationship with one man who either provides economic security or is on his way to doing so (he has "potential"). For a woman, commitment to this type of man means *achieving* this fantasy. *So commitment often means that a woman achieves her primary fantasy, while a man gives his up.*" Controversial but well-researched stuff like this is contained in an excellent book *Why Men Are the Way They Are*, by Warren Farrell, Ph.D.

1905

"Gift-Escalation"—a concept that strikes terror into otherwise stout-hearted men. Gift-Escalation comes from the widely believed phrase, "Give her an inch and she'll take a mile." Most men really *do* have great potential for being romantic, but they're afraid that women will want more expensive gifts every step of the way. So out of self-defense, they never even *start* being romantic. Here's news for you guys: About 95% of the women out there are perfectly satisfied with what might be termed "Low-Level Romance." In fact, studies have shown that *not* making small romantic gestures is what builds-up resentment, which leads to demands for bigger and more expensive gifts!

{Thanks to P. Miller, of Boston, Massachusetts.}

1906

I knew the Truth way back in junior high: Long hair on women is much sexier than short hair. 99.9% of all men think so. Sorry, ladies, I don't want to get into the argument about the practicality of shorter hair—we're talking emotion and desires here. What about those fashion models with close-cropped hair? you ask. Well, I'll just leave you with this, from *Cosmo*: "I've watched men thumb through magazines when they think no one's looking and, inevitably, they flip right past every boyishly coiffed beauty without a second glance. But show them a shot of long-haired Cindy Crawford or well-tressed Claudia Schiffer and they're transfixed."

1907

From a woman writing in *Playboy*: "I'm from the panty-hose generation; I grew up snickering at ladies in garter belts. I thought being totally undressed was sexy; he thought being partially undressed was sexier. I kidded him about it; he mentioned his craving less often. He was hopeful; I was firm. We dropped the subject. [She finally decides to humor him, and she buys a white garter belt.] . . . The vision in the mirror takes my breath away. Now that I have actually seen myself in it, I am feeling doubly lascivious . . ." [Don't take *my* word for it, ladies . . .]

1908

How do some guys express love?—They fix the toaster. Many men were taught to nurture and care through their *actions*, through problem solving. *I think that men need to be given more credit for this.* While I *do* believe that most guys should learn to talk and listen better, I *also* believe that women need to learn to meet us half-way.

The Way Women Think

1909

"Why Can't Men Be More Romantic? Maybe we'll never get what we want from men, maybe we want what we can't get. Maybe the question should be: Why can't women be less romantic?" This is from a 1983 *Redbook* article that I've been using in my Romance Class for years. Playwright and novelist Julia Cameron has a distinct viewpoint on this romance business. I don't think I can improve on her words—so . . .

"It would be nice if men were more—oh, all right, *romantic*. But I think it would be a lot nicer if we women were less so. Just as an addiction to sugar can obscure the natural sweetness of a pear, an addiction to Romance can obscure the natural sweetness of the pairing that we're a part of. I'm not suggesting that we learn to do without romance. What I propose is that we devise a New Romance to go with our changing lives. The Old Romance dictates long-stemmed roses, candlelight, filmy peignoirs and leisurely lovemaking. The New Romance substitutes daffodils bought at the commuter station, a high-intensity bedside lamp so your working late doesn't keep him awake, and a date to make love two days from now when you both have met your office deadlines . . .In the Old Romance, passion is a male prerogative; submission is the appropriate female response. This notion places men and women in enemy camps, endlessly negotiating a series of concessions through a series of bribes. The New Romance acknowledges female desire, and the fact that we may like to bestow burning kisses as much as we like receiving them."

1910

A lament from a guy I know: "If you miss *one* anniversary, you pay for it for the *rest of your life!*" While this isn't true for *everyone*, let it serve as a warning to you guys. {More words of wisdom from the wise Observer of the Human Condition, Courtney M., of Boston.}

1911

One hundred women were asked, "If you want to be alluring, what do you wear?" Here are their answers:

39 said "Lingerie"
28 said "Perfume"
12 said "Sexy dress"
6 said "Nothing"
4 said "Low-cut blouse"
3 said "Miniskirt"

No, this one wasn't *my* poll—I got the info from one of my sharp-eyed romantic informants who happens to watch *Family Feud*! {Thanks to Sally, from St. Louis.}

Gift-Giving

1912

Two very cool (and heavy) table-top books: *The Art of Giving*, and *Only the Best: A Celebration of Gift-Giving in America*, by Stuart E. Jacobson. Gorgeous photographs accompany the text that describes a wide variety of gifts given and received by some of the world's rich and/or famous and/or notable people.

1913

Is there a "hidden agenda" behind your gift? If so, be careful—you may be tainting all of your future gifts and gestures. That health club membership doesn't say "I love you"—it says "You're too fat!" That microwave doesn't say "I appreciate you"—it says "Cook more often!" *Don't turn your gifts into attacks!* The gifts, presents and gestures that are most truly romantic are those that are purely motivated, freely given, and genuinely heartfelt. [End of lecture—Class dismissed.]

1914-1915

As I noted in the first book: *Don't* give cash as a gift—*unless* you do it in an unusual or creative way. Well, some of my readers have done just that: They've come up with some ideas that are creative, if not downright unusual!

$ "Long-Stemmed Twenty-Dollar-Bills." {B.J.T., Boston, Massachusetts.}
$ "The Hundred-Dollar-Bill Single Rose." {Alice & Jim H., Grenada, Mississippi.}
$ "Origami Money"!! {Jennifer Beals, of Chicago, Illinois.}
$ "The Great Toilet Paper Roll of One Hundred One-Dollar Bills!" {Betty S..}

1916

Here's a way to add a little extra touch to books or other gifts and presents: Attach a "CardaPeel" to it. CardaPeels are a line of unique gift cards printed on self-adhesive labels. They make great bookplates, and they also double as gift tags or shipping labels. They come in seasonal designs, and can be found in bookstores and giftshops. And they're just 99¢ apiece.

1917

If you believe that the giftbox is just as important as the gift itself, you've *got* to get one (or both) of these books: *The Decorative GIFT BOX Book* and *The William Morris GIFT BOX Book*. Each book contains 20-some exquisitely designed press-out boxes for every gift giving occasion. Motifs include birds, florals, fruits and foliage, plus geometric designs, medieval prints and Egyptian symbols. Each book is just $20, via the gift catalog of the Museum of Fine Arts, Boston. Call 800-225-5592.

1918

Make sure your gifts, gestures and activities appeal to different parts of your partner's personality. We all have these different aspects to ourselves that need some attention: Logical, playful, emotional, childlike, classy, public, private, elegant, casual, sexual, sensual, serious, silly, artistic, practical, outrageous, showy, shy, creative, insecure, selfish, parental, adult, and loving. Over a year's time, you should cover all these bases.

1919

You don't have to wrap *all* of your gifts to her in the traditional paper-and-bow manner. Last year for Tracey's birthday I got her a new, fancy umbrella that she'd spied in a store. I hung it, unwrapped, from a hook in the ceiling in the hallway. She was delighted to see the umbrella, and had to—of course—open it. When she opened it, out fell a second gift—this one from Victoria's Secret. (The old "Gift-Inside-Another-Gift-Trick"!)

Couple-Thinking

1920

Many people fail to communicate not only because they're on "different wavelengths," but because they don't even recognize that there are different ways/methods/modes/styles of communication. Most of us assume that everyone thinks and communicates the way we do. Wrong-O!

- ◆ Some of us tend to be logical most of the time; others are more emotional.
- ◆ Ask yourself if you're speaking from your "Adult, Parent, or Child" self. (Concepts from Eric Berne's classic book *I'm Okay, You're Okay*.)
- ◆ Are you listening as well as speaking?
- ◆ Are you listening "between the lines"?

1921

Healthy relationships are partnerships of equals. Healthy relationships are growing, dynamic, evolving, spirited and unpredictable things. Healthy relationships have room in them for both dependence, independence, and interdependence—all swirling around in ever-changing patterns!

1922

Being romantic will not—and *should* not—prevent fights. That's not its purpose! Healthy, fair, air-clearing fights are just as important to maintaining a good relationship as romance is. [I hope you people don't really think that Tracey and I never fight. *Hah!*]

1923

"Resonance": When you're just about to call her, you're reaching for the phone—and *she* calls *you*. When you send each other the same exact greeting card. This is *resonance* in a relationship . . . a phenomenon that *some* believe indicates that you're Soul Mates. {Resonance, newly-defined by Joe D. & Pam K.}

1924

* ♣ "If the no-fault concept can be applied to insurance, surely there is room for it in relationships."
* ♣ "Relationship problems should be recognized as they occur, but dealt with when the possibilities of cooperation are greatest."
* ♣ "The means for correct resolution of an issue is always the same: The individuals must bypass their separate ego positions and gently unite."

{Some gems from *A Book for Couples*, by Hugh & Gayle Prather, as quoted in *Marriage Magazine*.}

1925

Love creates an "us" without destroying a "me," says Leo Buscaglia, in *Born For Love*.

1926

Lou Heckler, a business consultant and professional speaker, and his wife, began their married life with the conscious goal of spending as much time together as possible. Thus, they structured their lives to be as flexible as possible. They viewed many of their roles as interchangeable: raising the kids, household chores, financial obligations, etc. And, over the years, Lou has progressively reduced his travel time from 14 days per month, down to 10—and he's now aiming at 8. Best of luck!

1927

One of the best "courses" on relationships is the *Pairs* program. It's an intensive 16-week, 120-hour course for couples (married or unmarried) at any stage of their relationship. *Pairs* is designed to help couples learn new skills for preventing marital breakdown. The program focuses on communication, conflict resolution, bonding, emotional expression, family systems and their role in relationships, sensuality and sexuality, contracting and negotiating. *Pairs* founder Lori Heyman Gordon is the author of *Love Knots*, which describes the "mental road blocks" that couples often encounter during the course of their marriages. Her newest book, *Paths to Intimacy*, describes the *Pairs* program. For more info, call the Pairs Foundation at 800-842-7470, or write to 3705 South George Mason Drive, Suite C35, Falls Church, Virginia 22041.

Off-the-Wall

1928-1929

Write "I love you"...

- ❤ On the driveway with a piece of chalk.
- ❤ On the car windshield with a piece of soap.
- ❤ On the eggs in your refrigerator.
- ❤ On her computer.
- ❤ On his underwear in embroidery.

1930

The Ka-bloon card! The world's first inflatable greeting card. You open it up, push the button—and ...*Pow!*—A heart-shaped balloon inflates! Just 10 bucks, at card shops or through the *Lighter Side Catalog.* Call 813-747-2356.

1931

And now, for the man who has *everything*—except a tie that plays lovesongs: A blue tie with red hearts on it that plays *Let Me Call You Sweetheart.* Just $20, from the Expressions Catalog. Call 800-624-8957.

1932

How about a custom-made wall calendar—made from 12 of your own photos!? Candid Calendars will turn your photos into a full color, 11x17-inch wall calendar for only $19.95. Call them for a free brochure: 800-328-8415.

1933

Dig through your basement or closets for an old, unused board game—one with a "spinner" for moving the game pieces. Glue a piece of blank paper over the printing on the spinner, and re-label it. You're familiar with *Wheel of Fortune* . . . well, we're going to create a *Wheel of Romance!* Divide the wheel into 8 or 12 pie-shaped sections. Then, write-in various romantic activities such as: "Breakfast in bed," "One sensuous massage," "I'll do the dishes," and "One candlelit dinner." If you want to keep it simple, just tape the spinner to the refrigerator door, and give it a whirl every once in a while. Or, if you like to get elaborate, create your own "Romance Game"—complete with rules and a game board! (If you can't find an old board game, make your *own* spinner!)

1934

Be a genie: Grant your lover three wishes.

> *"I learned my passion in the good old fashioned School of Lover Boys."*
>
> ~ *Queen*

Myth-Busters

1935

Are you a victim of the "Happily Ever After" Myth? Most people won't openly admit to believing in fairy tales, but some of them have expectations of their partner that are based more on fantasy than reality. If you are continually disappointed in your partner, if he or she *never* measures-up, if you often use phrases like "I didn't think it was going to be like *this*"—you just *may* be trying to live a fairy tale instead of a real life.

Partners *don't* end your problems—But they *do* provide you with support and love so you can get through life's challenges. *Don't* expect Prince Charming to arrive—he already married Cinderella (and then I think he divorced her to marry Snow White. You *see!* Things aren't even perfect in the fairy tales!)

1936

Y'know, now that I think about it, I believe it *is* possible to live "Happily Ever After." Notice that the phrase is *not* "*Easily* ever after"—it's "happily." (Once the fairy tale ends with "And they lived happily ever after"—we all assume that the couple continued to live and have many adventures that simply weren't captured by Mother Goose. My guess is that somewhere along the way these decidedly *un*happy adventures probably took place: The Prince has trouble making the mortgage payments on the castle. The Princess suffers from PMS. The Prince can't fit into his armor because of a weight problem. —But of course, all these problems are resolved, they live "Happily Ever After"—and they *still* have more adventures. Just like in real life. How about that!

Nobody ever said it was going to be *easy!* But I know many couples in very long-term relationships who are *happy*. That's not to say that they walk around with foolish grins on their faces all the time, or that their lives have been trouble-free! But many couples have mastered the ability to work things through, to deal with life's ups and downs, while at the same time maintaining their peace, their calmness and their happiness.

I think that living "Happily Ever After" is a reasonable goal.

1937

Constant togetherness may actually stifle romance! Familiarity doesn't really breed contempt, but it *can* breed boredom! Mature couples trust each other to be apart. It allows growth and change to take place, it gives you new perspectives, and it allows you to nurture your commitment to one another. The result will be the excitement of discovering each other anew!

1938

A thought I had one afternoon while listening to the radio in the car, driving in rush-hour traffic on Route 93 into Boston: Y'know, I thought, everyone says that men are unromantic, insensitive and uncaring. How can you reconcile that with the fact that all those thousands of love songs have been written, sung and recorded by *men*? Those songs express all kinds of feelings—from tender love to deep passion to undying love to passing fancies to hopeless longing to joyful celebration.

Romance resides in the everyday.

Custom Made

1939

This is one of my favorite discoveries of the past year:

Custom jewelry made from the decorative metal caps that top champagne corks!

Wouldn't it be *great* to give your bride earrings made from champagne caps served at your wedding? Or how about an anniversary pin made from the champagne caps from your romantic dinner? Or a necklace made from the champagne caps served at her surprise birthday party? Jewelry designer Cheryl Berez has many styles already created, and she'll also design something based on your ideas. Prices range from about $80 to $150+. Call Cheryl at 310-394-3922, or write to 852 15th Street, Suite 4, Santa Monica, California 90403.

1940

How about a custom-knitted sweater? You provide a design or a message, and Tanya Kudinoff will create a one-of-a-kind sweater for your lover. She also makes blankets—and even "message banners," great for hanging or framing. Call Tanya at Custom Knits, 818-336-4269, or write to 16074 La Monde, Hacienda Heights, California 91745.

1941

+ First, run out and get two fabulous books: *Griffin & Sabine*, and *Sabine's Notebook*, by Nick Bantock.
+ Second, use the format of these books to create your own special books of correspondence and memorabilia. Don't be in a rush to complete this project. Make it a work of art. Make it a labor of love.
+ Third, send a copy of it to me, so I can include your story in a future book! (See page 295.)

1942

Immortalize Spot, put Puffy up in lights . . . with a commissioned pet portrait!

- ✍ Pencil drawings for $100; oil renderings for $250. Richard Grant: 617-241-7797.
- ✍ Watercolors for around $65. Grraphics (!), Ruth Daniels: 617-859-8078.
- ✍ Private pet commissions of $1,000+. Jerry Freeman: 617-731-6720.

1943

Here's an example of a "crossover-gift"—something that's generally used in the business world but rarely used as a personal item. CorporateCandy is hard candy with custom "printing" on each piece. (Actually, the lettering on CorporateCandy goes all the way through each piece—it's not just printed on the surface.) The possibilities are endless!

- ✦ *Her name*
- ✦ *"I love you"*
- ✦ *"Happy Anniversary"*
- ✦ *Short messages*
- ✦ *Both your names*
- ✦ *"Will you marry me?"*
- ✦ *Pet names*
- ✦ *Secret messages in code!*

You can fit up to 16 letters or numbers on each piece. This custom work isn't cheap—but for that special person on that special occasion, it's a great deal! The minimum order of 50 pounds (approximately 4,000 pieces) costs about $380. Turn-around time is just three weeks. Call Gift Service Inc. at 800-562-4448 or 205-879-GIFT, or write to them at 3 Office Park Circle, Suite 310, Birmingham, Alabama 35223. • P.S. You can also get custom made chocolate mints, chocolate coins, lolly pops and gum!

1944

Create your own "Love Potion"! Many readers enjoy experimenting with a variety of liqueurs and spices. Favorite ingredients include B&B, Baileys Irish Creme, Grand Marnier, Cointreau, Fra Angelico; and spices such as cinnamon, cardamom and clove.

1945

This one's a "10" on the Cool Scale. How about creating your own MTV-like rock video!? From the Beatles to Guns 'n Roses—from rock to country! It could be a great shared experience. Or—if your lover is wild about a certain singer or group, you could surprise him or her with a video of you singing a top hit!

First, you choose your song. Then you enter a private video studio. You can lip-synch the song, or make your own audio recording to add to the soundtrack. Musical instruments and props are provided. You practice a bit, then do the taping. Then, professional production engineers perform editing magic, adding mixing effects and graphics, to create a professional-quality cassette!

SuperStar Studios are currently located in more than 30 amusement and theme parks and vacation resorts in the U.S. and Canada, including these popular spots:

★ Pleasure Island, Disney World, Orlando, Florida
★ Canada's Wonderland, Maple, Ontario, Canada
★ Busch Gardens, Williamsburg, Virginia
★ Six Flags Over Georgia, Atlanta, Georgia
★ Valley Fair, Shakopee, Minnesota
★ Kings Dominion, Doswell, Virginia
★ Cedar Point, Sandusky, Ohio
★ Great America, Santa Clara, California
★ Six Flags Over Texas, Arlington, Texas

Call or write Star Trax to get more info! 301-913-0203; 4837 Del Ray Avenue, Bethesda, Maryland 20814. (You can also record an audio cassette, if you'd rather.)

1946

Create a "Stay-In-Touch Kit." Contents include pen, paper, envelopes (pre-addressed), love stamps, a list of suggestions for what to write, a photo of you with a funny caption, directions to the post office, etc.

1947

Beautiful, hardwood hope chests are built by Vermont Carpentry and Crafts. Master woodworker Kevin Dwyer creates heirlooms of these chests by in-laying personal items, such as wedding invitations, letters or poems, into the wood. (His first such chest was for his wife.) The chests are usually cherry or maple, and are lined with cedar. Prices start around $375, and can top $1,000 for especially intricate work. [Not much to pay for a romantic heirloom that will be in your family for generations!] Kevin also custom designs and builds all kinds of furniture, specializing in Shaker-type pencil post beds. (He's also toying with the idea of creating custom-made *wooden* greeting cards!) Call him at 802-658-2342, or write to Post Office Box 1083, Williston, Vermont 05495.

1948-1949

* How about creating a custom-made T-shirt for your partner? You could create a "Pet Name" shirt, or one with a commonly-used phrase, or private joke written on it. Lots of little shops will make custom T-shirts. They seem to be popping-up in malls all over the place.
* Or—how about custom-made bumper stickers? Drop-in at your local copy shop. (And don't forget about their ability to take comics and blow them up to poster-size. They can also convert slides into printed posters. Imagine the possibilities!)

1950-1951

Re-living memories can be a great way to spark romance. Anything that helps keep those good memories alive will enhance your relationship.

+ Tony F., of Lafayette, Arkansas, writes a poem every year to celebrate the events, accomplishments and "funny things" that he and his wife share. He's got 23 years worth of poems!

+ One couple in New York City wrote to say that they sit down together on New Year's Eve every year and write "A Continuing Letter To Our Older Selves" which is now 137 pages long! Every ten years or so, they read through it! [Pretty incredible, huh!?] {Thanks to D.&T. B.}

1952-1953

Companies have logos—why not *couples*? Why walk around advertising Polo or Izod, when you could have a unique, nifty symbol emblazoned on clothing, stationery, etc.?! Find a graphic designer who specializes in symbols and logos, and give it a try! It shouldn't cost more than a few hundred dollars (depending on how detailed you want it, and how many revisions you may want). I came up with this idea while having my "1001 Ways To Be Romantic" logo designed. (See the cover of this book.) Imagine your names, or your last name, or some significant symbol or phrase turned into a unique image—a visual symbol of your love.

And if you'd like to get your logo custom embroidered on some high quality polo shirts, call the Queensboro Shirt Company. I had them do my "1001 Ways" logo, and it looks *fantastic*! Minimum quantity is 12 shirts at #36.95 each—but the price per item drops significantly at quantities of two dozen. They also make shorts, tote bags and umbrellas! Call them at 800-84-SHIRT.

1954

How about a full-length romance novel starring you and your partner as the main characters?! Evelyn Brown has written three novels into which she can insert your names: *Our Love* ("a California romance"), *Paradise Dream* ("A Hawaiian adventure") and *Lotto Love* ("They not only find romance, they win the lottery!") The Lover's Edition is just $60. A more customized version, the Postscript Edition, is $200, and includes a custom-written epilogue (utilizing answers to 30 questions about your lives and relationship. Questions like "What makes your relationship special?" and "What joke or secret sign do you share?") A great wedding or anniversary gift, don't you think? Call Evelyn Brown/Swan Publishing at 800-535-SWAN.

Different Strokes for Different Folks

1955

"Attention Wegmans shoppers! Cheerios are on sale in aisle 5, and you're invited to a wedding in aisle 7!" Not one, but *two* couples were recently treated to all-expenses-paid weddings by Wegmans Supermarkets and WVOR-Radio in Greece, a suburb of Rochester, New York. Every store worker was dressed in tuxedos, and every shopper was invited to the weddings!

1956

Personally, my taste is more the satin-and-lace variety—but recognizing the fact that different people have different tastes . . .

You've seen the catalog, now visit the store—STORMYLEATHER, at 1158 Howard Street (between 7th & 8th) San Francisco, California 94103, or call 415-626-1672. The catalog's just $2.

1957

Did someone mention *public sex*?! For some people it's an occasional game. For others it's an *obsession*. A friend of mine (who was there) knows a couple who once made love in a department store canopy/draped bed, while he and two other friends kept the salespeople distracted. Yikes! {R.E.H., Ph.D.}

1958

If your lover is an engineer, a scientist, or just a science nut, you may want to get him or her the latest perfume from those romantic folks at MIT. They tell me that *Kelvin!* (the first unisex fragrance) was discovered by an MIT prof who was studying cold fusion. [Kelvin is the scale used to measure very cold temperatures.] This wonderful spoof of celebrity fragrances is appropriately bottled in a 25 ml. volumetric flask. Just $19.95, from the MIT Museum Shop. Call 617-253-4462, or write to 265 Massachusetts Avenue, Cambridge, Massachusetts 02139.

1959

A member of Hell's Angels actually wrote to me, challenging me and my readers to come up with a more *permanent* way to express your love than getting a tattoo of your lover's name! *Yikes!* {B., Philadelphia.}

Little Things Mean a Lot

1960-1964

10 Romantic Props Everyone Should Have:

1. Two crystal champagne flutes.
2. A great champagne on ice: Perrier-Jouet or Dom Perignon
3. A tape of romantic music (vocals).
4. A tape of romantic music (instrumental).
5. The recipe for his favorite meal.
6. Two tickets to the theatre.
7. A book of erotic stories.
8. Many candles.
9. His/her favorite perfume/cologne.
10. $100 cash.

1965

"Love Stamps" are "only the beginning" according to several creative Romance Class participants. They use *all kinds* of postage stamps to spark their romantic impulses. Some people write poems or whole letters on the theme of certain stamps, while other simply jot one-liners . . . such as:

- ✉ "Fly me to the moon" to accompany various space stamps.
- ✉ Simple flower-poems along with floral patterns.
- ✉ All kinds of cartoon balloons putting funny words into the mouths of various distinguished personages pictured on stamps.

{Tip 'o the hat to Jan Allen, Peter Tetly and A.B. Atkinson.}

1966

How do you know when it's *really* True Love? When you're watching TV together with a pint of Ben & Jerry's Heath Bar Crunch . . . and as he feeds you directly from the carton, he gives you all the biggest chunks of Heath Bar. {These wise words from Linda L. & Jeff L., in Colorado.}

1967-1970

Pay attention to those details!

- ✓ Don't just hand her a pack of gum—unwrap it for her!
- ✓ Pull-out her chair for her—at *home*, for *every* meal!
- ✓ Hold the car door for her—*always*!
- ✓ Place a mint chocolate on his pillow.

{Thanks to Rod McGarry, mentor and professional speaker, from Worcester, Massachusetts.}

1971

Hands and feet! Give her a foot massage. Or a hand massage. Or a manicure. Or a pedicure.

1972

Make love under the stars—while in your own bedroom! "Starry Nights" is the name of a package of glow-in-the-dark decals of stars and moons. Kevin Dwyer, of Williston, Vermont, once snuck into his lover's apartment and pasted 'em all over her bedroom ceiling!

1973

When she's talking on the phone, lightly kiss her on the neck, then walk away. Repeat every five to ten minutes.

1974

Wrap a gift extra-special: Use five different-colored sheets of tissue paper. Sprinkle-in confetti in the shape of stars and hearts. Tie it with satin ribbon. Affix a fresh rose to the package.

1975

Little things *do* mean a lot. It's very often the small, seemingly insignificant things that do us in. Petty annoyances can build-up and defeat couples who were once ga-ga in love. Pay attention to those little details—they're not really so little!

> *"All the things that "go without saying" . . . can build up a mountain of miscommunication."*
>
> ~ *Leo Buscaglia*

Actions Speak Louder...

1976

Add these ingredients, in any combination or measure, to your next romantic gift or gesture: Anticipation, intrigue and surprise. Mix well, don't do it half-baked, and serve with a flourish!

1977

Sometimes, the best thing you can do to help your relationship is to *help yourself*. Needless to say, romantics need positive self-esteem, a lot of self-confidence, and a sense of power about themselves in order to be able to give freely to their partners.

One of the most effective self-empowerment seminars around is the "Unleash the Power Within" weekend seminar created by master motivator and bestselling author Tony Robbins. This seminar has the potential to turn your life around *quickly*. Tony's central message is that you *do* have the power to banish your "limiting beliefs" and overcome your fears, doubts and worries in all areas of your life—in your work and in your relationships. This dynamic, inspiring weekend has helped 150,000+ people to transform their lives. Various types of seminars range from around $500 to $1,000+ (depending on length of the seminar and its location—from short sessions in local hotels, to the 9-day marathon seminar in Hawaii that costs $5,600!) For more information call 800-445-8183, or write 9191 Towne Centre Drive, Suite 600, San Diego, California 92122.

Making Beautiful Music...

1978

Create a Valentine's Day *concert*, just for the two of you. Record an hour's worth of your favorite romantic music. Print-up a program. List the song titles, along with some personal commentary about the significance of each song to you, or why particular songs remind you of her. Send her an invitation to the concert. Dress for the event. Serve wine and cheese.

1979

And George Winston has finally "completed the year" by releasing his long- and eagerly-awaited album *Summer*. Also from the master of solo piano:

> ❧ *Autumn* ❧
>
> ❄ *December* ❄
>
> ❀ *Winter Into Spring* ❀
>
> ◎ *Summer* ◎

1980

If you'd like to *literally* make beautiful music together, and if you both can play the piano, you could while away the hours playing some piano pieces for four hands, such as Mozart's *Sonata in F, K.497*; Ravel's *Ma Mere l'Oye*.

1981

The folks at Victoria's Secret will not only help you *dress* romantically, they'll help you set the mood with a little classy classical music, too! They've commissioned the London Symphony Orchestra to record a series of "Classics By Request." There are now *five* volumes to choose from. They include best-loved selections from all the great composers: Mozart, Beethoven, Liszt, Handel, Ravel, Tchaikovsky, Prokofiev, Mascagni, Boccherini, Haydn, Mendelssohn, Grieg, Donizetti, Bach and many others! CDs and cassette tapes are available—at any Victoria's Secret store, or through the catalog: Call 800-888-8200.

1982

Has she seen all of her favorite singers in concert? Has he heard all of his favorite symphonies played live?

1983

You can sing to your sweetie with back-up music by some of the biggest bands of all time! Just get a cassette tape of popular music with the vocals removed! I've found two sources for you:

- ☞ MMO Music Group, 50 South Buckhout Street, Irvington, New York 10533.

- ☞ Song and Music Systems, 3900 East Whiteside Street, Los Angeles, California 90063.

Newsletters Galore!

1984

To Us! The Newsletter for Committed Couples is a wonderful, warm and information-packed bi-monthly newsletter written by a couple that practices what they preach. *To Us!* presents articles by bestselling authors, tips on communication skills, ideas for inspiring romance, and suggestions for enhancing the passion in your lives. (You may have caught editors Faith and Danny Boyle on Donahue last summer!) Six issues for just $12! Write to Innovisions Unlimited, 5405 Alton Parkway, Suite A344, Irvine, California 92714.

1985

Perceptions is a quarterly newsletter of "sensual self-expression." It's comprised of 44 pages of erotic photographs, articles, fantasy, poetry, short stories, drawings, commentary and review—all submitted by subscribers! $3 for a sample issue; $10 for a year's subscription. Send to Post Office Box 2867, Toledo, Ohio 43606-0867.

1986

Romantic Traveling is for lovers with wanderlust. This quarterly newsletter gives you specific recommendations and reviews of romantic destinations, elegant restaurants, and specific hotels, inns and B&Bs. A sampling of recent features: "Romantic Inns of Northern New England," "Romance with the Kids Along," "Just for Singles," "Italian Originals," "New Zealand's Romantic Lodges." Just $15 per year (back issues at $4 each). Write to Winterbourne Press, 236 West Portal, Suite 237, San Francisco, California 94127, or call 415-731-8239.

1987-1989

And a few more travel-related newsletters for your consideration:

✳ *Travel Smart*: A budget-oriented monthly newsletter. $44 per year. Write to Communications House, 40 Beechdale Road, Dobbs Ferry, New York 10522, or call 800-FARE-OFF.

✳ *Gardens & Countrysides: A Journal of Picturesque Travels*: From elegant estate gardens to elaborate maze gardens of Europe; from spiritual gardens in Japan to gardening seminars! $75 for 10 issues, from Travel Publications, 401 Austin Highway, Suite 209, San Antonio, Texas 78209, or call 512-826-5222.

✳ *The Educated Traveler*: For lovers who want to pursue special interests like photo safaris, bicycle tours, "pub crawls" [!] and painting workshops. $75 for 10 issues. Write to The Educated Traveler, Post Office Box 220822, Chantilly, Virginia 22022, or call 703-471-1063.

✳ *Travel With Your Children*. Help for the harried! For a sample issue send $1 to TWYC, 80 Eighth Avenue, New York, New York 10011.

1990

Duos, a seven-issue publication subtitled *Choosing to Live as Lovers*, explores one major topic in each issue. These topics are: "Caring and Pleasure," "The Climate for Love," "Wooing and Romance," "Creating an Intimate Island," "Awakening Your Senses," "Choosing to Play and Be Happy," and "The Educated Heart." The cost is just $25. Write to Stratton & Company, 3125 North Main Street, Soquel, California 95073, or call 408-464-1780.

1991

The Mature Traveler is a newsletter for those over 50 who are on the go! This monthly publication tells you about senior discounts in the travel industry, including some just for their subscribers. Romantic places that have offered senior discounts in the past include Spain, Switzerland, U.S. National Parks, Vancouver Island, Alaska, Mexican resorts, and various cruises. Just $21.97 per year. Write to Post Office Box 50820, Reno, Nevada 89513.

Godek's Choices

1992

When you're in Boston . . . Have dinner at the most romantic restaurant in town: The Hungry i, on Charles Street. [That's where Tracey and I went for dinner after I proposed to her.]

1993

I was reminded of *this* one recently when Tracey was interviewed for a magazine article . . . This is the note that I'd included with the very first pink rose I ever sent to her:

> *Every person, all the events of your life*
> *are there because you have drawn them there.*
> *What you choose to do with them*
> *is up to you.*

~ From "The Messiah's Handbook," from *Illusions*, by Richard Bach.

1994

When you're in Rochester, New York . . . You've *got* to stop at the Parkleigh. It's the coolest gift shop/specialty store I've ever seen. They're always doing something fun, like sampling coffees and chocolates, or providing live music—from guitars to string quartets! They're always at the cutting edge of new products and ideas, from greeting cards to finely crafted items. Stop in at 215 Park Avenue, or call 800-333-0627.

1995

After telling 12 years' worth of Romance Class participants about sending their Valentines cards to Loveland, Colorado, to be specially postmarked, I've finally spoken with the Mayor of Loveland. Little did I know how that town goes *all out* for Valentine's Day! In addition to getting your envelope postmarked, it will be hand-stamped with a unique four-line poem/cachet. (And they write a new one every year!) This great, romantic tradition has been going on since 1947! The Loveland Chamber of Commerce, which organizes this romantic project, reports that more than 300,000 Valentines are handled every year, headed for all 50 states and 104 foreign countries!

Here's the deal: Enclose your pre-stamped, pre-addressed Valentine in a larger First Class envelope and mail it to: Postmaster, Attn: Valentines, Loveland, Colorado 80537.

1996

Make a WANTED poster of her—like something out of the Olde West. Fray the edges of a sheet of parchment paper. Glue her photo in the center. Write a headline and some copy: "WANTED: Tracey Godek, For Stealing My Heart! Last seen driving a wild Honda toward Montreal. Reward: My eternal love. Signed, Sheriff Gregory." {Concept by Peter C., of San Diego, California.}

1997

The Award for the Best New Catalog of the Year goes to . . .

*The **thirty**something catalog* (!)—"The spirit of the award-winning TV series **thirty**something lives on in the wonderful lifestyle fashions inspired by Michael, Hope, Elliot, Nancy, & Co. Featured are eclectic items blending classic styles. Included are Gary's jacket, Elliot's wacky neckties, Melissa's funky-type sweaters." There's a one-time $3 charge, which includes a $7.50 certificate! Call 800-241-9111, extension 316.

1998

The Award for the Best New Book of the Year goes to . . .

Born For Love, by Leo Buscaglia. Subtitled *Reflections On Loving*, that's *exactly* what the book is: Nearly 300 short "love-essays" that explore and reveal the many facets of love in our lives. You can read the book straight through, or read individual items in any order that suits you. It's an inspiration, an education, and sure to generate some intimate conversation.

1999

Instead of actually *being* romantic on Valentine's Day, why don't you use the day as a chance to re-dedicate yourself to the ideals of Love? *Make a Valentine's Day Resolution.* You could resolve to call her more often. Be more considerate of him. Listen to her better. Give him more of your time. Stop making excuses. Reserve weekends for each other.

2000

Godek's analysis of U.S. national holidays—wherein we reveal their true meaning: New Year's Day—Hangover Recovery Day. Martin Luther King Day—Not a real holiday yet (unfortunately). Memorial Day—A glorification of war. Labor Day—To honor working people (many of whom have to work on that day. I don't get it.) Thanksgiving—A celebration of gluttony. Christmas—We celebrate the Savior's birthday by overspending.

I think our holidays need to be revised, re-structured and re-defined. What kind of "holiday" is it when most stores are open? Don't those people need a holiday at least as much as our loyal government workers? I don't get it. Maybe I'm just dense or something. Anyway . . . On *my* proposed holidays, *everthing* will be closed—even 7-Elevens! It will be illegal to carry a briefcase. And lovers will be encouraged to . . . um, well—to do whatever lovers are *supposed* to do with time off together!

Here, then, is my modest proposal for a *revised* list of national holidays:

New national holidays

- ☆ January 27: *Mozart's Birthday*
- ❤ February 14: *Valentine's Day I* (The Traditional Winter Holiday)
- ✲ March 20 or 21: *Spring Equinox* (Day & night are equal lengths)
- ✓ March 31: *Hug Day* (Leo Buscaglia's birthday)
- ✳ June 21 or 22: *Summer Solstice* (The longest day of the year)
- ❦ August 14: *Valentine's Day II* (The Summer Holiday)
- ➤ September 22 or 23: *Autumnal Equinox* (Hobbit Day, too)
- ✦ November 7: *Sadie Hawkins Day*
- ↦ December 22: *Winter Solstice* (The shortest day of the year)
- ✤ *First Snowfall Day* (A variable holiday)
- ☞ Bonus holiday: *Leap Year Day* (February 29th)

2001: A Romantic Odyssey

2001

Set out on an odyssey of love. *Make these ideas **your own**.* This is only the *beginning!*

2002

Respect him
Give to him
Trust him
Care for him
Share with him
Laugh with him
Love him
Romance him

✦ ✦ ✦

Know her
Love her
Appreciate her
Remember her
Talk to her
Listen to her
Cherish her
Romance her

Book #3—
and Beyond!

The Newsletter!

Get a *free* one-year subscription to a unique publication from Yours Truly:

Would you like to be a part of the *third* book? It's tentatively titled:

LoveStories—
Outrageous & Inspiring & True
Romantic Stories

I'm tremendously inspired—and often touched—by stories shared with me by Romance Class participants, audience members at my keynote speeches, audiences on TV & radio talk shows, and folks who write to me.

So I invite you to send me stories about how you met your mate, how you got engaged, married, celebrated special events or expressed your love in a *special* way!

Ideas for book #4 are welcome, too! [*Lord help us!*]

1001 Ways To Be Romantic—
The Newsletter!

It's a $25 value, and it's full of creative, unusual and wonderful ideas, gifts and gestures [what *else* would you expect?!].

Sign-up yourself, your spouse, your boyfriend/girl-friend, your parents, your friends—*anyone* who needs a good swift kick-in-the-pants, or would appreciate receiving lots of great romantic ideas on a regular basis!

P.S.—And as long as you're writing, why don't you send-in your favorite creative ideas, great gifts, special gestures?! I'll credit you by name! [This isn't just a newsletter, it's a *conversation!*]

~ G.J.P.G.

Please send your LoveStories & newsletter requests to:
"LoveStories" or "Newsletter," Post Office Box 226
Weymouth, Massachusetts 02188-0001

Love Coupon

1001 *More* Ways To Be Romantic
Number 1779

✦

This coupon entitles the holder to an *entire weekend*
of Romance! What's your pleasure?—The issuer of this coupon
will grant your every wish!

✦

A gift to _____

A gift from _____

Love Coupon

1001 *More* Ways To Be Romantic
Number 1676

✦

This coupon entitles the holder to "Romantic Evening #1":
Music by Glenn Miller; watch the movie *Casablanca*;
sip champagne; candlelight—of course; and formal wear!

✦

A gift to _____

A gift from _____

Love Coupon

1001 *More* Ways To Be Romantic
Number 1001

◆

This coupon is a romantic "blank check": The holder is entitled to choose *any* romantic item—except numbers 274 to 280—from the first book, *1001 Ways To Be Romantic*.

◆

A gift to _____

A gift from _____

Love Coupon

1001 *More* Ways To Be Romantic
Number 1360

◆

This coupon is good for one "choreographed" lovemaking session! Choose your favorite romantic/erotic music, and then make love to match its moods & rhythms!

◆

A gift to _____

A gift from _____

Love Coupon

1001 *More* Ways To Be Romantic
Number 1091

———✦———

This coupon entitles the holder to one evening on Lover's Lane—
or a *reasonable facsimile*
of the activities associated with that particular locale!

———✦———

A gift to _____

A gift from _____

Love Coupon

1001 *More* Ways To Be Romantic
Number 1439

———✦———

This is an "ABC" coupon. Here's how it works: The
coupon *holder* chooses a letter. Then, the coupon *giver* turns to
page 138, and chooses an activity beginning with that letter!

———✦———

A gift to _____

A gift from _____

✦ Index ✦

Romantic Things To Do Today

_____

_____

_____

_____

_____

Romantic Plans for Next Week

_____

_____

_____

_____

_____

Romantic Plans for Next Month

_____

_____

_____

_____

_____

Romantic Plans for Next Year

_____

_____

_____

_____

_____

My Favorite Ideas from the Book

_____

_____

_____

_____

_____

A Few of My Lover's Favorite Things

_____

_____

_____

_____

_____

Romantic Ideas from Magazines, etc.

_____

_____

_____

_____

_____

Notes for Writing a Love Letter

_____

_____

_____

_____

_____

Order Form

1001 WAYS TO BE ROMANTIC

Available _now_:
- ☞ Softcover: *1001 Ways To Be Romantic* ($11.95)
- ☞ Hardcover: *1001 Ways To Be Romantic* ($18.95)
- ✦ Newsletter: "The Romantic Idea Newsletter!"—*Free!* See page 295!
- ☞ Softcover: *1001 **More** Ways To Be Romantic* ($11.95)
- ☞ Hardcover: *1001 **More** Ways To Be Romantic* ($18.95)

Available soon:
- ➤ Tapes: Romance seminars on audio cassette tapes & videotapes
- ➤ 1994 daily calendar: *365 Ways To Be Romantic*

◆

Call Toll-Free
800-444-2524
Extension 65

For fastest delivery & credit card orders
(*Overnight delivery available—for those romantic emergencies!*)

◆

Or fill-out this form & mail it
along with a check or money order:

- ➥ (_____) Hardcover books @ $18.95 each ....$_____
- ➥ (_____) Softcover books @ $11.95 each.................. _____
- ➥ Shipping: $3.75 for the 1st book.............................. _____
-     plus $1.50 for each addt'l. book .... _____
- ➥ Florida residents please add 7% tax .... _____
- ➥ Total ....$_____

Name_____

Address_____

City_____State_____ ZIP_____

Please mail orders to:
Casablanca Press, P.O. Box 226, Weymouth, MA 02188-0001